The
SOUTHDOWN
Queen Marys

A Souvenir

Julian Osborne et al

ISBN 1 900515 25 3

Original edition entitled 'The Southdown PD3s'
published 1985 by Capital Transport Publishing
ISBN 0 904711 69 2

Design and layout by Julian Osborne
Graphics by DTS Publishing
PO Box 105, Croydon, Surrey
Printed by Unwin Brothers
© Julian Osborne 2004

British Library Cataloguing in Publication Data. A catalogue record for
this book is available from the British Library.

Early Queen Mary Days Worthing Summer 1963, the last year I voluntarily wore
a tie. Mary numbers had been going in notebooks for about a year when this photo
was taken. Continued opposite. *(Loraine Osborne)*

Author's Note

In an earlier piece about Southdown's Queen Marys, I averred
that the real reason that I had chosen to write about them was that
they had always been there and were thus almost an 'easy' topic
Somewhere at the back of my mind I envisaged writing a follow-up
some years later when all but a handful had gone ..and I believe the
time for that follow-up is now. The story is not quite over but it's
now time for a souvenir. Of 285 buses built 40 years ago about a
fifth survive – a truly remarkable testament to good design and good
maintenance and not a little affection from owners and users! – but
most are now in some sort of semi-retired, heritage role, albeit that
they are some of the most active of such vehicles.

It is intended that this souvenir should be a definitive work so
readers may find pieces of text and pictures that have also appeared
elsewhere – they are essential to the historical narrative but there
is much new or revised(even corrected) information and many
previously unpublished photos. In addition, some pictures previously published in black-and-white are now in colour.

I am indebted to my financiers; and to my contributing authors
for the specialist knowledge and different styles of writing that
they bring. Although not credited in the text, my publisher, Mike
Davis, was also the source of all the original material for pp. 91–
96.

I am grateful to all the people who have assisted me in 40 years
of Queen Mary enthusiasm: the owners of them who allowed access
and photography and often chatted as well (this has included every
owner of a Mary mentioned in the text except some of the Barnsley
yards but including the Barnsley yard of the Askin family who were
always helpful to enthusiasts) and the many people who assisted
my researches and travels plus all those who helped put the book
together by trawling their memories or notes, finding or processing
photos or manipulating computer software or proof-reading – or
checking things on actual Queen Marys.

All key contributors appear somewhere in the book – in the text
or as photographers. Thank you all.

I hope you enjoy this book and find it a fitting tribute to these
much-loved buses.

JULIAN OSBORNE   MAY 2004

COVER PICTURE: In the seventies many Queen Marys worked from the former
Brighton Hove & District garages with the result that for much of the decade the
centre of Brighton was serious Queen Mary territory: in this picture, taken on Easter
Saturday 1974 the bus behind is a "BH&D" one whilst the one in front, with its full
blinds, works the one town service performed by the "real" Southdown garage
at Edward Street and this unusual juxtaposition of the two buses is included to bring
a smile to the faces of all my old colleagues at Conway Street garage (see p.61)

FRONTISPIECE: The clippie works her way round 404's full upper-deck *en route*
to Beachy Head on Friday June 2nd 1968.(Alan Snatt)

Contents

Whilst we aim for this book to be definitive, we know loose ends
remain. We would be interested to hear from anyone who can change
or enlarge the story. We also acknowledge that in an ensemblepiece
the odd bit of confirmatory repetition will be found. Photos
credited SEC are courtesy The Southdown Enthusiasts Club. Photos
credited "Authors' Collection" have no indication of photographer
on our copy – if they're yours, let us know! Uncredited photos are
by Julian Osborne.

Julian Osborne has been interested in buses since he was 10 in
1962. Now semi-retired from a career in civil aviation management,
he has been contributing to bus publications for twenty years - with
latterly a specialism in customer service issues, his comments
informed and sometimes embarrassed by the experiences described
on pp 49 to 63.Other CVs:p.128

Introduction

Much later. Pool Valley July 7 1996. In my adolescence these buses had taken me to school and on pleasure trips, their activities assiduously studied and documented; later they had provided the forum for learning a lot about life when I conducted them as a student – and then they lingered to remind me of my lost youth, rekindling my interest with a myriad latter day uses. Concluded on p.128 – but worth reading the book first!

On July 7 1996, a remarkable gathering took place in Brighton in Sussex – for a moment around two in the afternoon the old bus station by the pier filled with the sorts of bus that used it 30 years before. Eventually they stood in a line, Leyland O600 engines chugging happily away with ageing men and women looking misty eyed upon a recreation of their youth; or maybe just excited at their ability to assemble such a scene in 1996. What was remarkable was that so many of these vehicles from another era had survived to create this nostalgic scene. Even more remarkable is the fact that they were just a small percentage of the survivors of these fine vehicles. Some had remained behind at the rally site at Shoreham, others were parked up or in use all over the UK and others were unable to join in the day of nostalgia because they resided in other parts of the world.

Strange, then, to think that these buses were once new. Indeed so revolutionary on the 1950s south coast was their layout that they were known for some years as 'new buses' by the locals. My first recollection of one in the flesh, as it were, is in Portsmouth, where most of the early ones worked, on a visit to see a colleague of my grandfather who took early retirement on gloomy medical advice and eventually lived past ninety. They gradually infiltrated Worthing, my home: initially this was on trunk route 31 but by the time I took up notebook they were running locally as well.

In 1957, Southdown Motor Services was, to many enthusiasts, the finest bus company in the world. It maintained a fleet of exceptionally well-appointed service buses, operating a grid of services, covering Sussex and east Hampshire, which were carefully timed to give connections almost everywhere routes met; it also ran a large fleet of luxury coaches on touring and express work.

The excellence of its organisation and performance did not immunise Southdown, however, from the harsh economic realities of 1950s bus operation and, as it became apparent in mid-decade that demand for

bus travel was falling away from its post-war peak, the Company in common with other operators began to look for ways of economising to ensure continuing viability. One-man-operation[1] was then only considered feasible on lightly loaded single-decker routes and attention was directed towards buying larger crew-operated buses which had enough capacity to absorb peak loads. Such vehicles could eliminate the need to keep buses solely for duplicate work at periods of heavy demand. At this time many operators started to use rear-engined buses to achieve this aim, but Southdown mistrustful of the mechanical reliability of such machines, preferred to specify front-engined models of the newly-permissible 30ft length. As a concession to various trends introduced by the rear-engined vehicles, the traditional nature of Southdown's new buses was disguised with a full front and forward entrance.

Thus, between 1957 and 1967, Southdown took delivery of 285 Northern Counties bodied Leyland PD3s. The buses were built to the maximum permitted dimensions of the time, 30ft by 8ft, and were fitted with the Leyland O600 engine. Nos. 813–912, 953–977, 400–429, 250–315 and 346–369 were PD3/4s with synchromesh gearboxes; 913–952 were PD3/5s with pneumocyclic gears. Both versions had air brakes. All had NCME FH39/30FD bodies, except 257, and those on 400–429 were convertible to open-top.

These vehicles were destined to become Southdown's last two-manned double-deckers. Their unsuitability for one-man operation – eventually the most widespread choice for reducing operating costs – looked set to condemn them to an early grave but, as it turned out, they all had long and interesting lives – albeit much of them after sale by Southdown – and examples travelled to far distant parts of the world. Indeed, as late as 1985, the majority continued to perform all sorts of tasks in various parts of the globe and many survived into the 1990s. Nonetheless, the two hundred and eighty five never operated together, owing to the destruction of 939 in a tragic accident in 1965.

The origin of their Queen Mary nickname is the subject of much discussion – see p.21.

FOOTNOTE: [1] This phrase and the later one-person-operation are abbreviated in the text in many places to OMO and OPO.

3

The Queen Marys batch by batch

Above: TCD

Photo: SEC

Above: VUF

We acknowledge other nomenclature:
Southdown themselves always called
them by their numbers for instance – as
will be apparent in Bruce MacPhee's
contributions.

Photo: SEC

Below: CD

Above: XUF

Below: Semi-automatic

Photo: Malcolm G. Chase

Photo: Southdown

Above: Convertible

Photo: Chris Warren

Above: CUF

Photo: SEC

Below: FCD-D   **Above: BUF-C**

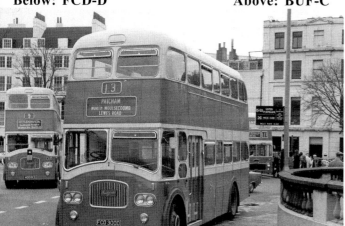

Photo: Richard Maryan

Below: Panoramic

5

February 17th, 1960

One of the 20 new Leyland PD3/4 buses with Northern Counties 69-seat bodies now being delivered to Southdown Motor Services. Similar to 30 already in service, they have now been followed by the ordering of a further 50 of these chassis

Tiger Cub and Avenger coaches, and Titan front-entrance double-deckers added to the Southdown fleet

Fleet modernisation in Sussex

THE buses and coaches operated in Sussex and along the south coast by Southdown Motor Services Ltd., have always been held in high regard for their standard of comfort and general appointment. In addition, the company has constantly pursued a policy of progressive replacement of its vehicles thus ensuring a low average fleet life and up-to-date bodies and chassis. The latest additions comprise two types of coach and a further batch of double-deck buses.

The new buses are, in common with the latest trends, 30 ft. long models with front-entrance bodywork. There are 20 in the currrent delivery, generally similar to 30 delivered over the past two years for use in Portsmouth and Brighton. The chassis is the Leyland PD 3/4 and the bodywork is by the Northern Counties Motor and Engineering Company Ltd., of Wigan. It seats 69 passengers and has an electrically-operated sliding passenger door under the control of the driver. The entrance is designed for two-way flow to facilitate rapid loading and unloading of passengers simultaneously. The buses of this type at present in service are used on inter-urban services in the Portsmouth area and town routes in Brighton.

The new coaches consist of 15 Harrington Crusader-bodied Commer Avengers and 15 Leyland Tiger Cubs with M.C.W. Fanfare bodywork. The Commers are for day excursion and private hire duties and seat 35 passengers on fixed seating with adjustable footrests. The chassis is powered by the Rootes two-stroke diesel engine. The Leylands are for the company's range of British Beacon Tours which cover itineraries to the Highlands of Scotland, Wales, Eire, Devon, and other popular areas. The M.C.W. bodies are built at the Addlestone works of Weymanns Ltd., and seat 37 passengers. Deflector ventilators are fitted to the side windows to obviate draughts and there are also front and roof vents fitted.

Additions to the Southdown coaching fleet for 1960. Left: One of 15 Commer Avenger chassis with Rootes two-stroke diesel engines and Harrington 35-seat bodies for day excursions and private hire work. Right: Over 800 Southdown buses and coaches are of Leyland manufacture including 15 new Tiger Cubs with M.C.W. Fanfare 37-seat bodies, for extended tours of Britain. The more powerful Leopard single-deck chassis has also been specified and 30 are to be delivered

More Tools for the Job

THE YEAR 1958 has seen a number of changes in the composition of the fleet, ranging from conversion from coach to one-man operation, to the introduction of 69-seater front entrance double-deck vehicles.

Earlier in the year we carried out a conversion on the ten Beadle coaches from 26-seater coaches to 31-seater one-man-operated buses. To do this it was necessary to mount the ticket machine on a bracket on the existing engine cover, additional seats were fitted and spaced as required, and the entrance door was motorised by fitting an appropriate gear with a floor-mounted motor.

Our latest conversion to one-man operation is now taking place on the 1500-type single decks, which, as our readers know, have the entrance behind the near-side rear wheel arch.

This entrance is being boxed in, the former step well is modified to contain the batteries, and a new front entrance is being formed. The partition on the left-hand side of the driver has been re-built to house the motorised Setright and the "Syro" change-giver, and a pair of glider doors, electrically operated, completes the structural modification. The 41-seats have been re-spaced to give comfortable leg room and each vehicle is fitted with a microphone and loud speaker.

The 69-seater front entrance double-deck vehicles are a new feature in our fleet operation. The chassis is a Leyland PD. 3/4, and the bodies have been built by Northern Counties Engineering Co., of Wigan. The engine in this chassis is the well-known "600" 9.8 litre fitted with C.A.V. pneumatic fuel injection pump, the gearbox is synchro-mesh in third and top gears, and, of course, air pressure brakes are standard on this chassis. We have continued our policy of fitting "Syndromic" automatic lubrication to these chassis, this arrangement ensuring correct and even lubrication to all moving parts.

The Northern Counties' front entrance double-deck body presents a particularly pleasing appearance, formica having been used extensively in the interior finish. The driver's vision to the near-side through the unglazed bulkhead is excellent, and his control of the door operation should not only improve the loading and unloading, but also be a major factor in the reduction of platform accidents.

W.G.A.H.

BUSES ILLUSTRATED

Vol. 8, No. 43 • September 1958

Published MONTHLY by Ian Allan Ltd
CRAVEN HOUSE, HAMPTON COURT
EAST MOLESEY, SURREY

Editor: E. J. SMITH

...been completed to Southdown Motor Services of 15 Leyland PD3/4s with Northern 813-27). They are in keeping with the modern trend in having front entrances. Seating is for 39 upstairs and 30 in the lower saloon. Fifteen more of these ...urfleet Transport Photos.)

The photograph above shows one of our latest double-deck vehicles, 24 of which are now coming into service, and together with double-deck 315, complete an order for 25.

The body design has in fact been based on double-deck 315, which was shown and briefly described in our October, 1966, issue, and which was the vehicle we exhibited in the Commercial Motor Show.

The chassis is the latest Leyland PD3/4, and the bodies are again being built by our friends Northern Counties Motor & Engineering Co. Ltd., Wigan, and include the extensive use of plastic materials — Warerite on the lining panels and Formica on the bulkhead panels.

Standard heating and ventilating, however, is used in these last 24, and again "Rotavent" ventilators have been fitted above the large side windows in both saloons, to ensure that a constant flow of fresh air is always available.

In addition to all the controls now coming more easily to the driver's hand, special attention has been paid to heating the driver's cab, and to additional insulation in the bonnet top for noise suppression.

Even at this early stage, we have received a number of complimentary reports on these vehicles, both from our own staff and the travelling public.

W.G.A.H.

Every Queen Mary was shiny and new once. Here are various trade announcements and brand new 251 and 277 glistening in the sun at Portslade on Saturday 3rd April 1965. Not only did they look new, they smelt new – all fresh paint and unsullied plastic.

The first batch: Southdown 813–827 registered TCD 813–827 (delivered May–December 1958)

The TCDs were Southdown's first double-deckers built to the new maximum permitted dimensions of 30ft x 8ft. Their chassis type followed standard Southdown practice – a long line of Leylands punctuated periodically by some Guys. The choice of body manufacturer was less predictable, and the standardisation on that firm which followed even less so – the Company had sampled a variety of body-builders since the war and particularly since the cessation of body-building by Leyland itself.

Like all but one batch of their later sisters, the TCDs were Leyland PD3/4s. Features of this chassis, stressed in an article written for driving staff when the first examples arrived, were the Leyland O600 9.8 litre engine with C.A.V. pneumatically governed fuel injection pump, the four-speed gearbox with synchromesh in the top two gears, and the air pressure brakes. Southdown specified 'Syndromic' automatic lubrication to ensure even lubrication of all moving parts.

Like all their later sisters, their highbridge bodies were constructed by Northern Counties of Wigan (NCME) to a design involving a sturdy lower saloon built directly onto the chassis and a lightweight upper deck lifted on afterwards. They were metal framed with timber inserts, to allow the attachment of exterior panels by woodscrews, this being normal practice with Southdown. All panelling was sheet metal except for some fibreglass bits like the domes above window level (which were single-skin); floors were of plywood. Mudwings were made of steel, this batch being unique in that respect.

As mentioned on page 3, these bodies featured full fronts (possibly their most distinctive feature) and forward entrances – Southdown hoped that driver proximity to the doors would improve loading and unloading times and help reduce platform accidents. However, their faith in this change was not total with this first batch: they had a duplicate set of door controls where they had been on earlier buses–on the platform.

The bodies also featured a lot of side ventilation – virtually every window had an opening section – but little at the front. Heaters consisted of small radiators supplied with engine cooling water and electrically driven fans to assist the heat transfer; separate units heated each saloon, the cab and the windscreen. The fan switches were inside the cab (separate ones for each saloon on the bulkhead, cab heater/demister one on the door control panel) but the taps for the hot water to the heater units were under the bonnet and turned on or off by workshop staff at either end of winter.

For the first time on Southdown buses, extensive use was made of Formica in the interior finish – the fascia panelling at the front of each deck and the staircase panelling was of this material, the former featuring a wood pattern and the latter a basically cream design. The saloon lining was of patternless brown fabric and the ceilings and domes were painted cream. The cushioned seats and seat-backs were finished in Southdown's standard brown moquette. Conductor access to the number blinds was from the upper-deck, and at the back involved rummaging behind the rear seat. Access to the rear destination blind was from the lower saloon, but the front one, which could not be operated from the outside as it could on halfcabs, was reached from the cab and came under the driver's control.

Fleet numbers 813-827 represented a straight progression from a fleet of PD2/12s which started in 1950 with number 700. Successive PD3 batches continued this sequence.

Body Modifications

The first five TCDs to arrive, which were numerically the last of the batch, had three features (black offside staircase panels, front indicators behind the front-axle at window level and exposed water filler-caps) which later disappeared. 818 and 814 arrived with cream staircase panels and the rest entered service with alterations to all three features that were to become standard – cream offside staircase panels, front indicators at the front corners below the driver and filler-cap flaps. The early vehicles were brought into line – filler-caps had been done by December but the staircase panels and indicators took longer in some cases. Eventually, all the TCDs ended up identical to the following VUFs in these three respects. Early TCDs also had single-piece windows in their nearside cab-doors – these were subsequently replaced by arrangements incorporating a small opening portion.

828–842 (VUF 828–842)
(delivered February–April 1959)

The VUFs introduced one or two further modifications to the Queen Mary body. The most significant of these was a switch from brown seat moquette to green; the pattern also changed from an abstract design to a more functional check. Saloon lining remained patternless brown. Other changes were that the gutter above the upstairs emergency exit was reshaped to sweep downwards at each side and that, in what was to mark the start of a long-running activity, there were modifications to the ventilation arrangements. The middle and rear side-windows no longer featured opening portions and the small ventilator in the offside dash panel (next to the sidelight) was also dropped from the design. From 828, the Marys only had cab door controls. Wings were now made of fibreglass. All the TCDs and most of the VUFs were later fitted with dome ventilators.

843–862 (XUF 843–862)
(delivered November 1959–February 1960)

Northern Counties produced a slightly redesigned front for the next batch of PD3/4s – the XUFs; this included body alterations concerned with ventilation. An outward opening portion was fitted in the nearside windscreen and in the front upper-deck windows. These latter were something of a mixed blessing, producing a pleasant effect at the front, but anything up to a gale further back; opening them on anything other than a baking summer day was a sure way of getting into conversation with one's fellow passengers! The small sliding ventilators above these same front upper-deck windows were retained, despite these innovations and the fitting of a large ventilator in the dome. A new design of front indicator also featured.

863–912 (2863–2912CD)
(delivered October 1960–May 1961)

The Queen Mary body design continued to evolve with this large order. Two 'Pearlescent' perspex panels were included in the roof to give additional light, and fluorescent saloon lighting was also introduced on some of the batch, including 863, the 1960 Commercial Motor Show exhibit for NCME. There were four tubes downstairs and six up, some being located on the ceiling

TOP: 827 when newly-delivered at Portslade Works in 1958 and below in Brighton in the early sixties, just before losing its rear blind display. Note the position of the flashing indicator in the first picture. The short bay amidships is a curiosity. Northern Counties employed equal length side windows on almost all their other 30ft-long bodies but here appeared to merely stretch a 27ft design. The London Transport RML displayed a similar characteristic a few years later. Contemporary literature suggested that this feature was for "structural reasons". *(SEC/John Bishop)*

ABOVE: Last of the VUFs numerically was 842, and soon after delivery she is seen at South Parade Pier, Southsea, with 1948 all-Leyland PD2/1 344 and a Portsmouth Corporation TD4 open-topper behind. Like the previous batch, the VUFs' radiator grilles were painted, apart from the surround and, sometimes, the central vertical bars. *(SEC)*

LEFT: XUF 854 at Hilsea shortly after delivery, with, in the background, a Park Royal rebodied TD pulling out of the large Southdown garage there. The XUFs had grilles of the same pattern as those before, but in unpainted stainless steel; these continued unchanged for all subsequent batches. Provision for having two blinds in either big box – one for ultimate destination and one for route details was available on the Queen Marys from the start (251 opposite, 827 p.9) but none were fitted thus before 1961. Initially Queen Marys used single blinds and left the number boxes blank as on 854 here. Some of them were later found using blinds like those shown on 842 and 854, with or without the numbers blanked off, in conjunction with an active triple route number box (280 p.33). The division bar (which defined the limit of the apertures and also stopped light from shining through between the two blinds) was sometimes removed when single blinds were fitted and sometimes not. Single blinds remained in use into the seventies. *(SEC)*

ABOVE LEFT: This is the interior upstairs of Show exhibit 863 when new and described by Buses Illustrated as possibly the sleekest vehicle at Earls Court. How many of this batch had interior fluorescent lights is not clear – Southdown publicity in 1960 said, "some". *(Southdown)*

ABOVE RIGHT: 895 towards the end of her Southdown days in the early seventies. QMs delivered in 1961/2 (864-912 and the PD3/5s) originally had large flat-glass mirrors with thin pressed-steel bases, which proved unsatisfactory. The 1964 deliveries had mirrors of equal size, but with convex glasses in sturdy cast-alloy bases, being an enlarged version of those fitted up to 1960. This style quickly became universal throughout the fleet: 895 has one here. As it spread, you could see earlier ones on later buses –952 on p.11, 878 on p.22; 879 on p.25 has one of the unsatisfactory ones. Shortly before the CDs arrived, Southdown had reintroduced the practice of fitting a Southdown scroll plate to radiator grilles: the CDs had them from new and they eventually spread to all Marys. *(David G. Savage)*

and others on the cantrail. The only adjustment to the heating and ventilation arrangements on this batch was the disappearance of the small subsidiary ventilators above each of the front upper-deck windows. Once again the chassis remained unaltered.

913–952 (6913–6952CD)
(delivered October 1961–June 1962)

This was the only batch of Queen Marys to differ substantially from the basic chassis specification. Designated PD3/5, they had a completely automatic 'centrifugal' clutch, which began operating at approximately 500rpm and transmitted full engine torque at 750rpm, through an epicyclic 4-speed gearbox, with pneumatic control. All the driver had to do to change gear was move a small lever; the bus did the rest, all gears being air-operated through cylinders provided with restrictor valves. This made for a very comfortable ride, the Chief Engineer believed, asking drivers to observe carefully the instructions in the cab. Drivers found, however, that producing this smooth ride was slightly trickier than implied (see p.42).

There were new body features as well. All the batch had fluorescent saloon lighting – in the cantrails. They also had fluorescently illuminated advertisements – two cantrail ones in the lower saloon, and the main 'tweendecks one outside on the offside. The front indicator design changed again, and rubber wings were

introduced, being fitted to all subsequent deliveries. There were also some detail changes to the basic PD3 specification during the construction of this batch (see p.10).

The chief features to be noted in day-to-day operation of the semi-automatic Marys were: a distinctive clattering rattle of the centrifugal clutch when idling at stops or in traffic (despite anti-rattle screws) and a disinclination to move off on hills. This first came to light when buses would not depart from Copse Hill request stop in West Dene, Brighton while working on the 12 route diagram.

As a result of these failures, modifications like different fuel pumps and lower ratio diffs were tried and tests carried out with modified buses *fully laden* with Works staff. In this condition, regardless of modification, it was found that they would not even climb the hill with a rolling start. This became the subject of some discussion between Southdown and Leyland. A 5-speed box was put in 952. Southdown, whilst acknowledging that 952 performed better, decided to live with the others as they were and just not order any more. It abandoned plans to use them on Route 12 and swiftly reallocated some examples from Brighton. Some did however remain at Brighton and Eastbourne until the mid-sixties when it was decided to rationalise the situation and concentrate all the batch on the flatter terrain at the western end of the network. In 1966/67 the remaining eastern semi-automatics, bar 952, were involved in a large-scale swap for western CUFs.

BELOW LEFT: The purpose of this after-dark shot of a PD3/5 was to demonstrate the illuminated advertisement panel. It also illustrates the Southdown advert on the staircase panel, a feature introduced with this batch which became common throughout the Queen Mary fleet, one style superseding another as time went by.*(Southdown)* **BELOW RIGHT:** Last days of full rear blinds Worthing c.1963. Conductor access to the number box when in use was interesting. The upper rear seat was in three parts with the centre section hinged to allow access to the winding gear. The conductors had to use their head to hold the seat up while they wound and "needed tact when approaching a terminal, where a number change was required, at night and needed to lift the seat when it was in use by a courting couple!" 869 spent most of its career at Worthing but by 1969 was not a drivers' favourite, it being "hard to get a smooth gear-change" – despite the easiness of clutch adjustment (remove bellcover and protective panel beneath and there's the flywheel); some Marys always seemed less popular than others with drivers because of running maintenance issues (see pp 42-3).*(Jim Jones)*

Body Modifications 1963/64

In the summer of 1963, No. 906 appeared with a bulkhead window partially separating the driver and engine compartment from the platform. Communication with the driver from inside the bus was still possible, but now involved curling round the bulkhead window. The rationale behind this innovation does not appear to have been publicly stated but it seems likely that it was designed to restrict contact between the driver and anyone else in the bus and possibly also to reduce draughts in the cab and noise in the lower saloon. Whatever the reason for it, the innovation started to spread through the fleet and most subsequent versions featured larger windows than the prototype fitted to 906 – making contact with the driver difficult with the doors open.

Soon after the programme of bulkhead alteration began, a further modification to the PD3s started to appear. At the turn of the year, rear destination blinds fell rapidly out of use and their apertures were soon boarded over. The indicator box assemblies in the rear panelling then began to be inverted so that the still extant number boxes could be reached from the lower saloon. Many of the defunct destination apertures eventually acquired advertisements.

The 1964 deliveries had bulkhead windows and single rear boxes (for route numbers) fitted as standard. By the time they started to arrive none of the earlier Queen Marys was displaying rear destination details (848 was the last, operating thus until March 1964) and the programmes of bulkhead modification and rear display inversion were well under way. These programmes were carried through fairly rapidly, but as always there were a few stragglers; four non-inverteds for instance, were still around at the end of 1966. The longest-lived straggler seems to have been 938 which in early 1967 had still not received a bulkhead window, nor had her rear blind boxes inverted.

ABOVE LEFT: The negative of this photograph is filed under 840 in Southdown Enthusiasts Club records; it shows the original open bulkhead, before the aperture was partially glazed, from inside a Queen Mary. On p.18, the interior view of 362, which had a bulkhead window from new, shows how the earlier vehicles like 840 were modified and **ABOVE RIGHT** we see the interior of preserved 294 with your author in a fairly typical post-bulkhead window conductorial stance, although the most common curled-round-window one required the doors to be shut. *(Vincent Tweed)*

LEFT and BELOW: Changes to rear destination equipment: at Fareham 849 shows the initial blanking-off of the destination box while 934 alongside shows the inversion of the destination and number boxes which followed. 827 shows the original facilities. Subsequently advertisements appeared in the disused destination boxes; most of these were for Southdown but one or two others did appear. Lower saloon emergency doors on earlier cars were latched by weighted handles, which had to be lifted to open or close the door. QMs from 913 on had sprung pull-handles; these doors could be slammed shut. *(Michael Dryhurst/SEC)*

BELOW: By chance straggler 938 appeared in an ideal position to illustrate this piece when Passenger Transport went to photograph Pompey's buses only main shopping street in 1967. *(Passenger Transport)*

Queen Mary's Intimate Details   *Contributed by Bruce MacPhee*

You may already know all about the PD3, but for those who don't, here are a few details:

In 1927, Leyland launched Mr. Rackham's Titan TD1, which set the standard for double-deck bus chassis until the advent of the Atlantean (which set the standard for most of those since). We are not interested in the Atlantean (and neither were Southdown) and so will go on to say that the Titan PD3 was the direct descendant of the TD1. By now, we had oil-engines, (part) synchromesh gears and (marginally) better brakes, but there was no point in the Titan's history at which every component was different from those of the preceding model. In fact, one small item continued unchanged throughout – the sump plug! Other long-serving components were rear hub bearings and seals, used from TD3 to PD3 and beyond, and the PD3's steering box was first used on the PD1. PD3 brake shoes were the same size as those of the PD1, which might explain a lot!

Basic details of our PD3 chassis were as follows:

wheelbase:	18ft.6in.
engine:	O600. 6-cyl 4.8in. bore x 5.5in. stroke 9.8 litres, 125 bhp @ 1,800 rpm
clutch:	16¼ in. dry plate, mechanically operated, with four-stage adjustment for wear. (PD3/5: 16¼ in. dry plate, engagement by centrifugal force acting on rotating bob-weights)
gearbox:	4-speed constant-mesh, synchromesh 3rd and top. ratios: 4.95, 2.63, 1.59, 1:1. (PD3/5: Wilson direct-selection, air-operated epicyclic ratios: 4.28, 2.43, 1.59, 1:1)
final drive:	9in.-centres, underslung worm. ratio: 5.4:1
steering:	Marles cam and double roller. Ratio: 28.5:1
brakes:	direct air-pressure, type-16 diaphragm actuators manual adjustment.

("16" refers to the effective working area of the actuators. By comparison, Tiger Cubs and Leopards had 20's on the front axles and 24's on the rears; this might explain a bit more!)

Air-pressure systems were mostly of Westinghouse manufacture and chassis electrical equipment alternately CAV and Simms, the early batches and Panoramics having CAV.

Optional extras specified by Southdown were Tecalemit 'Syndromic' automatic chassis lubrication and Frankmann oil dispensers, where the engine sump was topped up automatically from a reserve tank via a float chamber. Smiths magnetic-particle fans were fitted to later cars. The fan was mounted on the water pump in the usual way but 'free-wheeled' until a pre-determined temperature was reached. Electrical coils were then energised, which magnetised iron filings contained within the unit. This locked the fan to the belt-driven hub of the pump, thus becoming driven at the same speed.

Standard items deleted were rear dropframe extensions (the body overhang was cantilevered), bonnet and mudguard components (PD3/4 and /5 were nominally 'exposed radiator' models) and on later chassis, brake back-plates (mostly being discarded on the earlier deliveries).

Minor differences divide the PD3/4s into two groups: 813-912 and the rest. 813-912 were fitted with d.c. generators (dynamos) and pneumatically governed C.A.V. 'N' type fuel pumps. Later cars had alternators and 'NNL' pumps with 'SF' mechanical governors. The changes occurred within the PD3/5 batch (exact numbers not known). Even when making these small distinctions, and leaving out the two specials, 257 and 315 (which were the same animal but with some vital organs in different places), PD3/4s delivered from 1964-67 formed the largest group of mechanically similar Southdown cars (143 total), closely run by Tiger Cubs 1000-1114, 620-644 (140). In contrast, the 113 PD2/12s had two different gearboxes, three diffs, three fuel pumps and two types of spring shackling arrangements – in different combinations. Also, the PSU3 Leopards must be divided into those with or without air suspension, in-line or DPA fuel pumps and UHV or conventional heating/cooling systems.

This might be an opportune time to examine the reasons for our PD3/5s' poor showing on hills. Comparing the 1st gear ratios from the foregoing, we can see that the figure for the PD3/5 is roughly 85% of the PD3/4's and, all other things being equal, this indicates that it would only have 85% of the other's tractive effort. When it came to re-starts, all other things were *not* equal; the centrifugal clutch had to be taken into account.

If a vehicle with conventional transmission is required to start on a steep hill, near the limit of its ability, the driver can increase the revs beyond the speed at which maximum torque is developed (900 rpm in the case of the O600), and slip the clutch as required. A centrifugal clutch begins to engage at a lower engine speed and will hold it there until the vehicle gets under way. As the engine cannot, therefore, reach the speed of maximum torque when starting from rest, it has less chance of getting under way in any case. Compounded with the higher 1st gear, this would have seriously reduced the PD3/5s' gradient ability.

952 had a 5-speed gearbox; this had the same ratios as the other PD3/5s, but with an additional crawler gear, so nothing would have defeated it. I have seen no mention of this option in Leyland spec sheets of the time, other than for the Worldmaster, so assume that this might have been a "one-off".

From a PD3/4 spec. sheet, I notice some conflicting details of the synchromesh box which might explain some of the confusion that surrounds this unit. I quote: "The gearbox is of the constant-mesh synchromesh type. All gears are in constant mesh with synchronising cones determining the correct relative speeds of the 4th and 3rd speed gears". So far, so good. It then continues, "Dog engagement is used for 1st and 2nd speed gears". This is again true, but it repeats what is already implied. If 1st and 2nd are in constant mesh, they *must* be engaged by dog-clutches. "All gears are ground and the 2nd, 3rd and 4th speed gears are in constant mesh, 2nd and 3rd speeds being helical gears to promote quietness in operation." Wait a minute! It said, just now, that *all* gears were in constant mesh! What about 1st? Is that *not* now in constant mesh and are they also implying that it is a straight-toothed gear?

There is no point looking at a service manual or other illustrated Leyland publications for guidance; even the latest ones show the early 'synchro 2nd' box that was superseded in 1955, while spare parts manuals, although providing line-drawings of everything from engines to drop-frames, somehow managed to ignore the gearbox! The world's largest commercial vehicle builder evidently did not see fit to provide accurate information about this major item, in large-scale production from 1955-67!

From experience, I can categorically state that in *all* of Southdown's PD3/4 gearboxes *all* gearwheels (except reverse) were helical and *all* forward ratios were engaged by dog-clutches, assisted by synchromesh for 3rd and top. (If, while stripping your PD3 gearbox on the kitchen table, you observe a large straight-toothed gearwheel on the mainshaft, this is *not* 1st gear; it is a wheel which meshes with the reverse pinion only). Here endeth the lesson.

.........and something about her immediate family

The Leyland O600 engine, introduced into the passenger range with the PD2 in 1947, proved to be an efficient and trouble-free unit and continued to serve with few modifications right to the end of Titan production.

Its newly designed gearbox had synchromesh engagement for 2nd, 3rd and top, being one of the first British heavy vehicles with this feature. Unfortunately, the gearbox was much less reliable than the engine and a large number of PD2s were off the road during 1948 due to this. As an interim measure, Leyland quickly adapted the PD1 constant-mesh box (popularly, but not strictly accurately, referred to as 'crash') to fit the O600 engine. This combination was fitted as an option to many PD2s from 1948-50, including the last 30 or so of Southdown's '300' PD2/1s.

From 1950, a modified synchromesh was apparently found to be satisfactory and this continued to be produced for the next few years. Southdown, however, took a long time to trust synchromesh after the initial troubles, so insisted on the PD1-type 'crash' box for their Titans delivered over the next few years, *i.e.* PD2/12s 700-764.

In 1954/5, Leyland redesigned the 1st and 2nd gear assembly of the synchro box and deleted the synchromesh from 2nd gear. This box, discussed at some length earlier, was fitted to Titans from then on; in Southdown's case: 765-812 and all PD3/4s.

The standard axle-ratio for post-war Titans was 5.4:1, there being one higher and one lower ratio as options but all of Southdown's were of this standard. As with most conventional double-deckers, the final-drive, or 'diff' was the underslung-worm type, where a hardened steel worm drove a phosphor-bronze wheel. This gave a lower transmission line than a spiral bevel type and was much stronger. Nevertheless, Leyland progressively increased the size of the unit to keep ahead of increasing weights, viz: TD1-2: 7in. centres; TD3-PD1: 7½ in; PD2: 8 or 9 in; PD3: 9in. In contrast, Guy kept to one size from Utilities up to the Mk.V: 8in.

If we were to put PD3 362 over the pit and PD2/1 362 over the one next to it, how much difference would we notice between these vehicles, delivered nearly twenty years apart? Under the bonnet, the O600 engines are virtually the same but one drives an exhauster for the vacuum brakes, the other has a compressor for air. The fuel pumps are different; the product of the 'sixties will not last as long as the old one but we can't tell that just by looking at it! On the other side of the engine, the new car has an alternator instead of a dynamo and unchanged, on top of the engine, is the familiar 'bomb' air-silencer.

Lifting the floor trap in the saloon, we note that the swinging-link flexible engine mountings and the gearboxes look identical. Not having the benefit of X-ray eyes, we will not see that the older car has synchromesh on 2nd gear, whereas the PD3 does not.

Underneath the PD2, a vacuum servo mounted on the chassis frame operates the rear brakes through rods and controls auxiliary servos on each swivel-axle for the fronts. The PD3 has four small brake chambers; one for each wheel, fed from the air reservoir through a brake valve mounted on the side of the chassis. We notice that the air reservoir is very small compared with the vacuum tank on the PD2. The PD3's unloader valve maintains the air pressure system at between 85-112 lbs./sq.in. Atmospheric pressure averages 14.68 lbs./sq.in., this pressure supporting a 29.9 inch column of mercury, vaguely remembered from the days when we dealt in old money. With the exhauster set to draw a maximum of 27 inches, the vacuum braked vehicle will have an (inverse) effective working pressure of only 13lbs./sq.in. Thus it can be seen that a large tank of nothing is equivalent to a much smaller tank of air.

A two piece propshaft takes the drive from the gearbox to the worm diff; the shaft is longer on the PD3 due to its longer wheelbase and the axle is of the same pattern but a heavier unit. The 'Syndromic' pump is driven from the propshaft via a belt; dozens of small-bore pipes radiate from it, taking oil to lubricate spring shackles, steering ball joints, king pins, etc. Greasing is done manually on the old '300' but not the shackles; these are steel and rubber 'Metalastiks' requiring no maintenance. We notice that both cars have the rubber-bushed stabiliser, bolted to a chassis cross-member and back axle, designed to eliminate rolling. I do not notice the silencer, so bang my head on it; then stumble from the pit, having said a rude word.

How much did the driver's place of work vary between the two? Very little, in fact; the structure designed for the PD1 continued virtually unchanged to the end of Titan production. For our two '300s', the steering box, change-speed, pedal-gear and handbrake were identical items and the square Smiths instruments were housed in the same panel. Although similar in appearance, the PD3's speedo was electric and at 20mph, it would read something like 20. The PD2/1 had a mechanical-magnetic instrument; at the same speed, it wavered from 0–40. Flanking the speedo, were an air-pressure gauge (vacuum on the PD2) and an engine oil-pressure gauge. This was always blanked-off at overhaul; what the driver couldn't see, he wouldn't worry about. Completing the comprehensive instrumentation was a "no-charge" warning light on the bulkhead-mounted control box; not exactly in the driver's line of vision!

By the 1960s, it was realised that drivers should be comfortable if they were to work safely and efficiently. Thus our PD3 had a seat which could be adjusted in vertical and horizontal planes independently; not too remarkable today but an improvement on the early post-war type which had a single adjustment: up and back to down and forward. With the early type, a tall driver had to choose between stooping to see under the wiper motor or driving with his knees in his ears; a short man could either see over the steering wheel or reach the pedals. The PD3 driver had a few extra switches to play with: an extra wiper, cab heater/demister, separate heaters for upper and lower saloons, buttons for the electric doors and a switch for the flashing direction indicators, which self-cancelled by means of a timer.

In the days when drivers gave, and others expected to see, hand signals, there was an often-quoted cynical remark that bus drivers only ever signalled with four inches of their fingers. Those who complained would not have known (nor would have cared!) that an 8ft. wide Titan chassis was essentially the same as the 7ft.6in, apart from the front axle and parts of the rear; thus the driver sat in the same place; 3in. extra on each side. This was particularly noticeable on 315 and those later, with their parallel cab sides - someone once asked me about the new bus where the driver sat in the middle! So, if you were ever annoyed by a four-inch signal, it might not have been the driver's fault; it could have been as much arm as he had to spare!

LEFT: 952, the only Southdown 'decker with a 5-speed gearbox at Glen Rise, Tongdean. It will soon descend Copse Hill, the ascent of which had embarrassed its sisters. When the other "one-leggers" were exiled to the West, 952 remained at Brighton, but seldom worked the 12 road in latter days. It carried its illuminated advert for Ford dealers Eastbourne Motors throughout, however and one wonders if they received much business from the residents of Worthing and Chichester while it made up Edward Street's contribution to the 31! *(Michael Dryhurst)*

953–977 (953–977CUF)
(delivered March–July 1964)

Possibly as a result of the experience with the semi-automatic CDs, 1964 deliveries saw a reversion to the PD3/4 chassis.

Body refinement continued however. The CUFs had bulkhead windows (slightly narrower than most retro-fitted ones) and number-only rear blind displays as standard. Compared to the previous batch, they had twice as many head and fog lamps, while their sidelights were of rectangular shape. Later arrivals sported single-pane fully-opening drivers' windscreens. The grab rails on either side of the doors were angled outwards to give easier access. Skirt panels were deeper between the axles, eliminating the need for lifeguard rails, but were upswept behind the back axle to prevent grounding on inclines and cambers. Sliding windows were altered to reduce rattle. The use of wood-patterned Formica was extended to saloon lining panels and seat-backs: this was a particularly imaginative and attractive response to the vandalism problem. The six smoke extractors on the roof were arranged more symmetrically from this batch on. The CUFs also featured illuminated advertisement panels on the offside like the preceding semi-automatics. Nos 973 and 977, at least, entered service with fixed glass in place of their upper-deck front push-out windows, but they were soon brought into line.

The fleet numbering system, which had been continuous for the Marys from 813 (coaches in the way having been renumbered), broke down after these vehicles, as a further batch numbering more than twenty-three would have passed number 1000, and no Southdown double-decker had a four-figure number. The next batch was numbered in the 4xx-series, taking over the fleet numbers of the Guy 'Arab' Utilities that they had come to replace.

400–424 (400–424DCD)
(delivered March–June 1964)

The DCDs were delivered concurrently with the CUFs and were identical to them except for various features concerning the upper deck. The DCDs were convertible open-toppers and had rather specialised upper-decks designed to cope with lengthy exposure to the atmosphere and especially with a sudden downpour while they were operating unroofed. The seats upstairs were trimmed with water-repellent 'Everflex' material, the seat-backs and lining panels were colour-impregnated fibreglass and the blind box panelling was unpainted aluminium. There were drain-holes in the floor which ejected water through outlets over the lower deck windows and, via a surge tank in the cab roof, through pipes down the front corners; a roller-blind was available at the top of the stairs to protect the platform. Their roofs were also different, having squarer contours to retain overall height despite the joining strip and inside were double-skinned throughout with a cream coloured plastic known as Darvic forming the interior layer. The CUFs were the last Marys to have single-skin domes, two layers of metal for the main roof and painted ceilings: all the later Marys had a plastic Darvic 'skin' throughout the inside like the DCDs.

A sophisticated process of roof removal and storage was introduced with these vehicles. When operating in open-top form they were fitted with front and rear windshields and perimeter guard-rails on the upper-deck. When operating closed top, they became more-or-less standard Queen Marys but were distinguishable by their roof contours, the joining strip between roof and body (which always created the impression of a higher window level in the upper saloon) and the all-weather fittings on the upper-deck which made them a little more spartan there than most Southdown buses: downstairs of course there was the normal Southdown moquette luxury; the overhanging tree disclaimer also looked odd when they were operating roofed. Another clue was their advertless 'tweendecks panelling: as open-toppers they carried boards advertising the Beachy Head, Devil's Dyke or Hayling Island routes, as appropriate, and to avoid compromising these they carried no external advertisements on the upper deck. Presumably the same reasoning lay behind them not having illuminated advertisement panels. Because of their earlier delivery, more of this batch than of the CUFs had split windscreens. Stage carriage use of open-tops waned almost from the moment of the DCDs' introduction, but their convertibility continued to be an asset throughout their long careers.

425–429 (BUF425–429C)
(delivered May–June 1965)

In 1965, the convertible stock was augmented by the delivery of five vehicles. They were identical to the DCDs except for the 1965 innovations of quarter-lights, an extra Pearlescent panel and different seat moquette pattern (downstairs). See over for further details.

TOP LEFT: Reeking of new 'Everflex' No 413, seen at Worthing Pier, was Brighton's contribution to route 102 on Sunday 7th June 1964 only days after she had entered service. The overhanging tree disclaimer is visible. **TOP RIGHT:** In 1964 clapping eyes on a bus for the first time was very important to us spotters: known as 'copping' it entitled the vehicle to be underlined in our Ian Allan *abc*. In autumn 1964, I was close to having underlined the entire Southdown fleet and tension was mounting as the needs list narrowed to single figures. The double-deck part of that list had been increased dramatically earlier in the year by the arrival of the 50 new QMs and it was touch-and-go all summer whether the last double-decker would be one of them or some recalcitrant and elusive backloader. As it turned out, it was 409 and I photographed it to celebrate the sighting in Brighton's Edward Street garage on 19th September. **ABOVE:** At Whitsun 1964 Eastbourne's convertible Queen Marys ran alongside the Guy Arab utilities they were bought to replace – the Guys had been retained through the winter to ensure adequate cover for Derby Day in the event of any late arrivals amongst the DCDs and, as it turned out, some of them did make one last trek to Epsom Downs that summer before disposal. This picture was taken at Beachy Head. *(Jim Jones)*

BELOW: 424 was to remain in continuous use with Southdown and its successors for 38 years so this picture of her at Northern Counties when brand new in 1964 is of particular interest. Some DCDs were delivered with fixed glass at the front of the upper deck like 973 and 977. *(C. B. Golding)* **RIGHT:** 23 years into her Southdown career, she went to the Isle of Wight for the day. *(Brian Jackson)*

250–256/258–284 (BUF250–256/258–284C) (delivered March–June 1965)

This batch of PD3/4s started the new number series which had been inevitable since 977 got so near to the single-deck only area beyond 999. They slipped into the fleet unheralded in the Southdown house magazine, the only Marys so to do. Body modifications continued. The BUF-Cs saw the revival of experiments with ventilation: screw-out quarter-lights were fitted in all rear side-windows, and these vehicles also had a push-up roof vent in the rear dome. A revised seat moquette pattern, known as 'Cirrus', was introduced on the BUF-Cs. Other features were an extra Pearlescent panel in the roof (making three) and single-pane windscreens on all of them; they did not have illuminated advertisement panels. All the Marys were equipped and finished to Southdown's customary high standard, but from the BUF-Cs onwards the Company and Northern Counties really surpassed themselves. The driver of 278's second owner spent most of the Author's 1980 visit expressing amazement that a vehicle of such quality was ever intended for ordinary stage operation.

SEQUENCE LEFT: Using only the materials provided, convert this open-top bus into a closed top bus! On your marks . . . Queen Mary 425 in Portslade Works on Monday 15th June 1970, having attended The Derby, is converted to its roofed state for the rest of the summer and from a route 13 to an 000. *(Richard Maryan)*

BELOW: The new 'Cirrus' seat moquette can be seen in this view of 258 which was bouncing towards Brighton on a post-morning-peak-lull route 10 journey on 6th February 1970.

BOTTOM: Quite new 271 at Portsmouth. *(Roger G. Funnel)*

ABOVE LEFT: No. 257 in the eccentric fuelling position referred to in the text, during the summer of 1966. **ABOVE RIGHT:** Almost new in early 1966 on her first regular duty –on the 1/ 2 road. Whereas the sides of previous Queen Marys tapered in from the bulkhead to the front panels,the width of the windscreen necessitated this section of 257 remaining parallel. The front part of the top deck was also squarer and its front windows did not have the push-out vents that had been standard from 843.

Experimental bus registered BUF257C (delivered October 1965)

The last of the BUF-Cs to arrive turned out to be a little different from the rest of the batch. Her most obvious eccentricity was a wrap-round windscreen. She was able to have this because her radiator had been resited . . . and therein lay her difference.

She had a Clayton 'COMPAS' automatic heating and ventilating system. The radiator was removed from its normal position and placed under the stairs where it could act as a heat exchanger; the appropriate header tank was mounted above it. A hydraulic pump, belt driven on the engine, drove a reversible fan below the heat exchanger. At a water temperature of 140°F the fan came into operation and depending on the lower saloon thermostat, hot air was either blown in or out of the ducts built into the offside panels. The system functioned automatically, maintaining a constant temperature in 257 regardless of outside conditions. The temperature in the cab was controllable by the driver, using the hot water tap, through the two-speed heater and demister gear. There were also small ventilators above the windscreen.

All opening windows were locked shut apart from the rear quarter-lights and the push-up one in the roof. The front dome ventilator completed the fresh air provisions.

Soon after her arrival it became apparent that 257's experimental apparatus was a lot more effective at heating than ventilating the bus, and this led to the removal of the passenger seat nearest the radiator, reducing her capacity from 67 to 65, and the unlocking of her sliding windows; subsequently some of them were changed to Rotovents.

This, however, was only the start of it. Staff at Worthing Garage, where she spent most of her Southdown career, remembered her with a mixture of amusement and affection, recalling the continual battle to stop her boiling. At one point charcoal blocks were apparently put round the header tank but all was to no avail. To make matters worse, the engine's overheat warning buzzer overreacted to the problem to such an extent that drivers were eventually told to ignore it, as they tried to ignore the rush of hot air from the radiator which passed through the cab every time the brakes were applied.

Worthing drivers appreciated the better vision afforded by her windscreen, but spoke wryly of another of her eccentricities—the position of her heating apparatus dictated the fuel tank being sited anomalously on the nearside. This meant that she confounded the refuelling parade every evening by needing to turn round in the garage and come back facing the wrong way. Occasionally drivers would forget and sit there wrong side to pump, until challenged by the fueller.

From the passengers' and conductor's point of view she was a travelling Turkish bath, but at least the passengers were given some chance of coming to terms with her by the predictability of her daily behaviour. For the early part of her career, 257 was allocated one specific duty, Brighton Hove & District-style and operated it every day; those with strong feelings about tropical temperatures could therefore avoid her or seek her out, according to choice. One rather foolish young enthusiast presumed that such route allocation was so that her whereabouts were always known and assistance could be dispatched swiftly if she blew up, but it was probably just to keep one variable constant in the experiment she represented. During the time she was pottering about on Routes 5 and 6, your Author regularly joined her to go home from school at lunchtime; much merriment was occasioned by crews dashing off – into even sub-zero temperatures – gasping for air, as soon as she had stopped at her Durrington terminus. One always appreciated her balmy atmosphere on boarding, but was equally pleased to get off 10 minutes later.

LEFT: 257's rear view was the same as that of the rest of the batch – like 276 here. Horizontally split skirt panels aft of the back axle were a feature from 1965 and a new style of tail lamp (with separate direction indicator and stop/tail with chrome surround) was fitted for this year only. Compare these with the previous type (combined direction indicator and stop/tail with chrome surround) on p.9 and those on 1966/7 deliveries (combined but larger and with no surround) as displayed by 307 on p.44. One or two early Marys had the lights in a lower position (see 827 p.9) *(E. G. Haynes)*

ABOVE: One Sunday, soon after delivery, 296 is seen at Pool Valley whilst working a special 23 service to St Francis Hospital, Haywards Heath. This view clearly shows the tubular "Rotovents" in the side-windows, previous batches of Queen Marys having had "top-sliders". 296's upper blind, wound to the end where the white blank begins to show, is marked AD/62. "A" denotes Brighton area, "D" is (ultimate) Destination, 62 is the year of its compilation. Presumably, the lower blind is an AV/62 ("via" blind). D blind displays were 41"x5", Vs 41"x8". In the background are 257 and 401, the former on her regular route 9 working and the latter on the Arundel open-top service, reputed to be the longest open-top service in the world. *(SEC)*

285-314 (FCD285-314D)
(delivered March-November 1966)

The FCD-Ds were PD3/4s and showed no obvious signs of 257 influence, although they did incorporate further advances in heating and ventilation technique. Their main distinguishing feature was their possession of 'Rotovent' ventilators. Southdown used them because of the advantage of freshly introduced air being directed upwards in the vehicle, rather than blasting passengers in the face. Only four were fitted on each side – a considerable reduction on the seven sliders that had been standard since the VUFs. The now familiar dome ventilator was however retained, as were the push-out windows at the front of the upper saloon, and the driver's nearside front push-out; the quarter-lights and roof vent, introduced on the BUF-Cs, were also kept: the latter was, however, set further back on this batch. Additional consideration of heating and ventilation resulted in re-siting all controls in the driver's cab; the driver had always controlled the booster fans but from 285 onwards the taps for the hot water to the heater units were also under their control – by means of sliding levers in the front of the cab.

Further thoughts on driver comfort resulted in a couple of other minor innovations: better siting of screen wiper controls – on the door control panel – and painting of the cab instrument surfaces in matt green to reduce glare. In addition, to make garage staffs' jobs easier, the FCD-Ds introduced a full-depth grille panel which allowed easier access to the engine from the front. The vehicles had the same attractive interior finish as the BUF-Cs, with green 'Cirrus' patterned moquette seats and wood patterned Formica (sometimes referred to as Warerite) as seat backs and saloon lining.

Experimental bus, registered GUF250D
(delivered October 1966)

A year after 257 burst upon the scene, and after delivery of the fairly conventional FCD-Ds, another out-of-the-ordinary Mary, 315, appeared. Although part of the 1967 batch, she turned up early equipped with another experimental heating and ventilation system, after appearing at the 1966 Commercial Motor Show as Northern Counties' chief exhibit.

The main body structure of the last batch used components common with the latest design for rear-engined chassis with big side windows, but the fine detail was the same as on the other post-1965 batches. A transcription of the Show Catalogue will illuminate further: 'The construction of the body is, as Northern Counties standard, all-metal framed. Body length: 29ft 11½in; body width: 8ft 0in; height overall: 14ft 7in; seating capacity: 69. Indicator and route gears supplied by Reeves Engineering Company Ltd. Curved windscreens are fitted in the lower saloon, and curved windows in the front of the upper saloon. The cab signalling window is made by Awdest Engineering Company and the hinged rear ventilating windows are supplied by Auster Limited. No sliding windows are used, all the glass being of Triplex manufacture. The electrically operated double-folding entrance doors are supplied by Deans and Lightalloys. Overtons gears are used for the emergency door

BELOW: Shortly after entering service, 315 was observed getting wet in the Old Steine on Saturday 12th November 1966. Her body design represented a leap in the steadily-evolving Queen Mary style. 315 had a BET standard windscreen similar to 257 and also a BET single-deck standard rear screen at the front upstairs which meant, like 257, parallel sides the length of the bus. The back was also squarer and more upright than previous Marys

and the upper saloon rear emergency window. The floor covering in both saloons is Green Treadmaster, Ferodo Green Filled Treads and Nosings being used on the stairs. The Accles & Pollock tubular seat frames with stainless steel top rails are trimmed in a combination of Cirrus and Holdsworth moquette. The cushion fillings are Dunlopillo and rubberised hair is used for the squab fillings. On the seat backs Burmese Teak Warerite is bonded to the squab boards. The fluorescent lighting in the saloons is by means of Philips Transistors and B.M.A.C. Diffusers with Philips Tubes. C.A.V. equipment used on the body includes WS 1 windscreen wipers, rear stop and tail unit flasher lamps. Cream Darvic bonded to 20G aluminium is used for lining the ceilings of both saloons. Interior window finishes are in Darvic. Interior lining panels are covered with Warerite. Paint supplied by Blundell Spence is used for the body exterior. Clayton 'COMPAS' type Heating and Ventilating System is installed with Austers Rotovents. Stainless steel handrails are fitted throughout.'

An empty Coke can was also installed on the back seat upstairs after a group of not yet too socially-aware young bus enthusiasts had lunch on her on Saturday 24th September 1966. It is interesting to note that, building on the experience with 257, Mary 315's automatic heating and ventilating system included some opening windows; as with all deliveries at this period, they were Rotovents. She was not nearly as notorious as 257, but nonetheless the last of such major heating and ventilating experiments.

Body Modifications 1966

Not unconnected with the heating and ventilation experiments incorporated in 257, the FCD-Ds and 315 were the modifications made at the same time to some earlier Marys. During 1966 Nos 909, 943, 952, 955 and 250 were fitted with experimental dome ventilators; the last two received imposing-looking ducts, whilst the first three acquired Rotovent devices – 315 also subsequently received one of these, possibly from 952, as she lost hers. All the others retained these modifications for the rest of their careers and 955 was, additionally, temporarily equipped with some Rotovent windows during 1966.

346–369 (HCD346–369E)
(delivered February – July 1967)

The last Queen Marys (PD3/4s again) were the 'Panoramics'. The new numbering system, which started with 250, encountered difficulties here when it was not possible to book registration numbers coinciding with fleet numbers 316–339; to get matching numbers it was decided to leave this little group isolated from its fellows and the other member of the batch (315) as 346–369.

Their body design was similar to 315's but featured standard heating and ventilation, which meant the return of the radiator to the front and, therefore, a more traditional lower deck front end. Despite their conventional heating and ventilating system, the HCD-Es had fewer opening windows than 315: they had the same arrangements as the Show exhibit, but without the quarter-lights. In the cab, special attention was paid to the heating and to additional insulation in the bonnet top for noise suppression. The dash panel ventilator, which had been omitted on 257, the FCD-Ds, and 315, reappeared.

As a sign of the straitened times in which they were entering service the cream/green interface below the windscreen no longer took the form of a graceful curve, following the windscreen contours, but was a straight line.

Rare pictures of Panoramics in as-delivered condition:

LEFT: In May 1967, No 369 is seen at Pool Valley, accompanied by Park Royal bodied Guy (PUF) and Leyland (OCD) backloaders and semi-automatic Mary 917. Unlike the other Queen Mary batches, each door-leaf on the Panoramics had a single pane of glass.*(SEC)*

BELOW: At Eastbourne on 22nd April 1967, 365 is seen also with a PUF-registered Guy in attendance.

LEFT: Some years later some convertibles and 353 together illustrate the 1967 body modifications – maybe 353 actually has 406's window. The convertibles show the two types of opening windscreen with which this batch was delivered, and we can also see a later type of mirror; of the same construction as the 1964 type, but a slightly different shape. Experiments with earlier Marys aimed at giving the Panoramics lower fronts like 257 and 315 were not a success. There were two guinea-pigs (late 800s, W or C buses) - one had a Leopard radiator, the other had a cut-down PD3 one.(see p.42)

Body Modifications 1967

Despite the attention given to the Marys' heating and ventilating systems over the previous nine years, things were still not quite right on this last batch and in the autumn of their delivery year they received a modification: their front dome ventilators were replaced by push-out windows. These came from the offside upstairs front windows of the convertibles, which subsequently had a slightly piratical look when roofed. The transfer process was completed swiftly, and all the convertibles lost their windows, for the sake of uniformity, even though six need not have done. The gaps on the convertibles were initially filled with perspex; eventually one-piece glass windows were fitted. Two Panoramics, 357 and 356, subsequently reverted to more conventional dome ventilators (by 7/74 and 2/79 respectively) – this was possibly due to the old problem of draughts.

Final Flourish

The body style of the 1967 batch was the last development of the Queen Mary idea. No more double-deckers entered the fleet until 1970. Already by the time the HCD-Es entered service, large numbers of pay-as-you-enter single-deckers were being purchased and, soon after, government grants for one-man-operable double-deckers, and attendant difficulties in obtaining traditional chassis, finally persuaded Southdown to take the plunge with the rear-engined designs it had mistrusted for so long.

Body Modifications 1968

At about this time, the brown moquette upholstery of the TCDs began to look a bit dated and certain members of the batch appeared with elements of green interior trim. One of them, 823, apparently also appeared with painted rather than fabric covered lining-panels, but this is believed to have been an isolated incident.

Body Modifications 1972 and after

In the early seventies, many of the CUFs, Convertibles, and BUF-Cs were fitted with the FCD-D/Panoramic-style full-depth grille panels, and all surviving Marys received windscreen washers, to comply with the legal requirement introduced in 1972. Such other alterations as were made to members of all the batches most of which were of a very minor nature, are detailed at the appropriate places in the text. Detail modifications to, and variations represented by, individual vehicles were myriad and cannot all be listed, but a study of the photos will reveal much. Start with mirrors!

BELOW LEFT and RIGHT: These interior views were taken on 1st September 1979 near the end of the Panoramics' career; facing forward on 362 and backwards on 355. Most of the PD3s had interior numbers (in the lower deck). Unlike earlier deckers (and the TCDs at least initially), these were not gold transfers similar to the exterior ones but white plates made of plastic with the number in green. Convertibles alone had upstairs ones; these were gold transfers affixed to the dome ventilator.

Early Queen Mary Days

ABOVE: A late arrival, 815, at Hilsea shortly after entering service; she has the swiftly-introduced modifications of cream staircase panel, front indicator position and filler cap flap. *(SEC)*

Sussex is a beautiful county of rolling green downland and bracing sea air. Most of its population lives along the coast, which is largely urbanised, while the lighter inland settlement is concentrated along the river valleys.

In the post-war decades, there was a noticeable peak in Southdown's passenger figures in the summer due to the holiday trade, but sufficient resident population to justify a year-round intensive service to take them to work, school, shops, play, on visits etc. Because the Sussex

LEFT: A very early colour picture of a Queen Mary showing new 832, one of Brighton's first (all the TCD batch went to Pompey); check out the other classic delights in this Old Steine view: the Regent behind is Corporation HUF88 of 1947 and on the other side are trolleys and a Southdown Royal Tiger. *(Phil Tatt)*

ABOVE: No 836 negotiating floods in Southsea shortly after delivery. *(Southdown)*   BELOW: It must be 1959 with 837 there and 826 still has her indicator in its original position; it is believed the first five delivered had a number of differences like indicators as here, lower rear lights and no conductor's cupboard under the stairs – others are listed on p.6.   *(Michael Dryhurst)* BELOW RIGHT: Early Brighton days: VUFs on the Bevendean services. *(SEC)*

coast is an extremely popular area for retirement, an unusually high proportion of Southdown passengers were senior citizens. In 1958, the bulk of Southdown's services were operated by double-deckers with conductors, with a few lightly-used routes run by single deckers, some OMO. These operations were based on five centres which, reflecting the population distribution, were all in the south. From west to east they were: Portsmouth (actually in east Hampshire), Chichester, Worthing, Brighton and Eastbourne.

Most of the early Queen Marys were allocated to and operated in and around Portsmouth. At that time the city was a rather dreary maze of Victorian terraced houses – punctuated by lingering wartime bomb-sites – crammed onto Portsea Island with few links to the mainland. A post-war malaise was beginning to obscure the fact that Portsmouth was a city with a proud history, inseparable from that of Britain and the maritime strength on which Britain's power had depended, and with much splendour to be seen in and around her dockyard. This malaise resulted from a decline in Portsmouth's fortunes as she and the Navy mirrored Britain's changed and reduced role in the world.

This was, however, not without its benefits for bus operators, because it meant that Portsmouth did not share so fully in the South's general post-war affluence, with its increase in car and TV ownership (which latter was reducing evening traffic), and buses remained full; Southdown and the Corporation with which it had an operating agreement, ran very busy and profitable services in and out of the city. It was to these services that the first Queen Marys were allocated. The operating agreement precluded any protective fares, or restricted travel arrangements; thus any passenger could make any journey on either operator's bus.

For many years there had been a strict hierarchy of operations at Southdown's western extremity. New buses went onto the London Road routes; middle-aged machines covered the Havant Road services; and the old bangers worked the Fareham Road. Something of a stir was caused, therefore, when the TCDs were placed amongst the Fareham Road veterans – presumably this was where most duplicates could be saved (see Alan Lambert on p.21). The Fareham Road services as the name suggests, went to Fareham via one of two routes through Portchester, and periodically on to Warsash, the western end of Southdown stage carriage activity.

It seems that the original decision was to allocate the bulk of the second batch to Brighton, but the immediate loan of 830, 833, 836 and 837 to Portsmouth thwarted this plan. These buses were soon afterwards transferred officially to the depot, which thus ended up with over half the batch. Most VUFs also started work on the Fareham Road.

Brighton was thus left with a mere six VUFs, and their first duties were on the Bevendean services. Three XUFs – 843, 859, 861 – went to Brighton and the rest to Portsmouth; at both places they were initially allocated to the same routes as the TCDs and VUFs.

The first PD3s come to Portsmouth

Contributed by Alan Lambert

There was great excitement at Portsmouth depot early in 1958 when the Area Manager was advised that some new buses were being allocated to the depot. Not normally, perhaps, something to cause excitement, but these buses were going to be different. To start with they were 30 feet long (instead of 27), seated 69 passengers (instead of 54) and had front entrances. However, it was expected that because of their larger seating capacity, it would be possible to reduce the number of duplicate buses provided at peak periods.

Brighton and Portsmouth depots both carried a large number of vehicles that were used solely at peak times for schools, works services and stage-carriage reliefs. In Portsmouth there were some 50 of these buses, most of which were double deck but did include seven Royal Tiger saloons and of this total about eight were solely dedicated to workers at the Dockyard in the afternoons. In the mornings all buses before 9.00 a.m. ran round the 'Dockyard Wall' instead of Commercial Road and so dedicated reliefs were not required for the 'Dockys' to get to work.

The question was then, which routes to put them on? The routes out of Portsmouth were divided into three groups: Havant Road (excluding 31 which stood on its own), London Road (or 'over the hill') and Fareham Road (service 45). The Havant Road was really unsuitable, as all the routes inter-worked and at some point one would probably end up on the narrow roads round Northney on Hayling Island. The London Road was a possibility, but took a lot of vehicles, all interworked, leaving the Fareham Road which took 17 buses. Thus it was that 18 of these new PD3s were allocated to Portsmouth.

We did some surveys on the 45 reliefs and concluded that there probably could be some savings, in the peak. However deliveries were slow and although the first five entered service in July, only seven had been delivered by September when it was decided to make a reduction in the off peak frequency whilst retaining the same number of seats per hour by using larger buses. In the summer there had been eight buses per hour from Portsmouth to Fareham, but in September this was reduced to six per hour to Fareham, with two per hour turning 'short' at Cornaway Lane. This had the effect of saving one bus. In November the frequency was reduced again by removing the Cornaway Lane 'shorts' and this frequency of six per hour remained for many years, except in the summer high peak when it returned to eight per hour for a few months. It was actually not until early in 1959 that all eighteen buses were in service.

The buses themselves were unlike anything that had been seen previously. The chassis was broadly similar to the last batch of PD2/12 chassis that had gone before but were longer. The bodies, however, were by Northern Counties which was a bit of a surprise as the only Northern Counties bodies the Company had purchased recently were ten fitted to Leyland PD2/12 chassis in 1953. These latter vehicles were not very popular with crews as they were quite light and tended to bounce and rattle. However the new PD3's were much heavier and produced a much more solid ride. The drivers cab was full width and as there was no bulkhead window a piece of perspex was fitted behind the driver to deflect draughts but as some of the engine noise was dissipated into the saloon it was quieter for the driver. The intention was that as the conductor had many more fares to collect the loading and unloading would be under the control of the driver and he needed to be able to communicate with the passengers. The radiator cap was situated below the windscreen and was inset into the bodywork, as the radiator itself was hidden behind the full front, which had a false radiator grille. They were also fitted with a standard destination display with triple route number box above at both front and rear. These were fitted with a periscope to help the crews select the right display. In order for the conductor to change the rear number box he had to remove part of the back seat upstairs!

Several modifications happened fairly quickly. First the perspex screens and the periscopes were removed. Other changes meant that the radiator filler cap was hidden behind a flap and the flashing indicators were moved down to the front panels below the window line. Eventually the rear destination box was panelled out and inverted so that the numbers could be changed from downstairs! As successive deliveries were made, they gradually spread to other routes and more modifications were made, but it is often forgotten that it was Portsmouth depot who pioneered their introduction.

And finally, 'J.M.W.' writing in 1960 in the staff magazine 'Tweenus' that 'Conducting is Fun' claimed that 'the latest mobile blocks of flats' were known as 'Queen Marys' in Pompey. This came as a surprise to the staff at Portsmouth, but as it was quite obvious that the writer came from Brighton, it explained everything! This seems to have been the first reference to the nickname, but even so it was many years before it came into general use.

Whence Queen Mary?

I thought it was clear. Soon after they arrived, Pompey crews nicknamed them Queen Marys because of their anomalously large size. But Alan queries this and so does Mr. A Young who conducted out of Eastbourne until 1965 and tells me that the name was unknown there. It had definitely reached Worthing by 1970 - I think probably earlier - and was commonplace in Brighton when I was conducting in 1973/4 ("please can we have a Queen Mary?, they're much easier to conduct"). But it now seems that the contention that they were always known to their crews as QMs needs some fine tuning - although research confirms that the nickname is now pretty universal and the way things are going they may outlast all similarly named royal personages, ships and ECW LWL coaches to puzzle archaeologists in times to come with the origin of their soubriquet.

JMW said in 'Conducting is Fun' that the "latest mobile blocks of flats, known in Pompey as Queen Marys, have simply nowhere to crawl out out of the way when all fares collected, you want to be alone" (stand behind the driver, it goes on, and the steady unblinking gaze of the entire lower saloon will sooner or later give you a shocking inferiority complex no matter how you glare back). Perhaps here in that article we are actually looking at the origin of the nickname.   JO

BELOW: The Queen Marys' earliest known Southdown ancestor! The unique double-deck coach of 1950. *(Southdown)*

Queen Marys in their heyday the Swinging Sixties

The sixties were years of Queen Mary abundance throughout the network, when they were fully occupied on trunk services and generally extending their sphere of operations at the expense of backloaders. New batches arrived more or less annually, and as hair got longer and skirts got shorter, Marys became more plentiful, and took over more of Southdown's busy services, plus one or two less busy ones.

As we have already seen, at Portsmouth a hierarchy of allocation tended to operate. This was true of all garages; as new buses arrived everything else was downgraded and the oldest of all became surplus to requirements and were withdrawn for eventual sale. As we have also noticed, the placings of routes in these hierarchies were not absolute. Nonetheless, hierarchies are a helpful concept in getting some idea of what was going on as the Marys were delivered. Basically, new buses went on the busiest services—those that carried the most passengers—as they were best able to cope with the heaviest loads, but sometimes other considerations modified this.

TOP: The farthest point reached on the London Road was Petersfield, while other services peeled off all the way up it to terminate at such places as Waterlooville, Hambledon, World's End, Droxford, Horndean, Catherington and Clanfield. Brand new 970 is seen here bound for Catherington (Glamorgan Road) – the blinds have been arranged in the form of a brainteaser. You can trace the lineage of the Queen Mary body from 762 behind, through 882 at the back to 970. South Parade Pier Southsea. *(SEC)*

LEFT: Another terminus for London Road buses was picturesque Hambledon, birthplace of cricket where 878 was officially photographed in the summer of 1964. Certain services including the 139 did not run right through Portsea Island to South Parade Pier in Southsea but terminated instead at the Southdown garage near the Guildhall. *(Southdown)*

Demonstrators appeared periodically during the Queen Mary ascendancy, most of them being front engined types as one would have expected but none proved anything for the Queen Marys to worry about. 816 is nonetheless affronted to find AEC Renown 7552MX occupying the London Road stand at South Parade Pier in the autumn of 1963. *(T. V. Runnacles)*

Irrespective of the duties to which they were assigned, the Marys showed little tendency to change garages during the sixties (except for swaps connected with the PD3/5s) – they went somewhere and stayed there, and the backloaders displaced particularly the oldest examples, became involved in an increasingly frantic game of 'musical chairs' around garages in search of work. To study this in more detail we shall now take a journey across Southdown-land in the sixties eastwards from the Marys' first base at Portsmouth.

Sixties:Portsmouth

As already stated, operations in the Portsmouth area were busy and organised around three main traffic arteries: the Fareham Road, the London Road and the Havant Road. Buses on all three roads entered and left Portsea Island by means of the main Portsbridge; between there and Southsea, Portsmouth's seaside resort at the southern end of the island, they ran in droves via one of two routes: half of them went by way of Commercial Road and the Guildhall and the remainder went through Fratton. Between North End and Portsbridge all services used the same stretch of road, and these two miles were a Queen Mary enthusiast's paradise for most of the sixties.

The London Road

We covered the Fareham Road on the previous pages, so attention can be turned to the London Road group of services. Because of the surprise route allocation of most of the TCDs, VUFs and XUFs, this was not the first area of operation of Portsmouth Marys, as one might have expected. In fact, despite one or two odd early workings, it and the Havant Road were really joint second, for as Portsmouth's first CDs started to follow former practice and appear on the A3, other garages began to put their members of the batch onto Service 31. The London Road soon made up for its late start, however, and was served almost entirely by Marys throughout the sixties.

Amongst the trunk duties, the London Road diagram featured various satellite services worked by Queen Marys and their crews *e.g* Petersfield local service 142, or the hourly Clanfield trip which in late sixties' winters only worked between there and Snell's Corner on the A3, connecting at that point with northbound and southbound 42s. Density of population around the A3 allowed Portsmouth's London Road operations to be the Marys' only sustained success at inland penetration whilst they were with Southdown.

Between North End and Portsbridge all services used the same stretch of road, and these two miles were a Queen Mary enthusiast's paradise for most of the sixties. These pictures illustrate this except the **BOTTOM LEFT** which portrays: Connections will be made... The Snell's Corner rendezvous. The Clanfield short waited for the southbound 42 then crossed over the A3 to meet the upbound before heading for Clanfield.

Photo: John Allpress

RIGHT: Soon after delivery, 846 was photographed performing a 46 duty. (Alan Lambert)

BELOW: 299 pauses outside Hilsea in November 1969 after working an evening peak special duty.

BELOW CENTRE: Illustrating Southsea–Hayling Mary activity is 860, passing through Havant, Hayling-bound, on Saturday 18th February 1967, while 974 waits at the next stand pretending to be a single-decker on route 67.

An occasional diversion for Portsmouth Queen Marys was a spell of 'mileage balancing' within the joint operating agreement. Thus, 848 worked on Corporation route 3/4 at the beginning of 1964 and this special rostering caused her to be missed in the rear screen removal programme and become the last Mary able to give back destination details. Runs scheduled for open-top buses at Portsmouth required three vehicles – initial Queen Mary convertibles were 408, 415 and 423 – and involved only the service along the southern shore of Hayling Island. The main route to Hayling Island is a Havant Road route and to that artery we now turn.

The Havant Road

The Havant Road group of routes comprised the interworking services to Hayling Island and Westbourne – plus the separate famous marathon 31 route to Brighton. Queen Marys operated all of them in the sixties. In addition, Havant itself, was quite a centre of Mary activity, boasting various local services provided by them. The most significant of these local Havant services were those linking the town with the huge Portsmouth 'resettlement' estate of Leigh Park to the north; Corporation buses – Atlanteans from 1963 – connected it with the city itself. The Havant–Leigh Park services were the 46 and 68 – the latter actually progressed from one-man-operated single-deckers to PD3s during the sixties. Another local service worked by Queen Marys was the 49 between Emsworth and Waterlooville, most journeys on which spurned Emsworth as a terminus in favour of Havant; this route eventually interworked with the 68.

Finally, locally, there were the Havant–Hayling services. These were connected with the Southsea–Hayling service, for until 1965 the Southsea–Hayling diagram included them as well as journeys on the 43 route between Southsea and Westbourne; the 43s combined with the through Southsea–Hayling buses to give an even headway on the Southsea–Havant section. After 1965 the Havant–Hayling journeys more or less disappeared; the Havant–Southsea headway was maintained but all journeys were numbered as though they were Hayling services and erstwhile 43 trips terminated at Havant, the 43 surviving as a one-man-operated rump between Havant and Westbourne. In peak periods the Southsea–Havant frequency applied right through to Hayling Island and back. This set of alterations clearly demonstrates the masterly maintenance of regular headways and connections practised by Southdown in any route restructuring exercise.

The other Havant Road service was of course, service 31, the 56-mile, largely urbanised route between Portsmouth and Brighton, which boasted a 15-minute headway for much of its length; it was however half-hourly between Bognor and Littlehampton for most of the sixties, and short-workings were therefore found at either end. This route is somewhat difficult to deal with, as it traversed four of the operating areas and was worked by buses from garages in all of them. We will try, in each area, to discuss only the local allocation, even if we illustrate alien examples passing through. 830 here is not an alien, however, but a genuine Portsmouth PD3, returning from elsewhere to become a Havant Road bus. This shot was taken in Havant on Monday 15th December 1969. Because of different allocation considerations in different areas, type distribution on route 31 was quite wide. We could use the 31 to travel on to Chichester. Apologies for 830's lack of co-operation with our eastward drift.

FOOTNOTES:
[1] Codes carried on circular discs in cabs.
[2] Sub-allocation: In some areas subsidiary garages were operated more or less as autonomous units with their 'own' fleets sub-allocated from the main allocation. Such sub-allocation was fairly informal except at Littlehampton and Bognor.

Sixties: Chichester

Once out of the Portsmouth Corporation area, Southdown had almost a monopoly of bus operations until it got to Brighton. Independents were not common in the area and mostly involved only in coach hire and excursion work. Chichester, the county town of West Sussex, was more of a rural market town than any of Southdown's other traffic centres. Thrice-weekly one-man operated single-deckers to downland destinations were as typical as busy double deckers. With its Roman walls, magnificent cathedral, and fine market cross, not to mention its Archbishop's Peculiar, Chichester was an important and historic town like Portsmouth. Southdown's other three traffic centres were of newer significance – seaside resorts boosted by developments in transport like railways and roads.

Queen Marys came late to Chichester. The depot received only four of the large 1961 batch and did not really start to look like a 'Mary' operator until the semi-automatics arrived. Many members of the later batches were allocated there, however, and by Monday 15th December 1969, when the picture below was taken at the bus station, Queen Marys had monopolised the trunk routes around the city.

The earliest Queen Mary appearances in the area were on the 31 route – initially by other garages' PD3s, and then by Chichester's own 874, 875, 876 and 880. Portsmouth's 868 is seen passing the market cross – this architectural delight dates from about 1500 and is the best-preserved market cross in England. Subsequently Queen

ABOVE: 868 passing the Market Cross *(Southdown)*

BELOW: Gaps and bunching caused by traffic congestion were known in 1961. Here 45 minutes worth of 31s have coalesced at Chichester Bus Station one summer Sunday. *(Alan Lambert)*

BELOW: On Saturday 4th October 1969 No. 928 is seen picking up Selsey passengers in South Street.

CHICHESTER AREA GARAGES AND DORMITORY SHEDS (C)
CHICHESTER BOGNOR COMPTON MIDHURST PETWORTH SELSEY WITTERING
SOME SUB-ALLOCATION TO BOGNOR, WITH SOME VEHICLES CARRYING A B DISC.

Marys spread to the routes linking Selsey Bill with Chichester and its suburbs – first to route 52 to Selsey Town and then to the 53 to the Witterings. Marys also appeared on the Bognor local services between Pagham and Elmer at about the same time as these Selsey developments.

RIGHT: 422 on an autumnal 53 in 1968; its and 418's re-allocation to open-top route less Chichester in 1965 had emphasised the DCD's quickly reduced prospects of working topless. *(Alan Snatt)*

Chichester's Queen Marys were not employed to any significant extent away from the coast. The only developments in this respect were isolated appearances on the 22/60 route in 1967 and 1968 – this involved operating service 60 from Bognor to Midhurst, and then travelling through to Brighton behind the Downs on the 22 – and a brief period of Mary responsibility for the, by then, detached 60 service at the end of the decade.

RIGHT, BELOW RIGHT & BOTTOM LEFT: The picture of 294 climbing out of Cocking captures the essence of this last Queen Mary inland adventure but was actually taken in 1998. It is one of two non-contemporary pictures in the body of the book. The 60 entered Bognor by way of Nyetimber where at The Lamb it met QMs working on local services. On 19th August 1969, 929, on which I had climbed out of Cocking earlier in the day, met 875 Pagham bound.

RIGHT and OPPOSITE BOTTOM RIGHT: In central Bognor QMs were the main performers in the mid-sixties although working alongside backloaders – such as those in the February 1966 line up – for most of the time. *(SEC)*

BELOW: On now to Worthing on the 31 ...with 830 at Yapton still resolutely trying to go in the opposite direction. *(SEC)*

LEFT: As at Chichester, Marys made their debut in the Worthing area on the marathon service 31, being hailed in the Worthing Herald at the time as "new giant 69-seater buses". No 286 is seen in Ferring during August 1969.

Just a skeleton . . . firemen probe smouldering remains of bus smashed

The wrecked bus, wrapped round the train . . . after being punched 100 yards along the line from the crossing

Over the years, several Marys were written off after accident damage . . . only three of these by Southdown themselves. Fortunately, none of the other incidents matched the dreadful circumstances in which 939 started this sad little group. The Indian Summer of September 1965 gave balmy days but, of course, mist and fog when the sun was not up and normal autumnal temperatures prevailed. On the morning of Wednesday 22nd September 1965, visibility of 30-50 yards along the Sussex Coast produced difficulties for British Rail's electric train services as the timetable could not safely be adhered to. Confusion concerning the whereabouts of the 8.47am Brighton to Portsmouth led to the gates at Roundstone Crossing, Angmering being opened before that train had passed. Queen Mary 939, working the 9.01 31 from Worthing to Southsea was the first vehicle in the queue for the gates when the erroneous opening took place. She was driven onto the crossing and was immediately struck by the train. She was pushed 100 yards down the track, erupting in flames as she went. Three of her passengers were killed; miraculously the other six and the crew survived, as did everyone in the train. Heat from the blaze was so intense that parts of 939 became welded to the railway line: only her wheels and batteries were salvaged.

CENTRE LEFT: For the first eight years of her life, 954 underwent this transformation in the late winter months and travelled around extolling the virtues of Sussex holidays. The enterprise was the joint venture of nine Sussex resorts, which filled her interior with publicity displays of photographs, posters and information. She visited towns in the Midlands and the North of England and also, in some years, places in northern France. In this view Charlie Henley of Worthing assists a prospective Sussex holidaymaker aboard 954 in snow-covered Stoke-on-Trent during January 1966; his co-driver, George Gatterall of Brighton, looks on. (Southdown)

ABOVE: Another shot showing 954 in French dressing, at Portslade Works, in February 1966. (Southdown)

LEFT: Queen Marys visited France on three other occasions during the sixties. Passengers board 315 during her 1967 visit to Dieppe for the Sussex Normandy Fair. Queen Mary 429 in open-top form had attended this in 1965; 421 (as an open-topper) accompanied 315 in 1967; and 428 and 429 (both as open-toppers) went in 1969. In 1967, at least, the buses operated a service between the Casino and the Palais des Expositions – Autobus Dieppois provided the conductors and Southdown the drivers, who were allowed to drive onto the left-hand side of the road so that passengers could board from the kerb. The buses carried advertising related to the fair. (Frank Bunce)

Sixties: Worthing

One-third of the inhabitants of Worthing are over retiring age, whilst one per cent of them are actually over 90. This pleasant seaside town is also the largest centre of population in West Sussex and therefore represents one of the heaviest concentrations of old people in the country. It is a suburban, residential place and, in the sixties, Southdown was its sole bus operator. The first Worthing Marys were some 1961 PD3/4s – namely 879, 889, 890, 891, 893, 897, 898, 901, 903 and 906 – allocated there when new. They were followed by representatives of all subsequent batches.

Worthing's hierarchy philosophy was one that underwent some rethinking as the Queen Marys arrived. Worthing had six main uses for its buses, namely the routes to Pulborough and Horsham (1/2), the 31, the main town route complex, the Arundel/Littlehampton to Brighton inland services (9/10), the separate group of town services numbered 5/5A/6/6A and the Worthing–Lancing circulars (7/7A). When the Marys arrived in early 1961 the hierarchy was arranged as given in the list above, the 1/2 having recently received some new Guy Arabs and the others sinking through a career structure of PD2/12s, PD2/1s, PD1s, Utility Guys and rebodied TDs. With the arrival of the PD3s, the 31 and 1/2 swapped places. The disappearance of the TDs put PDs on the Lancing routes hauling the 7/7A to second place and depressing the 5s & 6s just as the 9/10 was overtaking the Town Services with PD2/12s displaced from the 31 by Queen Marys. From 1964 the PD3s increased the status of the Town Services which had been gradually slipping down the hierarchy. In 1965 the hierarchy had become 31, 7/17 (erstwhile 7A), 1/2, Town Services, 9/10 – with the 5/5A/6/6A being worked by crew Leopards. All the other routes were PD3 worked (some PD2s still worked on the Town Services, as did Guys, and routes 9/10). After 1966, OMO Leopards took over the 1/2; and the 31, Town Services, 5/6 and 9/10 saw Worthing PD3/4s increasingly mixed, regardless of age. PD3/5s remained on 7/17, and also appeared on 5/6.

Services scheduled for operation by open-top buses at Worthing attracted initially four convertibles (400, 401, 403 and 411) and involved the 34-mile service 102 from Arundel to Devil's Dyke via Worthing and Brighton. Shortly after the convertibles' delivery, this service went into a sharp decline, ending as a Sundays and Bank Holidays only service, not always worked by open-top buses. Incidentally, open-top workings between Devil's Dyke and Brighton via a different route were designated 27 and worked by Brighton vehicles and crews: this service also went into decline during the sixties. As a result of these declines, from 1965 onwards, some convertibles at all garages operated during the summer, on ordinary services, with their roofs on, some even being allocated to Chichester which had no open-top routes.

Some Marys were sub-allocated to Littlehampton for that garage's mini-hierarchy of routes, 31 and 9/10; these restricted opportunities, combined with the long-term sub-allocating to Littlehampton that was practised, meant that such Marys stayed on the 31 service longer than those at the parent garage. No. 893 was probably sub-allocated longer than any of her sisters; others were 901, and several of the semi-automatics: these latter did not of course work the hilly 9/10 route. Sub-allocation to inland Horsham was less definite and after the 1/2 route became one-man operated featured few Marys; 960 did however spend a long time at Horsham at the end of the sixties, for use as the school bus.

WORTHING AREA GARAGES AND DORMITORY SHEDS (W)
WORTHING DIAL POST STORRINGTON LITTLEHAMPTON PULBOROUGH HORSHAM STEYNING
DEFINITE SUB-ALLOCATION TO LITTLEHAMPTON AND HORSHAM; BUSES AT THE FORMER DISPLAYED W&L DISCS.

The complicated 9/10 services were a collection of changes and adjustments that had been made over the years. During most of the sixties they operated between Brighton and Littlehampton/Arundel via the foothills of the South Downs on the main A27, or 'Top Road', dropping into Shoreham and Worthing *en route*; in the early part of the decade their diagram included journeys on the 9A between Arundel and Angmering-on-Sea, and the 107 between Angmering-on-Sea and Worthing. The whole ensemble was

Photo: Chris Warren

ABOVE: The next Worthing services to receive Marys after Route 31 were the Lancing circulars, which eventually became a virtual monopoly of the PD3/5s because of their flatness; 948 is seen in Lancing in 1970. The PD3/5s were not trusted on the Town Services because of the periodic climbs to High Salvington in the schedules, nor were they allowed onto the hills of the 9/10 routes. The Author's recollection of them is that they were generally of a rather clattersome nature but study of contemporary notes has revealed that all vilification was reserved for one vehicle – 948 (*e.g* Saturday 18th December 1965 – "Vibro-massage on 948, 3d"). However, 948 was particularly popular with Worthing drivers. These gentlemen appreciated the PD3/5s in traffic – provided the terrain was flat – because there was no heavy clutch to keep down. **RIGHT:** Given Worthing's route hierarchy it was quite reasonable for the Queen Marys to take over the Horsham and Pulborough services from the Guy Arab IVs, known by virtue of their registrations as the PUFs, and they did so dramatically in one total operation, on Saturday 1st August 1964. However, contrary forces, such as too few passengers, made their stay on these services brief and preserved the coastal

pattern of Mary activity; one-man operated Leopards replaced them on Sunday 6th February 1966. Marys made an earlier attempt to work the 1s and 2s in January 1962 but were quickly switched to the 7s because they would not fit in Storrington garage. I believe that this issue remained when they returned in 1964 as I remember a school acquaintance telling me that the last 1 was never a PD3: I dismissed him, foolishly it would now seem, as an unreliable informant whilst secretly awestruck that he was out that late.

scheduled for one-man operation in 1967, but crew scepticism about the practicality of this resulted in only the interworking activities succumbing and the 9/10 service remained double-manned until 1973. Queen Marys first began to appear on these schedules in 1965, and did so regularly after the one-man operation of the 1/2 routes in 1966 produced a few with nothing to do. By 1967 they had almost a monopoly of the services. A further word is necessary here about multi-garage operation of routes. The 31 was not the only example of this, though the major one. Whilst Worthing and Littlehampton supplied most of the vehicles for the 9/10 services, Brighton did provide one or two; they were invariably of the same general type as Worthing's and long-term allocation of individual vehicles (883 and 258) was a feature in the late sixties: both had adverts for a carpet firm and use on these routes may have been a condition of the contract although 883's unpopular gearbox was also rumoured as a reason (see p.98). Brighton also co-worked the 102 with Worthing, provided a few buses for Chichester's 22 service and shared various routes with Eastbourne.

The Queen Mary heyday laid the foundation of my interest in these buses. Of course I didn't realise it at the time: they were everywhere and not nearly as interesting as the time-expired backloaders they were gradually surrounding. But we were beginning the sort of long association wherein nostalgia eventually blossoms and they were logging up in my subconscious all sorts of features that I would only appreciate after they had gone. One day I would appreciate their ubiquity. One day their just being there – their layouts, their fittings, their signs, their bells, their very ordinariness – would produce a nostalgic smile. One day I would regard warmly, the gurgle of their engines and the hiss of their brakes. One day I would remember fondly, boisterous trips home from school on them (having to vault the seats to get off them) and the many QM journeys undertaken on 'bus-spotting' expeditions around Southdownland. One day sitting in a packed PD3 crawling through Portsea Island's traffic congestion or clambering over the hills between Brighton and Eastbourne would seem less ordinary; as would a journey on a lighter-loaded Mary trundling around Worthing. One day, perhaps even the tedious droning of their saloon heater fans and the peculiarly ramshackle nature of 948, would be seen in a different light.

From Worthing one can move on to Brighton by service 9 or 10 as a change from the 31, although it means missing most of Shoreham Harbour, a surprise to visitors with its high warehouse walls, power station, ships and oil terminal in the middle of green and genteel Sussex.

ABOVE: For most of the sixties, fourteen vehicles were required to operate the main town route complex in Worthing. Although Queen Marys first appeared on it in 1964 (the author's first recorded sighting was of 871 so engaged on 30th January), they only had a monopoly of the workings in the last days of two man operation in 1970 and 1971. The two least profitable services in the complex were the 108 and the 3, as may be gauged from the sparse loads on 357 and 961 one Saturday in July 1969.

ABOVE RIGHT: Suburban Worthing is a sunny land of bungalows, flowers and old ladies; most of the bus clientele came from the last-named and it has to be said that the Queen Mary's two-step entrances were not a source of glee to them. This shot of 962, crossing The Boulevard at Durrington *en route* to the Pier, was taken during June 1967.

ABOVE: As well as the main town services complex in Worthing, Marys also worked the 5/5A/6/6A diagram. Before 1964 these flat and undemanding routes had occupied a place well down the local hierarchy. Then, in February 1964, less than a year after they had seen their last 'Utility Guy', they were converted to crew Leopard working with brand new buses; the odd double-decker soon began to reappear on these routes however – at first these were the previously standard depot geriatrics but, gradually, as such workings became more common, with the diversion of Leopards to country routes newly-converted to one-man operation, more modern types, including Queen Marys, began to appear. On New Year's Day 1967, the routes were officially reconverted to two-man double-decker working and also revised and reduced in frequency. This revision eliminated the 5A and 6A services, but projected the 6 along the last bit of the 6A route and a short distance beyond its old terminus at Ringmer Road. In the absence of supporting destination blinds, buses on these workings were supplied with additional window boards reading 'Littlehampton Road' to indicate the extra half-mile The boards soon fell out of use and for most of its 2-year two-man operated life the new route 6 deceitfully claimed that it terminated at Ringmer Road – but 252 on the first day (a normal working day in 1967) chugs up South Farm Road with the board still, after a couple of hours(!), in place. The new 5/6 service was largely 'Mary' worked – their advantage if replacing smaller buses when the frequency was reduced, was that they maintained roughly the same number of seats per hour. Undemanding in terms of loadings and road conditions, the routes were favourites for 'difficult' vehicles – 257 acquired a regular duty, and semi-automatics were common.

SCENES ON SERVICE 10:

LEFT: 972 descends Arundel Hill in August 1969;

BELOW LEFT: 252 approaching the *Horse & Groom* at Patching in December of that year;

LOWER LEFT: 898 further along the route in South Farm Road Worthing in October 1966;

BOTTOM: 253 crossing the main south coast railway line in Lancing. Sister route 9 crossed this line eight times. *(Roger G. Funnell)*

Cosmopolitan Suburban Brighton

Southdown's headquarters were in Brighton, our 'Queen of Watering Places'– the 'largest, grandest and gayest' of Britain's seaside towns. By 1960 Brighton had come a long way since Dr. Russell and the Prince Regent, and was the centre of a conurbation of 350,000 people, in which engineering was the largest industry. She had never lost the raffishness, the taste for the avant garde and the eccentric that characterised her early days as a resort, though, and this had allowed her to embrace all manner of different activities and ideas over the years – industry, housing estates, day-trippers, race-course gangs, dirty weekends, Mods and Rockers, Bristol buses, seedy terraces under viaducts, a University, candyfloss stalls and seafront vulgarity, trains made up entirely of dining cars, antique dealers, sloppy driving, retired barmaids, Hove, actors, people with funny political views, Belisha beacons (first in the country), old ladies with poodles, high-quality graffiti – to name but a few. "Staid Victorian Hove" might bridle slightly at the suggestion that it was embraced by Brighton, but it did occasionally

do something curiously Brightonesque like retaining the naval name for the requisitioned municipal swimming baths after the cessation of hostilities in 1945; only the HMS was dropped from the King Alfred. It is said that the British are a tolerant race; if that is true, then surely it is clearly seen in the hotchpotch that is Brighton. Part of this hotchpotch was to have three bus operators – Brighton Corporation, Tilling Group Brighton Hove & District (the main town operator) and Southdown.

What role did the Marys play in this splendid place? Quite an important one, as Southdown's Brighton area had a large number of our heroines. As with everywhere else, most activity was near the coast, and services there topped the local hierarchy so Queen Marys went there first. After 1960, they filtered more or less simultaneously onto local Brighton routes, joining the few early ones, and the busy interurban services along the built-up coast to east and west, but for a while were more prominent on the inter-urbans. The pictures on this page show westward interurbans.

The loads carried by Marys working on Brighton local services varied considerably but were rarely as great as those on the interurban services which could pick up and set down within the Brighton boundaries. This has an historical explanation. Southdown had a potentially very profitable concentration of town services around the Lewes Road, but as a result of the squabbling which characterised the relations between the three Brighton bus operators prior to 1961, its access to Western Road, the commercial centre of Brighton, had been blocked by the other two operators and all its services were forced to terminate in the Old Steine, half a mile's uphill walk away. With the formation of Brighton Area Transport Services (BATS) in 1961, to co-ordinate the activities of the three fleets the position became, prima facie, even worse for Southdown[1], for newly-created links between the Lewes Road estates and Western Road, and better connections between Woodingdean and the town centre were worked by Brighton Hove and District and Corporation buses, whilst Southdown's Lewes Road services continued to stop short in the Old Steine. Thus, Southdown's town services rarely carried as many passengers as their inter-urban routes in the Brighton area during the Queen Mary heyday.

ABOVE: 280 is seen here near the outer terminus of the 38, sporting a single blind well into the two-blind era. *(Authors' collection)*

Under the BATS rationalisation scheme, Southdown took over operation of Brighton Hove and District's legendary 38 service, which used to provide one of the few links between the Lewes Road area and the town centre, operating by an obscure 'back-alley' path, packed to capacity. Its transfer to Southdown, however, came in different times, and with competition from the new 49 route; for most of its time with its new owners it was a mere shadow of its former self. Marys appeared on it from 1967.

One other Southdown town service reached the town centre, and this one did carry some passengers. Soon after BATS was formed, Southdown took over the 15 so that Patcham 13s could turn into 15s and go to Portslade via London Road, Western Road and Hove's main shopping centre. Potentially the busiest of Southdown's town services, gaining access as it did to Western Road, the 15 was transferred from Brighton Hove and District soon after the 1961 agreement. It provided another Lewes Road–Town Centre link, albeit somewhat indirectly.

As in Portsmouth, Queen Marys occasion-

FOOTNOTE: [1]Only prima facie as BATS revenue was pooled to an agreed formula regardless of loads.

LEWES ROAD SERVICES WORKED BY MARYS WERE THOSE TO AND FROM: Bevendean (ABOVE)—These routes had received the original allocation of VUFs in 1959 but traffic had declined considerably 10 years later, as can be seen from the view of 955 in Bevendean in February 1969. *(Chris Warren)*
Woodingdean (BELOW LEFT)—Lightly-loaded Marys characterised this service (numbered 48 after the formation of BATS) for most of the sixties. No. 364, newly-fitted with a convertible window in her dome, was actually returning to Old Steine, when she was snapped at the end of Cowley Drive on Saturday 18th November 1967. *(Chris Warren)* **Coldean (BELOW RIGHT)**—The busiest of the Lewes Road services. Some of these 13s continued over the hill top at Coldean and came down the other side into Patcham, via the factories at Hollingbury, where later they changed to 15s. From 1964, Queen Marys replaced Guy Arab IIIs and Leyland PD2/1s on these duties. Before interworking and Southdown responsibility for the 15, a 13 in the shape of 902 meets a BH&D Bristol FS at Patcham in 1962. *(Michael Dryhurst)*

ally took part in joint agreement mileage balancing which was more systematic in Brighton and involved crews as well as buses. In November 1968, Southdown were scheduled to work normally Corporation 39 on Saturdays: on November 16th, 407 was on it with Bruce MacPhee at the wheel. Strictly speaking, there was no ownership of routes in BATS and any operator could appear on any route.

> **BRIGHTON AREA GARAGES AND**
> **DORMITORY SHEDS (A)**
> BRIGHTON, EDWARD STREET
> BRIGHTON, FRESHFIELD ROAD
> BRIGHTON, MOULSECOOMB
> HAYWARDS HEATH   LEWES   CRAWLEY
> BOLNEY   CHELWOOD GATE   EAST GRINSTEAD
> HANDCROSS   HASSOCKS   HENFIELD
> SOME INFORMAL SUB-ALLOCATION.

The only long-lasting successes achieved by Queen Marys on routes away from the coast in the Brighton area were on four sub-depot local services.

ABOVE RIGHT: Historic Lewes is the county town of East Sussex, and two vehicles were required to work its local 28 service. From the mid-sixties these were Queen Marys, but the traffic offered rarely required their full capacity. 861 in the garage in April 1970 is screened for the 28.

RIGHT: A very early inland PD3 duty was working the sole local service provided by Southdown in Crawley New Town, where London Transport was responsible for all the rest. It fell to Southdown PD3s rather than London Transport RTs to provide public transport for the Gossops Green area of the garden city. 887 was depositing passengers in the then uncompleted estate in the early 1960s.

Photo: Michael Dryhurst

BELOW LEFT: Queen Marys began to appear on the Haywards Heath local service in 1967. As may be surmised from this view of 346 arriving at the bus station in October 1969, two-man operation was not absolutely essential on most journeys.

RIGHT: One of the lightest of the Queen Mary duties in Brighton's hinterland was the 34 service, which carried small numbers of passengers along the lightly-urbanised Hurstpierpoint–Hassocks axis. On Tuesday 12th August 1969, No. 906 was engaged in this peaceful activity and is seen at Stone Pound; by that date she had acquired a single-piece windscreen. Haywards Heath, Hurstpierpoint and Hassocks are part of a chain of affluent London dormitory towns flanking the London–Brighton railway line.

The internal finish of these buses was a revelation' says Michael Dryhurst.

Photo: Sc

The Early Days

Queen Who?....................contributed by Michael Dryhurst

I didn't like them. I mean...who could? They were very fussy in appearance, almost archaic.

Do I hear murmurings of the word...sacrilege? Well, I gotta tell you, neither did I like 'Marmite' when I was forced to eat it at boarding school. Forced? Well, if you didn't eat it, you didn't eat, and Matron would remonstrate with one that there were 'starving children in Africa/China/Asia/Anywhere'. So I got to like Marmite, to such an extent that in my sexagenarian adolescence, I eat gobs of the stuff at least three times a week, obtained at the local English grocery store in Sacramento, albeit at $19.95, some £12.00 per large jar. And so it follows that I got to like the SMS PD3s, but the courtship took some while.

Photo: Michael Dryhurst

To this eye, the styling followed on from Southdown 700H, the 1950 Leyland Titan PD2/12 upon which was mounted a very stylish double-decker coach body by Northern Counties, the only body of four-bay construction to have been purchased by Southdown; to me, what made 700H special was not only the fact that it was a coach, but that it was full-fronted, of four-bay construction and compactly harmonious, on its length of 27½ feet. Added to which, the livery, the lower-deck standee windows and the upper-deck cove panel quarter-lights all added to the aura of a magic-bus, long before Brian Souter and his mates came up with that similar sobriquet.

And to lessen the hurt, I should admit that I've never been a fan of the RML. Why? That dumb bit of economic expedience, the half-bay, which brings us back to the Southdown PD3... And to me, the first batch was made less-appealing by the absence of push-out vents on the front upper-deck windows. And, in those balmy days of 1957, the fact that a) I was a Brighton lad and b) Southdown was headquartered in that town made unacceptable the original PD3s by virtue of the fact that they were allocated initially to the...

Portsmouth area! I mean, if this wasn't Brutus putting in the knife...know wot I mean?

One of the major regrets of my life is the fact that my parents didn't see fit to christen me Anthony Edward Carlton...Dryhurst. Oh, to have had those initials!!! A Southall groupie I hear you ask? You bet! So said because my first ride on a provincial 30ft-long bus was on a Regent V of Rhondda, which can be described only as... excruciating! So said because the next out-of-Town 30-footer was a Ribble Leyland Titan PD3 with Burlingham bodywork, on a journey from Preston to Blackpool; and 45 years later I still revel in the eye-opener that was that journey. Magnificent...!

In the late Fifties on the outer edges of London were being developed the 'New Towns', one of which was Crawley. In an effort to attract people to this area of north-west Sussex, that New Town Commission was making some attractive offers, such as a brand-new two-bedroom flat for a weekly rent of 30/- (One Pound Fifty Pence...!). I could never resist a bargain could I, even if it meant a daily round-trip of 52 miles to Shepperton Studios. So, I moved in to 25 Lavant Close, Gossops Green. Which was Southdown territory. And the Arab IV was being superseded by the PD3.

Even back in 1961 I was a crusading advocate of public transport, not so much because I was a life-long devotee of the bus but because you didn't have to be a member of MENSA to perceive that the unbridled use of private transportation would lead to...chaos.

So, on those trips from Gossops Green to the Town Centre I eschewed the Mini (My first brand-new car, purchased 09/59, de-luxe model, £525.00...), and I took the bus. Which was Southdown route 79, by now in the hands of the Leyland Titan PD3. Okay, so I wasn't bowled-over by their external appearance, but one should never judge a book by its cover...right?

The internal finish of these buses was a revelation, and the ride...was second to none. Simply stunning. Much is made of the contribution by Leyland to the modern bus, most notably its underfloor-engined FEC Tiger, rear-engined Cub and rear-engined Atlantean double-decker. But in retrospect, there was an element here of 'all that glistens isn't gold'. The simple (not said patronisingly) but robust engineering of the Titan PD3 tended to get overlooked because that's what it was; the fact that it was 30 years of evolutionary engineering also seems to have been overlooked. But not overlooked by Southdown.

The Southdown PD3 was a truly magnificent bus, and with the possible exception of that reverse staircase, truly user-friendly. If I was a maintenance engineer, I might question engine-accessibility, but in a final analysis, this bus was one of the all-time British greats.

What a great shame that they were delivered too late to wear a livery that included dark-green lining-out... But then as Bette Davis says to Paul Henried in 'Now Voyager'; "why reach for the moon when we already have the stars?"

QM PD3 RIP

Thanks for the memories.

LEFT: Marvellous though the picture on page 3 is, it has to be said that it was not in any way a realistic recreation — Queen Marys never succeeded in taking over Pool Valley. At their peak, they held the middle bays with the 12 and 31 and featured peripherally on the 9/10 and 38. They very occasionally appeared on other services but for most of the 60s other types — backloaders and especially later OMO single-deckers — surrounded them. *(David G Savage)*

BELOW & RIGHT: The Eastbourne Road ...downland meets the sea. 426 at Telscombe in October 1969, 368 on a Sunday variation at Black Rock in May 1968, the aftermath of White Friday in December 1967

The summer of 1967 saw one-man operation of most of the inland country routes based on Pool Valley. Backloaders were the norm until the end of two-man operation, and Mary workings were rare. East of Brighton were more busy services though.

The South Downs meet the sea to the east of Brighton, forming the magnificent Seven Sisters chalk cliffs, which culminate in Beachy Head. Valleys, as one would expect, intersperse the promontories. Along much of this switchback Sussex coast urbanisation has taken place, with the result that in the sixties an intensive bus service clambered over it. Buses from Brighton proceeded to Peacehaven Annexe, or onward to the channel port of Newhaven and the seaside town of Seaford, or still further to Eastbourne. The heaviest urbanisation was between Brighton and Seaford, and bus frequencies reflected this.

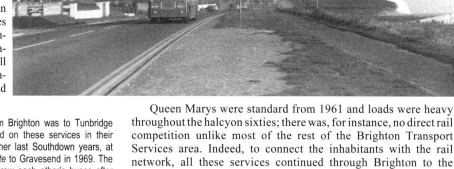

BELOW: After 1967 the only inland crew work from Brighton was to Tunbridge Wells and Gravesend. Marys occasionally appeared on these services in their heyday. Here is 813, reallocated from Pompey for her last Southdown years, at Maidstone & District's Borough Green garage *en route* to Gravesend in 1969. The routes were worked jointly with M&D. Crews would crew each other's buses after changes at Uckfield or Tunbridge Wells; unusual workings could result if substitutions took place in foreign territory and Southdown buses occasionally ended up on Gravesend local services. *(Frank Weston)*

Queen Marys were standard from 1961 and loads were heavy throughout the halcyon sixties; there was, for instance, no direct rail competition unlike most of the rest of the Brighton Transport Services area. Indeed, to connect the inhabitants with the rail network, all these services continued through Brighton to the railway station, most going on thereafter to the West Dene area.

Photo: F. W. York

King Winter descended on Brighton and Eastbourne on Friday, 8th December — when an icy blizzard caused chaos at Brighton and Eastbourne. Rottingdean and Exceat (on the Coast Road between Brighton and Eastbourne) were probably the worst hit, and it was not until Sunday afternoon that the last of eleven buses stranded on this section was eventually recovered.

Further west along the coast and inland, north of the Downs, the snow did not fall so heavily and despite long delays our drivers were able to keep the majority of services operating. Our cover picture was taken from the air during the Friday afternoon, and shows just how bad it was at Rottingdean.

After 1 p.m. on Friday the road became impassable and some 200 passengers had to spend the night and most of the following day as well at Rottingdean. The two Brighton and three Seaford crews stranded with their buses quickly set about finding accommodation for their passengers, many of whom were old and infirm. Young children were taken to the nursing home at the top of the hill out of Rottingdean, and the Police were assisted in making a list of people who required medical supplies. The tea rooms and local hotels stayed open to provide hot food and drinks.

The following morning everyone — police, bus crews and members of the public — set to work to clear stranded vehicles so that snow ploughs could get through, but some cars were a problem because the brake shoes had frozen to the wheel drums.

In Brighton itself services were suspended during most of Friday afternoon, but with the aid of a push from willing helpers, a few buses were despatched before services were finally suspended at 8 p.m. On Saturday things gradually became better and by Sunday were nearly back to normal. By the Monday afternoon Service 12 was again able to run right through along the Coast Road from Brighton to Eastbourne.

At Eastbourne, Chalkpit Hill on the Willingdon Road was impassable and north-bound traffic was diverted via Kings Drive. At one time on Friday afternoon buses were taking up to four hours to travel from Eastbourne to Willingdon. Further to the west, where the snowfall was lighter, there were heavy delays of up to three hours on Services 1 and 2, but the Worthing Town Services were able to keep going for most of the time. Some journeys on the London Service had to be cancelled, but by Saturday everything was nearly normal, though there were still delays.

At Portsmouth the trouble was caused principally by traffic congestion, rather than by snow, though this fell heavily between 10 a.m. and 2 p.m. There had been traffic incidents involving articulated lorries at Cosham and Fareham and at one time the queue of vehicles stretched bumper to bumper from Portsmouth Guildhall to Portchester Cross Roads. However, by 9 p.m. it had eased a great deal. This traffic congestion affected all services at Portsmouth, not least the Triumph Forces Leave Services, which eventually left Fareham some six hours late, although all the services were operated and arrived safely at their destinations.

Of the many letters of appreciation received it was particularly pleasing to have the commendation of the Chairman of the South Eastern Area Traffic Commissioners. His letter, three letters from the public, and a selection of extracts from others are reproduced on the next page.

Parts of the Southdown Chronicle White Friday coverage. Those of us west of Brighton might question the assertion in the second paragraph. Guy 531 maintained an hourly service on the normally twenty-minutely 6 past our house until approximately 20:00 though.

Ordinarily the trip from Brighton to Eastbourne was enjoyable and spectacular as your busy Mary rose and fell between the downland spurs beside the sea. On Friday 8th December 1967, it became a bit too spectacular when a blizzard of surprising ferocity rapidly brought havoc to the Sussex coast which was unused to such climatic phenomena. By mid-morning the hilly services between Brighton and Eastbourne had degenerated into chaos with buses stranded all along the route and crews negotiating temporary refuge for passengers at roadside hotels. The picture shows the scene at Rottingdean the following morning. Speculating about how the various vehicles got into their respective positions may prove diverting. Southdown had eleven buses stranded between Rottingdean and East Dean, five of them in and around the former. As can be seen, Brighton Hove & District were also in difficulties at the same spot. It was not until the following Monday that Service 12 was able to operate from Brighton through to Eastbourne again.

Similar chaos of varying degrees of intensity was found all along the coast on that day which passed into local folklore as 'White Friday'. In the flatter areas some buses did keep going but custom was minimal as everyone, having struggled home, stayed there. Ageing Guy Arab IV PUFs were suddenly rather popular again and appeared on all sorts of unfamiliar duties. Southdown was inundated with commendations of the exemplary behaviour of its crews, during a difficult few days. But enough of this. "Farewell old ocean's bauble, glittering Brighton" (Horace & James Smith, 1813) and on to Eastbourne, which garage supplied lots of the Marys necessary for the Eastbourne Road diagram.

Sixties: Eastbourne

At the eastern end of Southdown territory another large seaside town was the location of the last main garage. This was Eastbourne, a resort with much the same character as Worthing. It had a municipal operator though – the first municipal motorbus operator in the world it claims – and Southdown activity was thus more limited than in Worthing, with only open-top services operating wholly within the borough, and protective fares applying on other services while inside the borough boundary.

The introduction of Queen Marys on to Eastbourne routes began in the west and went east. They first appeared operating the big dipper over to Brighton and continued to do so throughout their heyday.

Next they appeared on local services – journeys on the Polegate–Eastbourne–Stone Cross–Pevensey Bay axis – and on the long route to East Grinstead. This inland adventure was short-lived (crew-operated Leopards took over in 1964) but Queen Marys working locally were familiar throughout the sixties. Semi-automatic problems may have brought some Marys off the 12 and onto flat local routes earlier than planned, but by 1965 PD3s were the norm on locals with representatives of all batches at work.

EASTBOURNE AREA GARAGES AND DORMITORY SHEDS (E)
EASTBOURNE, CAVENDISH PLACE; EASTBOURNE, ROYAL PARADE; SEAFORD; HAILSHAM; CROWBOROUGH; HEATHFIELD; UCKFIELD; SOME INFORMAL SUB-ALLOCATION.

East from Eastbourne, Marys were eventually to be found on the services to Hastings which were jointly operated with Maidstone and District: the 15 took the inland route via Hailsham and the 99 went along the coast; this latter only saw Marys in the summer as it was one-man operated in the winter. PD3s – Eastbourne and Brighton ones – also occasionally appeared (before OMO) on the network of joint Southdown and Maidstone & District services, known as the Heathfield Pool (which covered an area bounded by Tunbridge Wells, Hawkhurst, Hastings

TOP RIGHT: A typical payload boards 281 on a 12 journey in August 1970.

ABOVE: Protective fares still shielded the custard and blue corporation buses from Southdown competition within Eastbourne. *(Authors' collection)*

LEFT: 924 on the 92. *(SEC)*

BELOW RIGHT: Queen Marys working locally were familiar throughout the sixties – although they had to be timed carefully as they could not pass each other easily at certain points such as Coppice Avenue Willingdon on the 94. In this famous 1963 incident, 943 and 918 had drifted off timetable and become stuck together there: the situation was resolved by letting 943's tyres down. One timing an hour on the 94 was a full circle: 918 carried a special blind warning of the endless nature of this timing. *(Richard Creasy)*

BELOW LEFT: By 1965 PD3s were the norm on locals with representatives of all batches at work: convertible 419 is seen at the Bus Station with a Tiger Cub. *(SEC)*

LEFT: Whilst open-top services elsewhere dwindled, Eastbourne's contingent of DCDs continued to ply- and for most months of the year. On Tuesday 12th August 1969, in the soft light of early evening, 402 travels towards Beachy Head.

BELOW: In 1969 the most common type of relief work was support for a one-man-operated bus on the first, urbanised leg of a country route. Thus 283 had just helped out a Tunbridge Wells-bound single-decker as far as Hailsham on Tuesday 12th August.

and Brighton). A spin-off from these activities was the fairly frequent appearance of a PD3 on M&D local services in Hastings.

Another major activity of Eastbourne Marys was open-top working. The largest concentration of such workings had always been at the eastern garage, where Southdown had the licence for the exciting journey to the Top of Beachy Head. Whilst open-top services elsewhere dwindled, Eastbourne's contingent of DCDs continued to ply – and for most months of the year. Legend has it that Southdown, with commendable social conscience, instructed its conductors to keep watch for passengers buying single tickets to this sadly suicide-related spot ... no-one, however, seems to know what they were supposed to do if such a person were identified!

In its last few months before one-man operation, in the mid-sixties, Eastbourne Marys also appeared on the Newhaven local service, 26.

At all garages, Queen Marys not engaged on stage services would be used on a variety of miscellaneous activities, such as school and works bus duties, or relief trips ... a somewhat ironical use of Marys given the original rationale behind their purchase; still Marys themselves very rarely needed reliefs! In 1969, the most common type of relief work was support for a one-man-operated bus on the first, urbanised leg of a country route.

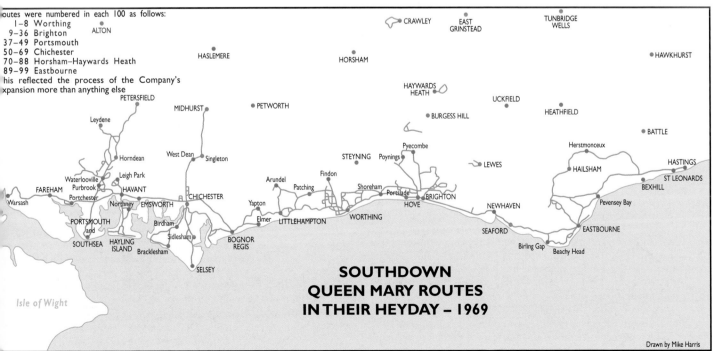

routes were numbered in each 100 as follows:

  1–8 Worthing
  9–36 Brighton
37–49 Portsmouth
50–69 Chichester
70–88 Horsham–Haywards Heath
89–99 Eastbourne

This reflected the process of the Company's expansion more than anything else

**SOUTHDOWN
QUEEN MARY ROUTES
IN THEIR HEYDAY – 1969**

Drawn by Mike Harris

A closet Bus Enthusiast remembers...........

Queen Marys? Ask me anything you like about the PD1 or Guy Arab but who on earth would be interested in Queen Marys? I mean, I push the wretched things about for six days a week – well, I did until recently. Thirty-five years ago? So it is! – doesn't time fly.

I cannot remember the first time I saw a Queen Mary for real, but a neighbour whose sister worked for the Company gave me a picture of one - it was from the cover of 'Tweenus'. I did not take this too seriously; perhaps it was one of those artists' impressions of how things might be in the future. What sort of Southdown bus had 45 on the screen anyway? Portchester and Fareham? They sound like made-up names! A school classmate later assured me that these things really did exist, and that there were now some at work on Brighton local services. Somehow, I managed to miss these as well, so the first I would have seen were those which were put on service 12.

What differences did we notice between these and the Southdown 'deckers we were used to? The full-front was most striking, and there were opening front windows on top, which even the space-age bus in the picture didn't have. Inside, green upholstery was something new and there was a long strip bell-push instead of buttons. The driver, always a remote and mysterious figure, was now among us and able to receive, "Good morning" greetings from passengers boarding and thanks from those alighting. Oh yes, of course, and the door was near the front instead of at the back.

None of this stretched the powers of observation you might say, but some found it mystifying. I remember an instance where the driver had drawn up with the doors perfectly level with the head of the queue. Ignoring the open doors, they walked towards the back and pushed and hammered on the body panels, expecting to be admitted via the usual entrance. Another time, a passenger managed to find his way inside unaided. He went to the back of the lower saloon, looked up, looked around, then asked the conductor, "Does this bus have an upstairs?" The bell-strip, which ran the length of both saloons, was convenient to use and had 'push once' labels attached, in case one could not guess its purpose. If its use was too daunting, one could ask the conductor, if at hand, for the next stop. Another way to stop the bus was to prod the driver with one's umbrella. The open bulkheads were later fitted with glazed panels, so drivers could concentrate on the hazards that lay ahead, safe from those that lurked behind.

My personal involvement with Queen Marys started at Southdown's Central Workshops at Portslade, where I was apprenticed. At various times in the following years, I also worked on them at Eastbourne and drove them on services covered by Edward Street and Seaford depots.

At Portslade Works, major overhauls (known as E-docks) were carried out at 300,000miles, service buses reaching this in 6-7 years running. D and C-docks (120,000 and 60,000 miles) were undertaken at both Works and Depots, while the shorter-interval B and A-docks were the responsibility of Depots only; the latter also dealing with running repairs and breakdowns. All mechanical and electrical units removed at the Depots were returned to the Works and reconditioned there.

When I started, overhauls of the first Queen Marys were well under way. There was nothing new on the mechanical side to give fresh problems; in fact their air-brakes were simpler to set up than

contributed by Bruce MacPhee

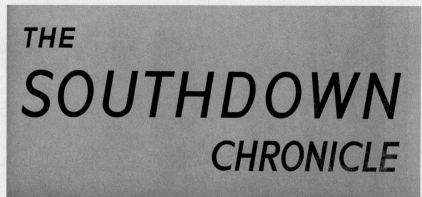

the linkages and automatic adjusters of the vacuum servo brakes on PD2s and Guys. The full-fronted body was the main hindrance. Whether working on the engine in situ or removing it for overhaul, these jobs were much more difficult than on the half-cabs, due to the restricted access. Working on the axles of buses was always a dirty job; after removing the wheels, one would brush the road-dirt from the wheelarch before squatting under it to dismantle brake gear and hubs. However much one cleaned down, there was always enough dirt left to fall down the back of one's neck! The man on the nearside front of a half-cab worked in comparative luxury; the mudguard could be unbolted, removing this inconvenience and giving him ample space in which to swing a sledgehammer when it came to removing king-pins. On the pits at Portslade, one fitter and his (semi-skilled) mate worked on the front of the chassis, and another pair on the back. In the stripping-down stage, the fitter traditionally worked on the nearside. As they used to say at sea: 'RHIP' (rank has its privileges!). Queen Mary's full-front ensured, however, that he had no unfair advantage over his 'oppo'.

Surely one of them must fit! 405 undergoes a tyre change at Eastbourne garage. Southdown, like many other operators, rented their tyres on a mileage basis, the tyre fitters attached to the major depots actually being employed by the tyre companies. When Eastbourne's tyre contract changed, Ron Firestone became Ron Michelin overnight.

After the mechanical work was completed on the pits, cars docked at Portslade Works would be reversed into the bodyshop for necessary attention. 933, photographed on 29th October 1966, would probably have been undergoing its second D-dock (i.e. 240,000 miles). As well as a side panel on the upper deck, we can see that the top-sliders of the lower saloon windows have been removed. The frames would have been stripped and new felts fitted; no rattling windows allowed in those days! After several years in service, reinforcement was sometimes needed where the platform joined the bulkhead and cab woodwork might need attention. Apart from this, Queen Mary bodies were largely trouble-free.

'Betsy' comes to Queen Mary's assistance. Less commonly referred to as 0181, Edward Street's TD5 wrecker carries the remnants of the Leyland lowbridge body from the TD1 wrecker that it replaced. *(Michael Dryhurst)*

Programmed maintenance work at Portsmouth necessitated a number of exchanges of service and garage vehicles at Hilsea during the day: on the evening of Thursday 27th November 1969, three of these were imposed upon fully-loaded peak-hour from-city workings, not entirely to the delight of the passengers involved. Here, 261, newly off School Contract 8, substitutes for 822 on a Hayling working.

Looking through my SEC fleetlist of 1969, I see that I "ticked off" 121 Queen Marys, so will have driven somewhat short of half the total. I do not remember all of these intimately but it is strange how insignificant details remain lodged within the brain, whereas important things that happened yesterday are completely forgotten. 832 went well, 834 was sluggish; 974 was good all round, 973 was awful; 908 did 53 mph (although it shouldn't have done!), 409 only managed 33; 911 fired on five cylinders when moving off, so did 973; 265, 282, 404, 900 had heavy steering – and so did 973. Of course, they "were all new once" and these defects would have occurred in service, but it seemed a long time before some of them were rectified.

So what were they like to drive? A road test of a Leopard published in a trade journal forty years ago carried the heading "That Solid Leyland Feel". This phrase could well describe our PD3s; whether you thought of "solid" in the positive or negative sense, solid they were! The large, thick-rimmed steering wheel, the organ pedal accelerator, which could accommodate the longest foot, and the clutch, requiring the strongest foot, added up to a sense of unpretentious dependability; this impression did not mislead.

The purpose of synchromesh in a heavy vehicle's gearbox was to allow fast and easy upward changes to be made, *not* to avoid double-declutching while changing down. Faster changes could be made with a "crash" box, if the clutch-stop was well adjusted, but this relied on the driver's deftness whereas the synchromesh took care of itself. The PD3 box had the worst of both worlds in that respect; being synchro, it obviously did not have a clutch-stop, but had no synchro on the gear where it was most needed! Starting on a hill in 1st, one had to "snatch" straight to 2nd. Not too difficult once one had mastered the art, but perhaps Leyland could have done just a little better.

Brakes were smooth and progressive in operation but gave the feeling that there was not much in reserve. Clutches had that familiar "judder" when moving off in 2nd gear, this being amplified by Leyland's carefully designed flexible-link engine mountings. Having ridden in and driven PD1s and PS1s, which have engines rigidly bolted to the frame, I seriously wonder how much was achieved by the later design.

The "epicyclics" relieved the driver of the heavy clutch and long lever movement to engage synchromesh gears. They therefore took less physical effort to drive, but more concentration was needed if a smooth change was to be achieved. With a manual box, an experienced driver would manipulate the clutch and gearlever almost without thinking; these being mechanical controls, would respond immediately to his actions. With epicyclics, he had no such control. The gearlever worked a number of valves, admitting compressed air to respective cylinders in the gearbox; these engaged the gears by means of brake-bands. Air-flow through pipelines is not instantaneous, so there would be a delay between a gear being selected and drive being taken up. Moving into neutral, it would take just as long for the air to escape, and therefore for the gear to disengage; if the air-lines were clogged with oil from the compressor, it would take even longer. I found that the only way to make a perfectly smooth upward change was to:

• keep the accelerator partly depressed while selecting neutral

• keep it there until one sensed that the gear had disengaged

• release accelerator

• wait while revs die down to right speed for next gear

• select gear and accelerate (not too much or bands would slip)

Naturally, the revs would not have died down to idling during the change, so the clutch would have remained engaged throughout. A rushed change would cause band-slip and standing passengers would pass down the car without even being asked. In short, the best way was to drive as one would drive a crash box when unable to operate the clutch; so much for progress.

There was more engine noise in Queen Marys' cabs than with our PD2s, but not as noisy as some other half-cabs. Although some later cars had extra insulation on the engine side-sheeting, they seemed noisier than 813-912. Leyland had introduced their "Power-Plus" goods range in 1960, with engines up-rated from their original spec. Some, but not all, of the modifications were eventually incorporated into passenger engines; whether or not this was the cause of them being louder, I am unable to say.

After dark, a driver could see little apart from reflections of the front-seat passengers. On later cars, an adjustable screen helped somewhat, but older ones only had a "concertina" blind covering all of the nearside. Dropping this would not make the driver popular, as neither conductor nor passengers would then be able to see where they were going.

The two "one-offs", 257 and 315, had their radiators under the stairs, allowing a lower dash and BET standard curved windscreens to be fitted. The possibility of having this cab layout with

ABOVE: Eastbourne depot's maintenance was as good as any in the fleet, although the driver of 973, seen crossing Newhaven bridge in October 1969, might have disagreed (see text). This 100 year-old manually operated swing-bridge was replaced a few years later. The new "state-of-the-art" electro-hydraulically operated bridge, built a few yards upstream, was not much quicker in operation and caused its fair share of problems, including a refusal to open if the weather was unduly sunny.

conventional cooling systems was explored, two of the later 800s being used as test beds. A Leopard radiator, shallower than the PD3's, was adapted to fit one, and the other had a PD3 radiator cut-down in height. However, in each case, the cooling capacity proved inadequate and the trial was abandoned. A little perseverance might have resulted in 346-69 looking like 315 rather than turning out as they did.

A convenient item taken for granted on Southdown was the front wheel step-ring, making access to the cab safe and easy. There were also two steps in the side-panels; you ignored the lower one, started with the right foot on the step-ring, left on the top step, then right on the door-sill. Many other operators' vehicles did not have a step-ring, having just a wheel nut guard-ring (not designed, nor safe to use, as a step), or none at all, in which case the top of the tyre served as the second step. If one were to use just the two steps in the body side, one could end up "wrong footed" and lined up ready to climb in the saloon window rather than the cab.

Considering their number and mileages involved, Queen Marys

seemed to be quite lucky in avoiding serious accidents. Other than the horror of 939, recorded elsewhere in this book, there were two other cases that I remember particularly:

839, on a school journey in Shoreham, went under a railway bridge, in the next road to, and slightly lower than, the one under which it should have gone, losing its roof in the process. When all was done, it returned to Edward Street and later that evening, I drove it back to Portslade Works, its last journey, there being cannibalised for spares. Why it should have made this "lap of honour" to Brighton and back is a mystery.

277 on service 12 had just climbed "Sanny" and was bowling along towards Eastdean. Steady rain now becoming a deluge, a car turned right across its path, becoming imbedded in the front. Perhaps the car driver didn't see it; sadly, he couldn't tell us. Any fatality involving a bus concerned not only Police but also Ministry of Transport. 277 had to be thoroughly examined, part of this being a brake test. Today, this would be carried out inside a testing station, on electrically driven rollers which measure brake force at each wheel. Then, things were simpler, a Tapley meter, measuring deceleration, would be secured inside so that it could not move. The driver would accelerate to 20mph on a flat stretch of road then, if all clear behind, brake as hard as he could. If the reading was satisfactory and the vehicle drew up straight, that was that. The flat stretch of road also had to be dry; days later, still no dry road to be found. The process of law could not wait forever, so it was decided to conduct the test in the Works. 277 was reversed to the end of the building and staff ordered to stand clear. The brake test was then completed to the examiner's satisfaction; a "crash stop" from 20mph is not *too* dramatic, even for a bus, but through the middle of the workshops....! 277 was soon repaired and back in service. It carried a reminder of this accident, a home-made grille, for the rest of its Southdown days.

"A stitch in time keeps the car in service", it doesn't quite rhyme but never mind. Small defects not attended to promptly, not only lead to more lengthy and costly repairs, but also cause frustration, bad feeling and rough treatment of the machine. What defects would one expect to find in a Queen Mary? Heavy steering for one! Not the lightest to begin with, maladjustment of kingpin thrust or lack of lubrication brought this on very quickly, more so than with a Guy or Bristol. The advent of radial tyres accentuated this problem, until everyone became accustomed to them.

The synchro on 3rd and top was virtually foolproof but these ratios could be stiff to engage. When a gearbox had been refitted after a clutch change, the change-speed linkage had to be readjusted; a fairly simple operation but often done incorrectly. With 2nd gear engaged, the lever should be to the left, against the reverse stop bar, otherwise there might be a danger of reverse being selected accidentally instead of 2nd. Adjustment fore and aft was not critical other than ensuring the lever did not hit the seat when in top gear and the seat wound forward. Many were not even spared this much time and effort, so instead of finding 1st and 2nd at the left of the "gate", the driver might need to bring the lever slightly to the right and fish around to find these ratios, just what he needed when changing down on a hill! Far from hitting the seat, the lever would often be set too far forward. With the hefty push to engage 3rd, the wrist would receive a painful knock at the steering wheel rim. Minor things perhaps, but more than a trifle annoying by the end of a long day!

The Leyland O600, not the liveliest, but very reliable, even when not receiving the attention due. An engine with a faulty injector might fire on only five cylinders until up to speed; this entailed 1st gear starts where 2nd would normally have sufficed and those of us with some feeling for machines were always aware of the damage done. Head gasket leaks were equally damaging and I can still sense the acrid stench of the sludge formed of oil, exhaust gas and hot water, as I topped up the rad .....of 973.

Much has been written about the surging caused by the pneumatic governors of some post-war Leylands (to me, "pneumatic" suggests air *pressure*, but in fact, the governor worked by varying degrees of vacuum, drawn by throttling the inlet manifold venturi with a butterfly valve connected to the accelerator). Apparently, some fleets had difficulties with this type but, in my experience, they gave precise control if correctly adjusted. Not so good were the SF mechanicals on later cars; they had to be removed at half the normal interval for overhaul. Gone was the steady idling of earlier types; when worn, they would "race" if facing downhill and stall when facing uphill. On the overrun, they would intermittently inject fuel, cancelling out any engine braking that might be hoped for.

As conditions deteriorated in the late '60s, countless changeovers were requested for defects but as I have hinted, not all were rectified. If drivers could have communicated with garage staff directly, things might have been different; serious problems could have been explained and hopefully dealt with. Receiving a message through a third party, e.g. an inspector, the garage might not know the difference between "genuine" and "crying wolf".

Taking over a 112 at Pool Valley, I had the novelty (perhaps not the right word for one of the *oldest* Queen Marys!) of 814, recently transferred from Portsmouth. As we swept up London Road, I noted how nicely it ran, but these thoughts were soon dispelled as it spluttered its way up Copse Hill. Reaching Dyke Road, it was then downhill all the way to Pool Valley (which it managed very well!). Not being a busy turn, and wearing rose-tinted sunglasses, I set off on the 1526 to "Saltdean, Peacehaven, Newhaven, Seaford and EASTBOURNE". The names on the "via" screen could be crossed off fairly easily, but the "destination" was more difficult. With few on board, Eastdean to Halfway Cottages might have been taken in 3rd gear, but we struggled in 1st.

- Pevensey Road – we drew up outside:
  "Changeover please, choked fuel filters; pass it on!"
- 1653 Eastbourne Pev Rd - Brighton Mill Rise
  (car 958, one of the best!)

Meanwhile:

- 1556 Brighton Pool Valley – Eastbourne Pev Rd
  (time of arrival: 1714)
- Pevensey Road – they drew up outside:
  "Changeover please, brakes!"
- 1723 Eastbourne Pev Rd – Brighton Mill Rise
  (a busy one, this!)
- Pevensey Road – phone call received:
  "Broken down, half-way up Sanny, car 814".

I meant: pass the message on to the fitter, not pass the car on to the next driver! Why do we bother!

Not *too* many broke down on service and I was lucky enough never to break down at all. Pulling into the Saltdean stop one afternoon, bound for Brighton, I found the clutch to be suddenly lighter; in fact the pedal did not seem to be connected to anything. Slipping into neutral just before we came to a halt and after a quick discussion with my conductor, I phoned through to Pool Valley. "Clutch linkage has come adrift, 974. Can you send a spare car to Black Rock for a changeover? I'll try to work through to there". Our passengers were advised where they could alight (anywhere facing downhill) and off we went (hoping not to be baulked on the uphill). Luckily, it was plain sailing all the way to Black Rock, where the "special" man was waiting with the changeover. "All change please". On our way again, ten minutes down with the horrible 911, but at least we had a clutch! Did 974 reach the garage unassisted? I have no idea; "Sufficient unto the day.....!"

As with any vehicle, our Queen Marys varied greatly according to their condition. They were once the mainstay of the fleet and even the less competent of drivers (who might "go sick" if faced with a Guy) managed them without too much difficulty. Standards being not quite what they were, Queen Marys still flogged on, seldom failing to complete their allotted work.

car to garage, book off 2355

car no: ..895...   remarks: ....OK................................

BELOW: In a 1964 Southdown Chronicle a Photospread reminds drivers of the seven bridges on Southdown double-deck services under which buses had to be driven off-centre – but occasionally weren't! – 884 hit Hassocks Bridge. There was a longer list of bridges under which highbridge double-deckers should never be driven but occasionally were – 839 hit Victoria Road Bridge in Shoreham.

ABOVE: Even though we knew this was a double-deck bus route, this bridge in Saffron Lane, Leicester was low enough to concern us when we picked 307 up in April 2000 (see p.119). We stopped and double-checked matters before proceeding.

FOOTNOTE: [1] Throughout the book I may use this as an alternative to Southdownland – apologies to Portsmouth.

Sixties: General

In 1967 various Queen Marys appeared in service proclaiming with large yellow advertisements that they did not want to be nationalised. This notwithstanding, in 1969 Southdown became part of the National Bus Company.

The year 1969 was also the one when Worthing's 889 found herself somewhat accident-prone. On Saturday 19th April 1969 she was standing at the Old Town Hall stop in the centre of town, setting down passengers, when the driver of a car transporter, passing round the adjacent roundabout, demolished her upstairs rear offside corner with the front car being transported. Recovering from this debacle, 889 returned to service in June. On Monday 20th October, however, whilst negotiating an experimental gyratory system at Tarring, she brought down the magnificent, copious wooden canopy of West Worthing Station wrecking the front of her upper deck in the process. Sadly, the canopy was not repaired but, once again, 889 was, returning to work in December. She was extremely lucky to receive all this attention: Mary 839, which lost an argument with the bridge in Victoria Road, Shoreham, in September 1969 was already too old to warrant repair, and an accident in which 884 became involved a few months later also resulted in premature withdrawal.

Several other Marys had been rebuilt during the sixties, however, and those that received noticeable body modifications were:

862 Extensively rebuilt after a fire in Clanfield Dormitory Shed, with fluorescent saloon lighting and offside illuminated advertisement panel – 1962.
854 Rebuilt without dome ventilator and rear destination box panel – 1965.
894 Rebuilt with upswept rear skirt panels and no rear destination box panel – 1966.
879 Rebuilt with no rear destination box panel – 1966.

Most of the repairs were done by Northern Counties. Other PD3s were also repaired during the sixties but emerged effectively rebuilt to their original design.

Queen Marys reached their Sussex[1] peak in the late 'sixties, with all of them (except 939) in service simultaneously – and interchangeable with no real hierarchies; as it happened, they were

Bishopstone, Seaford

Hassocks

Tongdean Lane, Brighton

Low bridges — where are they?

Any Southdown driver if asked to name the low bridges in this part of the country could probably list half-a-dozen without much difficulty, but he needs to be able to remember them in all weathers, in all traffic conditions and in plenty of time. For this reason photographs of seven bridges have been reproduced on these pages to act as a reminder. Double-deck buses must be driven in the centre of the carriageway under each of these bridges. Selham bridge has been included because a school contract double-decker operates on that route — the remainder being stage carriage routes.

Even lower bridges . . . .

The recent mishap in Queen Street, Horsham serves to remind us that there are more than seven bridges to think about, for the bridge in Queen Street is not on a stage carriage route and in any case has insufficient headroom to take a double-deck bus. The following is a list of bridges on stage carriage routes and roads adjacent to such routes under which DOUBLE DECK BUSES MUST NEVER BE DRIVEN:—

EASTBOURNE AREA
Jarvis Brook

BRIGHTON AREA
Brighton—The Deneway
Haywards Heath—Valebridge Road
„   „   Borde Hill
Horsted Keynes
Kingscote
Patcham—Mill Road

WORTHING AREA
Amberley

CHICHESTER AREA
Barnham

PORTSMOUTH AREA
Emsworth—North Street
Portchester

Portslade—Church Road
Shoreham—Kingston Lane
„   Victoria Road
Southwick—Grange Road
„   Southwick Station
Wivelsfield—Wivelsfield Station

Horsham—Queen Street

Bepton

Rowlands Castle

Bridges on routes or adjacent roads where joint services are operated are not shown.

Selham, near Petworth

Pulborough Station

Fareham

Friday Street, near Stone Cross

ABOVE: 868 awaits return to Southdown after its accident rebuild at NCME, in late 1965, alongside new 257. (C. B. Golding)

BELOW: 862 at Petersfield Station nine years after its rebuild. (Malcolm G Chase)

THE STORY of the big traffic diversions which came into operation on Monday is told on page 9. Valencia-road has assumed unexpected importance as a route for vehicles going west and north. Picture above shows traffic from Valencia-road (right) meeting with vehicles on the Tarring-road outside West Worthing Station.

HEAVY TRAFFIC, including buses, now diverted into once fairly peaceful Rugby-road.

NOW — no parking on the south side of Rugby-road.

coincidentally being used by the Author for unofficial field studies of the state of the British bus industry. These studies revealed that by 1969 a typical Queen Mary journey was made at a measured pace (i.e. rather slowly) and included some rather heavy-handed gear-changing, and the participation of about thirty-five passengers. The Queen Marys' Sussex peak came when they commanded all the trunk coastal routes. It is in the nature of peaks that there is a descent on the other side.

889's year with thanks to the Worthing Herald. The other Marys trying the Tarring gyratory are 897(?) and 255. (All news cuttings: Worthing Herald)

Observant readers will have noticed that the Mary concept – using big, two-manned buses to maintain capacity, sometimes at the expense of frequency—was not the only way of running services more economically being employed in the Sixties in an effort to come to terms with falling traffic. Services were also being cut back, and/or "restructured", and one-man operation introduced on an ever-widening scale. For a while all these solutions were being tried simultaneously, and enthusiasts smiled contentedly as traditional front-engined Marys continued to enter the fleet, increasing their number as the industry contracted.

In 1967 there began what optimists classified as a lull in Queen Mary deliveries. Instead of new Marys arriving and allowing the spreading of the type to inland routes, by releasing a few older examples at the lower end of the hierarchy to replace the remaining back-loaders, one-man-operated Leopards and Bristols appeared to supplant the Guys and Leyland PD2/12s on the main inland services.

This conformed with the pattern of Sixties economising – saving sometimes by one means and sometimes another but most often by a combination and it had seemed reasonable to suppose that at some point in the future more Marys would join the fleet – perhaps to replace the remnants of the backloader fleet or even to replace the earliest examples of their own kind; but by 1970 optimism was giving way to pessimism. No new Marys had been ordered for four years. Government grants towards the purchase of new buses, provided they had entrance doors in front of the front axle, facilitating one-man operation, had effectively rendered the Queen Mary concept obsolete.

The descent from a peak, of course, is not necessarily immediate,

and the big two-man bus concept was still alive. There were still plenty of busy routes on which the Marys could live out their lives, supplemented progressively by one-man-operable buses being worked temporarily with two crew. Or so it seemed. But the big two-man bus concept was not as healthy as it first appeared.

By 1970 it was no longer the same Southdownland which had welcomed the Marys 10 years or so previously. In 1960 Sussex buses were still relatively busy, but 10 years on, people were going to work, schools, shops, play, or visiting, much less by Southdown, and much more by car. This was partly due to increasing affluence and partly to continuing suburbanisation and dispersal of population, making the provision of a viable bus network more difficult; buses, being mass movers, need to ply amongst masses to be profitable. The holidaymakers too were coming by cars and using them, not Southdown, while they were there. All this meant that the decline in bus profitability, which began in the mid-Fifties, was by 1970 affecting not only the peripheral activities (rural journeys, duplicates, some off-peak trips, etc) but the main service buses on the trunk urban and interurban money-spinners as well. At the same time as this stage in declining profitability had been reached, there had been a simultaneous sudden change in the perceived potential of OMO stemming from the legalisation of single-crew double deckers in 1966. This was all bad news for the concept of two-man-operation and – given the difficulty of one man operating them – bad news for the Queen Marys. Their failure to spread to the inland trunk routes could now be seen as the beginning of the end.

As the big double-crew bus idea was dropped from the economy measures package, the Queen Marys became part of the problem rather than part of the solution to it, and immediately under threat from all the other remedies in the package. As well as from one-man-operation, they were at risk from restructuring, and reduction of service, as this was to start operating on a whole new scale in the Seventies. With the situation so parlous, the framework of Southdown operations in which the Marys had worked since new, required a complete review, and major surgery was going to be needed.

It looked as though the Seventies were going to pose a challenge for the Queen Marys and their operator.

The Challenge of the Seventies

The simplest solution was just to withdraw the Marys, and this was the fate which overtook many members of the early batches at the beginning of the Seventies. The most extreme case was 854, one of the first to go, which was sold in September 1971, having spent a mere 11 1/2 years with Southdown. This turned out to be the shortest period of service with Southdown of any Queen Mary not prematurely scrapped following accident damage. It contrasted markedly with the fleet life of the vehicles that 854 and her sisters had been purchased to replace, in 1960, but throughout the following decade we had been getting used to the shorter periods of service that a contraction of the fleet was making possible. Apart from the XUFs, the withdrawals of the early Marys were more or less in chronological sequence. After the first XUFs, inroads were made successively into the TCDs, VUFs and CD PD3/4s; the remainder of the XUFs followed. By the end of 1973 all but four of the oldest hundred had gone. The semi-automatics lingered a little longer, but most had gone by 1975.

The disappearance of the first 140 produced a rapid descent from the 1969 peak but not all the Marys just bowed out: some of them, and particularly the newer ones delivered from 1964, participated in other, more positive, strategies to try and stem rapid obsolescence and decline – to adapt to the Seventies. One of these was attempted conversion to one-man-operation. As we have already noted, this was not easy as it involved the driver in having to swivel round and conduct transactions across a noisy Leyland engine, but was considered to be worth a try.

Such experiments began in 1966 after Brighton Corporation successfully converted their half-cab Titans and 428 disappeared to the back of Portslade Works at the end of that year. Adaptations were made to her but were not tested in service, and she finally returned to normal two-man operation in February 1967. In 1971, with the challenge of the Seventies all round them, ten Queen Marys – 829, 831, 844, 953, 955, 961, 962, 971, 977 and 407 – took part in a slightly more determined attempt to adapt them for one-man operation. They appeared with various alterations, such as the removal of glass from the bulkhead window and transfer to the conductor's communication opening; installation of a ticket machine and change holding equipment in the new aperture; a reversing window in the lower saloon rear emergency exit, plus reversing lights and automatic warning horn; miscellaneous signs, an additional nearside mirror, a periscope, and a strip light in the cab. Some of these Marys were occasionally used in their intended role, usually on rural school journeys.

Reallocation in search of work was the only really successful strategy. Ten years previously, a number of backloaders displaced by the arrival of Marys had been transferred from garage to garage in a quest for gainful employment. In the seventies, some Marys were in much the same situation. One-man operated Bristol VRs were the replacing usurpers now and as they started to appear all over the system, some Marys escaped withdrawal by being transferred to fresh depots. With its large numbers of the older Marys, it would have been helpful if Portsmouth had become one-man-operated first, thus facilitating a simple replacement of TCDs and VUFs. As it happened, Worthing and parts of Chichester and Brighton were the first to be converted, yielding a large number of surplus middle-aged Queen Marys. Thus 1971 was a year of frantic reallocation as these vehicles set off for Portsmouth to replace the older ones on the city's busier services.

ABOVE: Queen Marys withdrawn in the early 1970s were sold to Frank Cowley, the Salford dealer, as was standard Southdown practice. This explains why 818 could be seen in Manchester on 11th April 1972.

RIGHT: Prior to sale, as was also standard Southdown practice, there were varying periods of delicensed storage with "no water in radiator"; hence these miscellaneous semi-automatics parked beside Hayling garage in the summer of 1974. *(Authors' Collection)*

RIGHT: The use of Queen Marys on one-man work was usually on rural school journeys. No. 971 was being so used when observed at Lewes during summer 1974. The extra riveted strip on the roof was part of an accident repair in 1966. *(D. Clark)*

RIGHT: A few Marys sought to cope with the seventies by prancing about in flambuoyant liveries. No.915 was the first bus in the NBC to carry an overall advert livery (for Roberts Off-licence between December 1971 and April 1975) and three of her sisters followed: 263 (illustrated here) for Rediffusion between February 1973 and February 1977; 270 for London & Manchester Assurance between February 1973 and April 1975; and 281 for Sapphire Carpets between November 1975 and February 1977. *(John Bishop)*

BOTTOM RIGHT: No. 927 found the seventies altogether too overwhelming and fell over. *(D. Clark)*

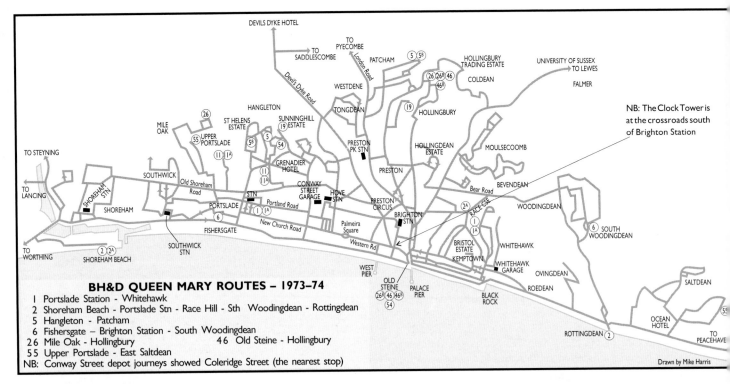

BH&D QUEEN MARY ROUTES – 1973–74

1 Portslade Station - Whitehawk
2 Shoreham Beach - Portslade Stn - Race Hill - Sth Woodingdean - Rottingdean
5 Hangleton - Patcham
6 Fishersgate – Brighton Station - South Woodingdean
26 Mile Oak - Hollingbury   46 Old Steine - Hollingbury
55 Upper Portslade - East Saltdean
NB: Conway Street depot journeys showed Coleridge Street (the nearest stop)

NB: The Clock Tower is at the crossroads south of Brighton Station

Drawn by Mike Harris

Brighton Hove and District crew routes in the seventies: Bristol Lodekkas and Queen Marys (this composite scene is at Hove Town Hall on 17th January 1974) carrying Brightonians and our many visitors (various of both with some buses August 1973 and 1974).

All Shift to Conway Street

After 1972, things settled down somewhat, but the stable allocation pattern of the sixties never returned and moves continued. With Portsmouth's requirements drastically reduced by one-man operation, a new focus emerged and many Marys found themselves moving to a new and rather alien environment.

From 1971, Queen Marys began to filter into what was to become the last bastion of crew operation within the Southdown network and save many Marys from premature withdrawal: this was the still extremely busy Brighton Hove & District system. Erstwhile competitor BH&D which operated most of the urban services through the still densely-populated streets of Brighton and Hove – including nearly all the routes along the chaotic main shopping street, Western Road – had been nominally absorbed by Southdown at the formation of the National Bus Company in 1969. With comparatively few one-man routes and a generally older fleet than Southdown, BH&D was able to welcome Marys to replace Bristol Ks and Lodekkas on the trunk routes of Brighton and Hove throughout the seventies. With increasingly little to do elsewhere, as restructuring and extension of one-man operation went ahead, more and more Queen Marys were transferred to BH&D duties and their strength built up so that by 1976 Conway Street and Whitehawk[1] garages had sixty-three PD3s between them, which was by then the largest single concentration of Marys in Southdown's area: it was the last bastion of crew operation.

As a slightly tangential illustration of this important development in the Queen Marys' careers, I would like to describe my experiences working as a conductor for 'BH&D' from Conway Street in 1973 and 1974. This is tangential for two reasons: firstly, because I shall talk generally about conducting and, secondly, because Conway Street crew-operated buses were not, of course, all Queen Marys – alongside them was a still sizeable fleet of Bristol Lodekkas. The PD3s were more popular than the Bristols with most crews because

their layout allowed the driver and conductor to communicate during the journey. This outweighed their rather ponderous nature, which was not best suited to intensive town driving and their lack of floor-to-ceiling stanchions, which made conducting them somewhat more of a balancing act. The driver could, moreover, see the platform so that ringing the bell became less of a necessity and they were 'rung off' in a variety of ways, including the bell, a coin tapped on the bulkhead window, a foot nudged against the bulkhead window from halfway up the stairs, shouts of "Ding! Ding!", or "Take her away, Jim!". Presumably things were even more informal in pre-bulkhead window days. The gradual infiltration of Conway Street and Whitehawk garages by Queen Marys during the period that I worked there contributed to the external appearance that BH&D was part of Southdown. However this was not really so; BH&D still operated more or less independently of the rest of Southdown, working its 'own' routes from its 'own' garages and employing its staff in its 'own' uniforms on straight, not split, shifts.

BH&D's methods of operation

Each BH&D bus and crew operated a specific duty – duties were identified by route and running number. There were, for instance, five Conway Street buses on services 1 and 2 (which interworked) and these duties were known as 1-16, 1-17, 1-18, l-19 and 1-20 (the other 15 were worked by Whitehawk garage).

FOOTNOTE: [1] 'BH&D's operations were based on two garages - Conway Street, Hove (their HQ) and Whitehawk in East Brighton.

ABOVE: The first BH&D Marys were five VUF-registered ones—830, 833, 836, 837 and 838—which were transferred in May 1971. Here is one of them–our old friend 830—in December of that year heading west along Western Road. Masked destination boxes to accommodate BH&D single-track blinds were a feature.

LEFT: The next BH&D Marys were a group of the 1964 CUF-registered vehicles drafted in for a month in the late summer of 1971. They were swapped for some XUFs, whose stay proved to be longer lasting, all but one remaining on BH&D strength until final withdrawal in 1973. The exception was the vehicle shown which, not having had her one-man-operation potential fully utilised, left Conway Street a year earlier. Despite the she was performing in a crewed capacity when seen using the size and weight of herself in the Old Steine on Saturday 1st April 1972. No. 844 was one of the XUFs delivered with TCD-style offside dash panel vents. *(Richard Maryan)*

BH&D still retained, albeit unofficially, its practice of allocating specific vehicles to specific duties, day in, day out. Incoming Marys joined in with this. The regular bus was known as the duty's service bus, and the situation on crewed routes at Conway Street during my time is outlined in the table below.

Duties left blank did not have regular vehicles, although many such duties with a different bus every day had drivers who would talk of a vehicle that they had not seen for months, as 'their' service bus. The system applied equally to one-man-operated duties – Brighton Hove & District did have some – and to Whitehawk garage.

Brighton Hove & District also allocated crews to specific duties. There were two shifts a day on each one; the early shift was identified by the suffix E, and the late one by the suffix L. Drivers operated one duty only – one week early, and one week late; thus they had a regular partner and the pair had a regular bus – their bus. Conductors were also allocated to one route and worked in pairs – one week early, one week late; but they operated all their garage's duties on the route, in sequence, thus working with each driver for a fortnight at a time. Crews were said to have a service on a certain route – they obtained one after a year with BH&D. Before that they were 'spares', and did not lead such predictable lives, being allocated duties on a day-to-day basis; itinerants such as me were also spares.

The Early Shift

By 6.00 am Conway Street was a hive of activity – revving engines, shouted insults, clatters of equipment being loaded into buses. I knew what duty I was on from a perusal of the Conductors' Duty Sheet the day before; one could also check one's driver's identity in advance by a similar study of the Drivers' Sheet. The vehicle was really the driver's responsibility and its identity often pretty predictable anyway, but on some early turns I would check this – on the actual day in this case: the bus could act as a rendezvous point, especially if one did not know the driver, and I often looked in the hope that I had been posted to a Queen Mary, with its facility for talking with the driver and fewer worries about the bell. There was a plan next to the Vehicles' Duty Sheet which showed where all the buses were parked; this became increasingly inaccurate as the morning wore on and drivers moved buses around to extricate their charges. By the time a crew came to begin late-

Conway Street Crewed Routes-Duties' Service Buses (Mondays to Fridays) Summer 1973

1/2	5	6	26/46	55
1-16	5-8 2058*	6-1 Never ran	26-12 278	55-3 846 then 969
1-17	5-9 2045*	6-2 Rarely ran	26-13 2076*	55-4 849 then 253
1-18 Never ran	5-10 2077*	6-3	26-14 2084*	
1-19 2081*	5-11 2082*	6-4 264	26-15 284	
1-20 2079*	5-12	6-5 2061*	26-16 Rarely ran	
	5-13 2073*:	6-6 261	26-17 272	
	5-14 2059*	6-7	26-18 Never ran	
			26-19	

Conway Street Crewed Routes-Duties' Service Buses (Mondays to Fridays) Summer 1974

1/2	5	6	55	
1-16 269	5-8 2058*	6-1 Never ran	55-3 969	These were then the main Queen Mary routes of Brighton Hove & District. Before 1973 they had occasionally appeared on others (such as the 19 – see 965 above) which were one-man operated by 1973. The 26/46 were partially OPO in 1973 and totally by mid-1974.
1-17 284	5-9 Never ran	6-2 Never ran	55-4	
1-18 Never ran	5-10 2077*	6-3 293		
1-19 2081*	5-11 2082*	6-4 264		
1-20 2079*	5-12 Never ran	6-5 250		
	5-13 2073*	6-6 261		
	5-14	6-7 287		

*Lodekka

Some semi-official lists may differ a little but this is based on actual practice.

ABOVE: The second BH&D Marys were a group of the 1964 CUF-registered vehicles drafted in for a month in the late summer of 1971. It was not normal practice to display intermediate point destination information at BH&D but some of these early transfers, like 965 here, did; 954 was seen showing Western Road using the Haywards Heath thoroughfare of the same name. *(Brian Jackson)*

LEFT: One of the last XUFs in Southdown service was 851 which is seen here grinding out of Rottingdean on Saturday 25th August 1973, a week before withdrawal, and experiencing the immense pleasure of being conducted by the author. Fortunately for the more sensitive readers, an influx of passengers has put me out of camera-shot, collecting fares. On coming across this photograph while preparing this book, I did recall Reg, the driver on this occasion, commenting when I returned to the platform: "'Ere, I've just had my picture taken". *(Jim Jones)*

that the notorious short-riders began to appear on the streets. Legend has it that BH&D made its fortune from the transport of people a few stops along the main commercial axis of the town – Western Road. One could often fill the bus with people travelling one fare stage at a cost of 2p. The tight system of staff rostering also assisted in the making of a fortune. From 9.00 am until lunchtime the bus got busier and busier.

starting duties like 1-17 or 5-14 they could spend quite a while wandering around looking for the bus. A drawback to the service bus system was that it occasionally led crews to assume that they would be using a certain bus without confirming that this was also the depot foreman's plan by checking the Vehicles' Duty Sheet.

Having signed on, collected your box, with ticket machine, audit waybills, paying-in bags, the duty's schedule, spare ticket rolls, clippers, Emergency bell-punch tickets (these were a bit of a pain involving punching old-fashioned style tickets and their use tended to be avoided –one might employ the "Honesty Boxes" on the platforms of the older Bristols or hit the Setright : most problems developed by the Setright Speed ticket machine seemed to be cured by hitting it), checked that the counter information entered on the waybill tallied with that on the ticket machine and prepared the back of your (and the late-turn conductor's) waybill for the entry of total ticket counter information at the end of each journey . . . you were ready for action.

Out onto the streets of Brighton we went ... 6.00 am and hardly anyone about ... with the usual problem for the first half-hour or so – the difficulty of giving change from the, as yet, small number of coins at one's disposal. Most of our early passengers were extremely helpful in this respect, tendering the exact fare often in useful small denomination coins, but occasionally difficulties could arise. Unless one carried an enormous float of one's own money (BH&D did not provide one) demand for certain coins could quickly exhaust one's supply early in a shift – early morning Factory Special 26s yielded a lot of people offering a 10p piece for the 9p fare ... a shortage of 1ps and a surfeit of tens, which could not be given as change, invariably developed at about the Open Market, much to the passengers' confusion. Sheer amount of requisite change could also stump us early in the shift. One morning in August 1974, starting a middle shift (a Saturdays-only phenomenon) at about 10.00 am with Mary 287, I was immediately confronted by two people seeking to pay their miniscule fares with five pound notes. The situation was relieved by one of their fellow passengers, who appeared to have a limitless supply of money and changed both notes.

Saturdays and Sundays were slightly different from weekdays in various ways of course. The summary that follows is based mainly on Mondays to Fridays.

The morning rush-hour was not usually too traumatic, as a number of extra buses (known to crews as 'Swingers'. Yes, duplicates for Queen Marys! But not just for them – swingers also supplemented smaller Lodekkas and served other functions like working school and works contracts or reducing gaps in the timetable, caused by crew shortages, at times of high demand) were run and, as long as one did not have one of the more outrageous school-runs, life was reasonably relaxed until about 9.00 am. Then Brighton really came to life, and all the extra buses returned to the garages, leaving the duty vehicles to cope on their own. It was at this time

Bus Crew Responsibilities

Responsibilities were pretty clear. The driver drove the bus, stopping at stops to deposit and uplift passengers. The conductor supervised loading and unloading and collected the fares. Jointly they were responsible for providing a safe, courteous and punctual service.

The general points about south coast bus passengers made earlier applied to BH&D except that, as town buses, their vehicles tended to see less of the holidaymakers. In 1973, BH&D was also suffering from a decline in custom, although apparently not to the same extent as the rest of Southdown. A feature of this was that the tendency for buses to become the carriers of those too old or too young to drive cars was becoming increasingly marked; many of our passengers came from these two categories and local factors exaggerated the phenomenon.

We have already mentioned the high percentage of old age pensioners in the Sussex coast population and Hove, being a flat town, had a particularly high concentration. The ranks of younger passengers were swelled, particularly in the summer, by the large number of foreign students who came to the local language schools to learn English, and turned Brighton into the youngest and most continental town in Britain. Amongst our passengers, the rest of the age spectrum was represented by a fair number of housewives and a smattering of other people. I did once carry Snow-white and one of the dwarfs, but I think they were going to a Fancy Dress party.

The Conductor's Job – Supervising Loading and Unloading

This aspect of the conductor's job showed all the elements of his joint responsibility for providing a safe, courteous and punctual service: safety, in ensuring that the passengers did not come to grief getting on and off, and that the bus did not become overloaded; punctuality, in organising boarding and alighting arrangements which ensured that the bus kept to time; courtesy, in the way the above was handled and associated passenger difficulties dealt with. Courteous intervention usually had a safety and punctuality bonus. Specific features were:

Overloading: One of the main reasons the conductor supervised loading and unloading was to prevent the bus carrying an illegal number of passengers. Passengers' beliefs about the capacity of our buses were amazing and at certain key stops, if there was no conductor to control things, they would crowd on until there was no room to move and the panelling was touching the road. There was obviously a safety aspect to this and also a punctuality one; sorting out the mess, at the stop, after it had occurred could be time-consuming, but letting it go resulted in the bus plodding dangerously along at a snail's pace—which additionally was mechanically detrimental.

Starting signals: Another important reason for the conductor to supervise loading and unloading, was to ensure that the bus left the stop only when it was safe to do so, whatever the load. Punctuality was also a factor here as the closer one monitored platform activity, the quicker one could give a safe starting signal

common practice when operating only as far as the garage to remove the number and merely display 'HOVE Coleridge Street'. This immediately elicited a delaying demand of "What number are you?" from the waiting customers, but did achieve the objective of drawing their attention to

and the less likelihood there was of having to stop again to sort out a platform accident. Courtesy was necessary when stopping overloading for the manner in which the conductor enforced the construction and use regulations had a direct effect on passengers' desire to co-operate and it stayed important as one pressed the bell – both to those on board ('Hold tight!') and to those who had missed you (stopping the bus again or deterring the flying leap).

Responsibility for a safe, punctual departure from stops was a little blurred on Queen Marys. The driver could see the platform and could, in theory, move off without a bell. Not all of them would however, and most preferred some sort of signal to go from the conductor. Given that busy stops usually required some involvement of the conductor in ensuring that overloading did not occur, any driver initiatives in this area were usually confined to slack stops.

Steep steps: Queen Marys were not greatly appreciated by our passengers carrying luggage or by our older customers because they had two steps to negotiate between pavement and floor level; the 'Lodekkas', with low platforms and, in some cases, special cutaway half-steps served the needs of these patrons somewhat better. Help from us was sometimes needed.

Checking things with the conductor: Boarding passengers were apt to quiz the conductor on various matters; here courtesy came to the fore but carried in its train punctuality considerations. Many of our passengers would, regardless of any information displayed on the front of the bus, question the conductor about its route. Delays multiplied as they tended not to check amongst themselves whether their particular query had been answered and the conductor became involved in a certain amount of repetition. There was some rationale behind such passengers' behaviour. Buses did occasionally appear with incorrectly set destination blinds and even if they did not, short-riders and visitors would find BH&D's rather cryptic destination details confusing and consider it prudent to check the routeing to the distant terminus. Also, for many of our elderly passengers, difficulty in reading destinations with failing eyesight, went along with a general need for reassurance that all was well.

The questioners were perhaps a more rational group than the contingent who put their faith in only half of the front display— boarding with reference to route number only, even on routes which regularly had short-workings. Occasionally more sophisticated members of this group would note the short-turning destination and then try and psyche us into being the sort of bus that they wanted, by such questions as the famous "1 You do go to Shoreham Beach, don't you?" . . . but the main body of this group would clamber happily aboard if the destination read 'ABU DHABI' provided the number was right. So widespread was this tendency that it was

the truncated working. Other non-standard short workings also removed their numbers. This practice was particularly baffling to foreign students, who more than anyone responded to numbers – to the extent of getting on buses going in the opposite direction every so often.

Passenger flow arrangements: The main consideration in trying to institute these was punctuality (speeding people on and off the bus to ensure maintenance of schedule), and the effort put a severe strain on courtesy. Success was slight once one went beyond mere exhortation to be businesslike about getting on and off. Difficulties in this area were symbolised by the 'both sides of the bar' phenomenon, which was particularly prevalent on the Queen Marys. They had entrances divided very obviously by a hand rail ('the bar'). The original idea behind this was to allow separated loading and unloading of each deck. However, the disproportionately heavy use of the lower deck led conductors to try to get different flow patterns across the platform. The favourite was a two-abreast boarding stream funnelling into the lower saloon. We sought to achieve it by standing on the platform, going blue in the face, beseeching people with the words "BOTH SIDES OF THE BAR, PLEASE. IT'S THE SAME BUS ON THIS SIDE" whilst the passengers, apparently aware of the original logic of the design filed slowly up one side only. This increased the amount of wheel-stop time, and even more so when the boarders waited for the disembarking crocodile to come down the same side. The reason most frequently advanced for not getting on both sides of the bar was not the original design, but a dislike of jumping the queue; also, of course, patrons knew that if they boarded in single file they stood a better chance of getting to a seat before the bus moved off. Our older customers in particular were unhappy balancing on a moving vehicle, and whilst we did endeavour to give them every consideration, it was not always possible, if schedules were to be maintained, to have everybody seated before we moved off ("Ooh, they don't give you time to sit down, do they?").

Whilst all the unloading and loading was taking place incidentally, the through passengers on board engaged in a game called 'Musical Chairs' whereby they all changed their seats and everyone moved a bit nearer the platform. This was obviously designed to get intending disembarkees near the exit and was thus helpful to the bus's schedule. From what has been said, it is clear that supervising loading and unloading often had to mean close platform supervision, which would have been fine had the conductor not also had the responsibility for collecting fares A balance between the two was called for to ensure safety and punctuality, and that was the art of conducting. Before we look at that balance, let us look at the business of collecting fares in more detail.

The Conductor's Job—
Collecting the Fares

The collection of fares may be broken down into several components:

Determining the journey being made: This was usually fairly easy but there could be problems. Foreign students, for instance, were not always awfully sure where they were going. The centre of Brighton is the Clock Tower; the English Language Centre, which most of them attended, was in Palmeira Square, which has as its centrepiece a Flower Clock. These similarities tended to confuse arriving students who would request carriage to such places as the Tower Clock or the Cock Flower (sic) and one could never be certain which they meant. Other visitors and even some locals could be pretty vague about their plans too. One old lady on a 6 stated her destination to me as follows: "Used to be Picture Palace .. ooh ... you know ... Bingo Hall now . . . along there . . . used to be Picture Palace ... well I know where I'm going!"

Or one might meet a late developer from the boarding enquirer group, like the little old lady who started her fare transaction on my 2 one morning (1-17E in the shape of 284) with the question "Am I on the right one?" and before stating her destination went on at great length about her previous experiences of getting on wrong ones.

Some passengers would not state their destination, but merely the fare they were paying – helpful on busy runs, eliminating the stage below – but with possible complications later on.

Determining the fare: Fares were on a graduated scale ranging from 2p to 9p, with fares above 2p reduced by 1p between 9.15 am and 4.15 pm Mondays to Fridays. Senior citizens of Brighton were entitled to travel for half-fare between 9.15 am and 4.30 pm and weekends (claiming this privilege with a pass and the immortal words "I've got a card"). Children between 3 and 14 could travel for half-fare at all times; those under 3 could travel free. Certain types of livestock were expected to make a contribution to National Bus Company funds.

Surprisingly passengers and conductors understood these confusing arrangements well. Divergences of opinion about the correct fare for the journey rarely emerged at this stage ... and except occasionally around 9.15, 4.15 or 4p (valid both peak and off-peak but for different journeys) this initial determining of the fare passed off smoothly . . . except with those of our passengers whose ages hovered around 14. At that age, hiding behind seats gave to more sophisticated methods of fare evasion as they became involved in the age-old game of trying to retain half-fare for as long as possible.

Enquiring how old they were made things far too easy and I eventually asked them what year they were born: quick thinking was then necessary if an untruth putting their age below 14 was to be produced. Mind you, by the time I left in 1974, the kids in Patcham were all automatically offering me a date in 1960 with their fares. Varndean School had a very helpful arrangement of changing blazer colour around the age of 14, which made it difficult for their pupils to lie about their age. Not that all youngsters were lying; one extremely adult-looking young lady who requested half-fare on New Church Road, was obviously used to world weary sighs of "Oh yeah, pull the other one" because she immediately produced a birth certificate. Incidentally, why bus companies had failed to notice that children were, in the seventies, no longer leaving school and earning at 14 is another matter!

Finding out whether any livestock fare was appropriate had its humorous moments: on Friday 20th July 1973 I was working 6-3E with 259 when a man boarded with a hamper, which he claimed during interrogation, contained a gorilla. This was all right as we only charged for dogs.

Receiving payment: Once the fare had been determined it was incumbent upon the conductor to relieve the passenger of some money and give them a receipt in the form of a ticket and any change due.

Passengers often found the conductor's change-giving difficulties hard to understand and usually suggested as a solution the possession of a large float. But how large? Coin in bulk is heavy and the conductor has to move around the bus. Within that constraint we did maintain a float, but a run on a certain denomination of coin could temporarily eliminate it from our cash in the middle of the day in much the same way as it could first thing in the morning, leaving the passenger trying to start again (reinspecting purse), in credit (worrying that we had forgotten we owed them 7p) or collecting coins (grudgingly accepting the amount in $^1/_2$ps).

To keep weight down we continually bagged the silver, which could not easily be given as change with such low fares, and locked it away, leaving mostly bronze as float. This arrangement made changing notes rather tedious and time-consuming: change for green ones usually had to involve fistfuls of bronze whilst change for larger ones meant unlocking bagged silver (we rarely had other notes to use instead). In most cases, therefore, passengers tended to get more than they bargained for. It was believed that the English Language Centre told its pupils to offer the largest unit of currency in their possession when they made a purchase so that they would get a lot of change and get to know the

One of the few KSWs to run alongside Marys for any time was this trainer. Conway Street garage. *(G. Smith)*

currency. If this was the plan it worked in spectacular style on buses: the only way I could change the £10 note proffered by a German student for his 5p ride on 292 one afternoon was to give him £9.95 in silver.

Whether one was tendered the exact fare or not, one always needed to check the offering for spurious coins. There was a remarkable number of Channel Islands and Irish coins in circulation, along with droves of old halfpennies masquerading as 2p pieces and smaller quantities of other unacceptable denominations. I would judge that 50% of these were handed over in all innocence by people who had had them slipped to them by someone else. One tried to intercept these coins at the time they were tendered, but we did not always succeed. I feel that I should not explain how we then got rid of them, although I would mention that a woman once became very indignant when her Canadian cent was parried: she claimed, in justification, that the conductor on her previous bus had given it to her.

There was pressure on the conductor to make sure that he gave the correct amount of change and did not retain any duff coins in his money, for, at the end of the shift, he had to balance the books ... and make good any shortages from his own pocket. Overs paid in were, incidentally, returned to us.

Hove's pensioners paid full fares, but were given a monthly allowance of free travel tokens: like the Brighton passes, they could only be used in the off-peak. Conductors had to bag them separately and they could not be given as change. On duty 55-4L's last journey one always ran out of change and one occasion found me surreptitiously handing over pensioners' tokens with the whispered enquiry "You got a granny?". It was never clear whether these tokens could be used to pay for dogs, but I usually permitted it if the dog looked elderly.

The most bizarre form of payment I encountered was undoubtedly a carton of yoghurt a woman bartered on Mary 264 one Saturday afternoon in August 1974, on the realisation that her husband had inadvertently driven off with her purse. It necessitated me obtaining a plastic spoon from the chemist at South Woodingdean shops.

Season Tickets: Many passengers avoided the three stages above by possessing Season Tickets. These greatly speeded the conductor's progress round the bus but once again the younger passengers had to be watched. Amongst those engaged in full-time education there was the phenomenon of the communal season ticket and one had to watch closely to see whether the passes were gradually being circulated amongst the group as one made one's way round. One conductor made all the children from one school hold their Seasons above their heads simultaneously as he checked them.

Ensuring that the journey paid for was the one actually made: However they paid, all passengers had to be monitored for this one. Season Tickets required careful scrutiny as the journeys attempted against them were not always compatible with the information printed on them – or in some cases, originally printed on them before unsubtle alterations by the holder (subtle changes we probably didn't spot !) Some of the foreign students seemed to think that Season Tickets for particular journeys were in fact Wanderbus tickets. Such possibilities of getting more than their money's worth also applied to non-Season Ticket holders: one needed to keep an eye out amongst the rest of the passengers, particularly those that had stated a fare rather than destination, for the inadvertent and the deliberate over-rider. Together these two categories made up a small but ever-present section of the travelling public. It was when they were approached that most divergences of opinion about the right fare for the journey, both on a practical and a philosophical plane, used to emerge. On busy journeys, the passenger who tried to avoid paying anything had also to be watched for.

The Art of Conducting

Whilst fare collection interacted constantly with courtesy, the combination with platform supervision was the only situation where it really affected safety and punctuality, and so we can deal with all that as one relationship. The relationship only became critical on busy journeys, when there was more need to be on the platform to prevent overloading and see clearly for ringing off, and more need to rove and collect fares. Balancing the two in a crowded bus depended on identifying the platform as one's base and knowing when to be on it and when to leave it, whilst ensuring that one could always return to it if one wanted to. Too far too soon and you couldn't get back in time to manage the platform –disembarkers would frustrate your return, fares could be missed in the leaving crowd and the bus was delayed as chaos reigned on the platform and seeing to ring off safely was denied. Not far enough soon enough and platform delays resulted from your fare collection thereon (pay as you leave) and fares were missed as

Brighton's bus drivers: safe, courteous and punctual.

passengers at the bus's extremities consulted late were tempted to forget exactly where they got on.

Before leaving the conductor's job it is perhaps worth looking a little more at the human relations side of it. We have seen that all aspects of the job require tact and diplomacy; the conductor's task was undertaken in a minefield of possibly explosive human reactions. Moreover the onus was on the conductor not to trigger any of the mines—somewhere in all that hurrying people aboard, answering repetitive questions, watching the coins being handed over, checking the journeys being made, it had to be remembered that you were providing a public service and that the customer was always right. Such consideration was not too onerous because Brighton's bus crews and Brighton's public generally got on pretty well together. BH&D's service bus system helped in this, allowing crews to get to know some of their regular passengers and a little bit of village-bus atmosphere in the big town. So there were friendly and interesting conversations on slacker runs, helpful tendering of the exact fare and sympathetic comments such as "I wouldn't have your job for anything" on busier ones. There were various other friendly gestures—helping hands, fares offered on the platform, sweets, waiting for runners (most of whom, by the way, went two stops!). Sometimes we gave the passengers directions and once the whole of 849's full load returned the favour in several choruses . . . that was the first time I did a 26 and neither I nor the driver (she was new too) had any idea where we were going.

The crew were jointly responsible for looking after the bus. This was mainly the driver's concern (things like sympathetic driving and not hitting things) but the conductor had duties here too, such as the prevention of overloading already mentioned. Another one was the deterrence of vandalism. This could have introduced strains into the social climate, but during my times as a conductor there was not much to deter. This absence of vandalism was partly a general south coast phenomenon, and partly because of the difficulty of aerosolling the ceiling on a permanently-packed bus. What little there was – anywhere on Southdown – was sorted in the body shop from time to time: new cushions, de-felt-tipping a panel.

The Driver's Job

The drivers rarely intruded on the conductor's minefield. They did their job in such a smooth and steady manner that even their most peripatetic passenger-the conductor – tended to take their expertise for granted. This was most unfair as they produced this smooth steadiness and kept to time regardless of any lack of co-operation from the bus, other traffic, Brighton's road system, topography, and the weather. Some BH&D 'driver stories' from my time there follow. Further descriptions of driving QMs appear on the following pages, on pp 42-43 and 111 and elsewhere.

On Thursday 6th September 1973 my driver on duty 6-6L suddenly found 261 coughing and spluttering in a rather unhealthy manner as we left Woodingdean. As she ground to a complete standstill, Vic whispered 'Don't tell the punters but I think we've run out of fuel'. Once the passengers were all safely dispatched on other buses we prodded about in the fuel tank and confirmed our diagnosis. How this came about was unclear but Bruce Macphee mentioned some duties at Seaford that required a very full tank to avoid a premature shift end and 6-6(first bus out in the morning and late in) may have been similar – and not filled sufficiently the night before. Mary 261 was incidentally a very wearing bus to conduct because of her superfast 'wham-shut' doors: not only were they very noisy but one had to delay ringing off to avoid taking the leg off the last boarder or alighter. 272 in contrast had "retro-active" doors –so slow, one felt one could start shutting them halfway through disembarkation.

On Wednesday 18th September 1974 we were in Whitehawk working duty 1-17 with Mary 278 (284 was over the pits having her brakes looked at) when we came upon roadworks which had narrowed the carriageway. A woman drove half-way through the constricted bit from the opposite end and then stopped and flashed her lights at us. 'What am I supposed to do lady?' Colin, the driver, asked no-one in particular 'Tip it sideways and come through on two wheels?' At least this car driver's intentions appeared to be helpful – unlike the gang who liked to play 'last past the bus' when we were pulling away from stops or those who pulled straight out in front of us, or those who parked on Bus Stops, or etc, etc.

One of Brighton's most distinctive features is its extreme hilliness and most routes involve buses and drivers in a certain amount of low-gear slog. Queen Marys from Southdown's Eastern Division, familiar with the town or the switchback route between Brighton and Eastbourne, were used to this sort of thing but those from the western end of the territory where things are generally flatter, must have found this constant hillwork a bit of a shock. Certainly it traumatised Chichester's 271. The extraordinarily steep Bear Road between the Lewes Road and the Racecourse, which was part of the 6 route, was a test for all vehicles and one that 271 frequently failed. The road had two steep sections, with a flatter stretch in the middle; it was the final grind up the second steep part that sorted the sheep from the goats. When well-loaded, 271 invariably turned out to be a goat, and it became necessary to organise a temporary disembarkation of the passengers to enable her to complete the climb. On the morning of Thursday 13th September 1973, Queen Mary 284, working her old service of 26-15, came upon 271 plodding slowly up to the Hollingbury factories on a special and promptly overtook her: I wish I had been on the kerb with my camera rather than conducting 284. Drivers always handled The Goat expertly so she never did worse than grind to a halt.

As an ex-Brighton car, 275 had no excuse for her performance on Wednesday 11th July 1973. She was chugging up Sutherland Road that morning *en route* to Race Hill when the climb suddenly became too much for her and a spectacular cloud of steam filled the cab. The brakes came on rather suddenly and the driver leapt from his seat to avoid being scalded. Gallons of water ran back down the hill but 275 calmed down and continued until temporarily crippled by a similar difficulty later in the day.

On Saturday 7th September 1974 it was gales that my driver had to contend with. 100mph winds had been a feature of the Channel for several days before, and they continued unabated that morning. Gusts rocked 253 (substituting for 969 on 55-3E) between Palace

Continued on Page 60

ABOVE: Hilly haphazard Brighton was not an easy place in which to drive a bus producing many tricky situations for BH&D's staff. Here we see the familiar problem of trying to extract a 6 from The Quadrant through cars queueing for the lower lights on top of painted instructions to keep the space clear; 293, the service bus on 6-3, was being negotiated through the mess on Saturday 28th September 1974. The Scimitar finally reverses.The item on the left is the famous Clock Tower; most traffic turns were banned at this point in 1977 in an attempt to reduce the mayhem – buses were exempt.

BELOW: The Goat on a rare all-day outing in September 1974 climbs into Churchill Square without incident.

Driving Queen Marys – a 1982 survey

In 1982, I spoke to some Mary drivers to get some idea of what they were like to drive. All of them agreed that they were solid reliable old tanks. Opinions as to whether this was a good thing or not varied considerably. At one extreme was the transport economist who drove buses for fun and said that driving a PD3 was 'delightful' because one could 'feel the steering, feel the engine, feel the gearchanges (even on a 3/5) feel the suspension' and overall feel one had especially with a full-width cab, 'a real, massive, heavy, workmanlike vehicle'. At the other extreme was the BH&D driver who could find little positive to say about them in comparison with the Bristols, mentioning heavy steering, heavy clutch-springs, the lack of escape from conductor-chatter and poor visibility in particular.

Most other drivers made similar comments tending to the former or the latter view seemingly in direct relation to how much or how little they had had to do with them. Another BH&D driver, but one who had had a Queen Mary for a service bus, said that they were nice to drive, holding the road well and that he preferred the immediate response of their synchromesh gears to the slower change of the Bristols' crash boxes. Older Worthing drivers with many years experience of PD3s described them as 'good safe workhorses that never let you down' but a younger colleague, overhearing the conversation, mentioned how noisy their cabs were and how unpleasant it had thus been to work them as one-man buses.

In summary my correspondents said:

STABILITY: The buses held the road well whatever the conditions.

STEERING: Slightly heavy.

GEARBOX: Synchromesh preferred to crash or automatic by many; clutches heavy.

PULLING POWER: A bit sluggish, particularly on hills. Top speed averages 42.

VISIBILITY: Multiplicity of pillars, crossbars and corners had to be got used to; visibility poor when raining.

DRIVER COMFORT: Windscreen cross-bars led tall drivers to drive with head bent. Distance between seat and pedals and the difficulty in adjusting seats (drivers adjusted them whilst sitting in them, damaging mechanism) posed problems for short drivers. None of the drivers specifically mentioned the brakes but Queen Marys were not noted for their ability to stop dead.

Crewing Queen Marys in 1996

Stephen Morris relates his experiences of driving Queen Marys

Life, they say, has it ups and downs. Back in 1979 the life of this particular writer was not exactly in the ascendancy, following a slightly disastrous year in Southampton. The year itself had been fun; Southampton is a great place to be and while my own local bus route was run by rather dull Atlanteans which photographed your money when you got in board, thanks to an ingenious fare collection system called Videmat which didn't work very often, the fleet itself was immaculate and there were still AEC Regent Vs running around the place, which added to the fun.

But the object of the exercise had been to emerge on an unsuspecting world with a piece of paper saying I could teach kids all they wanted to know about J. S Bach, Igor Stravinsky and other such similar things without which their little lives couldn't possibly be complete. Maybe I would have been more successful if I had applied myself more to education theory and less to Regent Vs, the local brew and a particularly fine curry house. But as the last hours of my final term ticked away and I knew I would never teach, something came up on the local television news. Anyone with a driving licence who presented themselves at Haywards Heath that Saturday could drive a bus.

Naturally this was something I had wanted to do since I was knee high to a gear lever. Arrangements were swiftly made and I duly presented myself to a large yellow training bus. It was, of course, a Southdown Queen Mary, 2880 (?) CD.

Southdown, it must be said, wasn't having a good day in Haywards Heath. What the TV had forgotten to mention was that Southdown was really interested only in people who wanted to go and drive for them;

and of course, all and sundry had turned up just to have a go on a bus. As I arrived a frustrated driving instructor announced that they wouldn't take anyone else out that day who wasn't interested in a job with Southdown. 'I've come all the way from Manchester!', I protested, not entirely truthfully, but Manchester is where I should have been by then and I had gone to a lot of trouble to have a play with a bus. And that seemed to swing things.

There were four of us to have a go; myself, a fellow student who was going to be a teacher and not a Southdown bus driver, a lady of 70 plus who had driven ambulances in the war, and also wasn't intending to be a Southdown bus driver and another chap who didn't seem that way disposed either.

I agreed to go first. It was certainly highly daunting; the PD3 had looked big from outside, but seemed huge from the cab. Visibility was not clever, especially as my eyeline was higher than the top of the windscreen. I expected it to be heavy, which it was, but not as heavy as I had expected. Yes, you do have to double-declutch, said the instructor, apparently not convinced that I could. Neither was I, but I managed it, though what struck me was how slow everything was and how much time you needed to take for everything; accelerating, changing gear, steering and stopping. But it was tremendous fun. I had driven a bus, everyone else had crunched the gears, and I could die happy.

Well so I thought. Not having made the grade as a teacher was the best thing that ever happened to me and I soon found myself writing about buses, in the amazingly privileged position as a professional bus enthusiast, and plenty more chances would come my way to drive the things.

As it happened, many of those opportunities involved Leyland PDs, most of them PD2s and with the occasional PD1 thrown in for good measure. I trained on not one, but two PD2s, one ex-Portsmouth, the other ex-Nottingham, on which I passed my test. I soon found they were not as huge as I first thought, you could hustle them along more quickly than I had thought and it was actually quite easy to crunch the gears. But never a Queen Mary came my way, until I was chatting to Julian Osborne towards the end of 1995.

He was excited, as he always is when Queen Marys are involved. Julian is usually one of those highly respectable people with a job in the airline industry and a home in Worplesdon, Surrey. His tonsorial appearance gives him the look of a serious, wise old sage (can sages be anything other than wise, outside a juxtaposition with onions?), and he is terribly proper. But once the subject gets round to Queen Marys, he is a 20-year-old student again, mis-spending his youth with a Setright round his neck, earning a few coppers to supplement a meagre grant. He throws out statements which to anyone not understanding Queen Marys might suggest he is a Russian spy talking in code, like 'I've just discovered 274 in a bog in Benbecula', or words (and numbers) to that effect. And I, as a mere Northerner, rack my brains and think what on earth 274 might look like, other than having a flat front with too many windows.

Julian's excitement was that he had got involved with the next year's Coastline rally which was to involve the biggest extravaganza of Queen Marys in living memory—for 15-year olds anyway. I explained that a Queen Mary had been the first bus I had ever driven, and I hadn't driven one since, and wouldn't it be fun if...

And so it was arranged. Thanks to Queen Mary owner Chris Pearce, Julian and I would crew his 294 on a special service for the rally. 'We'll be doing the 2', said Julian, the tone of his voice implying that reference to '2' should immediately put the wind up any would-be driver. Again, as a mere Northerner, I didn't understand the significance of '2' and thought no more of it, assuming that nothing could be easier than a gentle potter along the coast road between Shoreham and Rottingdean.

It was felt that some route learning might be a good idea, and so in April 1996, when I was in Brighton for the coach rally, Chris Pearce turned up in his 294. The run along the sea front, as I expected was a doddle. But then we turned left in Rottingdean, along a road not wide enough for a PD3 and the cars coming the other way, and began to climb, and I finally – and belatedly – got the joke. For those who don't know it, the 2 involves a tortuous route through a housing estate on the north face of the Eiger.

So what of this PD3, whose acquaintance I was renewing after 17 years? Well, to some extent it was very much a PD, though one of the easiest I had driven. The nice thing about old buses is that they all have a character of their own. This isn't sentiment; one modern bus does seem not unlike another to drive – and most these days are highly competent machines – but one PD-type Titan can be very different from another. With its extra weight and size, you might expect a Queen Mary to be heavier than a smaller PD2 to drive; not so with 294. Steering was solid, as you would expect, but it was one of the lightest Leylands I had driven, without power steering that is. It bowled along the sea front in fine style, and the way it romped up hills almost as if they weren't there, showed it to be in fine fettle.

Most of the PDs I have driven have had vacuum brakes. In true Leyland fashion, they stop the bus eventually. I assumed the air brakes of the PD3 would be much keener, though they weren't; they felt exactly the same as Leyland's vacuum brakes. This is not a bad thing; an air-braked AEC or Daimler of the same vintage could pull up on its nose if you hit the pedal too hard, whereas the Queen Mary still gave a nice, smooth, if noisy, stop.

The other notable thing about 294 was its excellent gearchange. Leyland 'synchromesh' gearboxes of that period have synchromesh only on third and fourth gear, so presumably the Trades Descriptions Act had not been in force by then. Leyland had proudly introduced its original PD2 with a box with synchromesh on all but first but it was troublesome and they had had to go back to the drawing board, even having to build some early PD2s with an earlier style of full crash box. Having latterly driven a 1951 Manchester PD2 with one of these synchro-second boxes, it's a shame Leyland couldn't get it right; the difference that gearbox made was incredible, with a superbly easy and completely foolproof 'knife through butter' change that was streets ahead of the thing in most PDs.

The 'proper' way to change from first to second on a PD is to double-declutch, waiting until the bus has almost come back to a standstill before attempting to select second and almost defeating the object of using first gear at all. In fact they were designed to start in second in most situations anyway, with first only there for emergencies, and normally 294 was more than happy to start in second. Often you get a very embarrassing clutch judder starting thus, but there was little trace of this with 294.

But if you do need to use first there is another trick; it involves going up to about half revs in first, pushing the clutch to the floor and snatching the lever back into second without lifting the pedal. It usually works, but 294 was most reluctant to let me do this, almost every attempt resulting in a horrible gnashing of teeth and not a lot else. It did in fact have its own little trick, which was shown to me numerously, but I really couldn't quite get the hang of it. Normally it wouldn't have been much of an issue, but given the ferocious gradients on route 2 the ability to use first gear would be essential. Indeed on the way up from the shops at Woodingdean the road gets so steep that it is necessary to go right down the box just to keep mobile; seldom have I had to select second on the move on a PD, and having achieved this without mishap on 294, I sighed with relief – until I realised it was still losing speed rapidly and would quickly die altogether if I didn't drop down to first. To my eternal relief, a swift double-declutch with bags of revs did the trick, first fell in silently and we kept going.

This of course was without passengers, and as the rally – when we would repeat the exercise *with* passengers – wasn't until the first week of July I had three months of sleepless nights in front of me.

The day of the rally started with the writer being rostered not to drive 294, but Wallace Arnold's open-topper, 425 on a 'mystery tour'. What the public may not have appreciated is that not only was the tour a mystery to them, it was also a mystery to the driver, but never mind. As one might expect from a vehicle owned by an operator so highly respected as Wallace Arnold, 425 was in beautiful condition and was mechanically first rate – if a little down on power compared with 294. Indeed with a load on first-gear starts were actually the order of the day; second gear starts were greeted with the revs dying almost to the point of extinction. And, lo and behold, 425's gearbox was of the same mind as 294's on the subject of snatch changes from first to second. With a load of passengers on, and the trip having been billed publicly as 'being driven by the editor of *Buses*', I felt it wasn't the time or place to experiment with snatch changes which can be very noisy and not awfully effective if you get them wrong, so I had little choice but to go through the very slow motions of double-declutching for each change – but at least they were quiet and hopefully gave the impression that I knew what I was doing.

Otherwise the drive was largely uneventful, apart from losing much time in a traffic jam and getting slightly alarmed as I dashed back to make up time; the interesting way in which cars were parked near a set of small traffic islands at one point meant we performed a magnificent 'Queen Mary slalom', and I doubted my ability to steer the thing fast enough at one point. Meanwhile the bus lurched merrily from side to side and I think the passengers thought it was all part of the fun. *(WE DID! J.O.)*

At last the time came to drive 294 on the route 2 etc, though the first part of the exercise was to stuff the old Pool Valley bus station with as many Queen Marys as possible, which made a stirring sight and even more stirring sound. It rained, but somehow that just added to the atmosphere and no-one seemed to mind too much. What we hadn't done on the route-learning bit was to pull into the bus terminus at Rottingdean, which is a bit small and involved about a seven-point turn, at which point 294's steering showed how very heavy it actually was.

Despite the extra load, 294 coped just as well with the hill climbing as it had done before, and again I managed those critical downchanges without a problem, though the conductor got a bit perturbed as I raised both hands in exultation at this feat. As we were down to about 4mph, it didn't seem to matter too much!

Continued on p.111. Some related pictures overleaf.

RIGHT: Diners watch askance as 294's seven-point turn brings its rear regularly towards their lunches! *(Andy Izatt)*

Photo: Andy Izatt

Photo: Andy Izatt

Photo: Andy Izatt

Mountaineering around east Brighton on the 2 was always fun except perhaps for the driver. Most of these pictures show preserved 294 reprising QM days on the route during the 1996 Rally...or in 1998. (The first gear incline was Shipley Road and 294 ascends it in the four lefthand pictures. At the top the road appears to drop vertically away behind whilst in the previous picture the viewpoint of a 6-year-old gives some further idea) but 409 (mid-right p.59) was on the top ten years earlier at another rally and 415, 290 and 412 were genuinely on service in 1979, 1978 and 1980 respectively. The pictures take you generally westward from Rottingdean to central Brighton.

Photo: Tim Osborne

Photo: Gary French

Photo: Andy Izatt

The western end of the 2 had its moments as well and buses at work on it can be seen on pages 61, 74 and 76. I liked working the 2. There were some duties at Whitehawk which were solely Shoreham Beach-Rottingdeans but most duties involved shorts or 1s so the chance to 'do a Rottingdean' was always nice. 1-17 did two Portslade-Rottingdeans as its evening. The isolation of Woodingdean led occasionally to minor social unrest and the periodic withdrawal of late journeys. In early 1974 kids running out and hanging on the exterior handles as we pulled away from stops was briefly a problem both sides of the downs.

Pier and Black Rock, as we set off on our first trip to Saltdean, but could not attack with full force until we got out onto the exposed cliff by Roedean. Ron, the driver, tested for a safe speed as one gust hit us and a second very nearly toppled us. 'I thought that was it – she's going over' he confided encouragingly. The wind swung round and for the rest of the morning it was only the westbound journeys that were affected in this way. Each one began with a fraught layover at Bannings Vale, with the wind howling round the vehicle, and then involved ten minutes on the top of the cliff being blasted and biffed all over the place by the gale. Whilst fanciful notions of being blown off the cliff occurred, the real danger was that in all the buffeting the driver would lose control of the bus – not that that was remotely possible with as steady a professional as Ron at the helm. That morning we did not carry many passengers – the section of the 11.43 from Portslade into town was the busiest journey – and much revolved around Saltdean stories. One passenger said that a bus had been seen to go up on two wheels the day before. A shopkeeper at Saltdean said that a Corporation driver had ordered all passengers downstairs and, weighted with 16 standing, proceeded. Ron said that he did not mind where they sat. We saw a very lightly-loaded Corporation Atlantean jumping about all over the place, a look of intense concentration on the driver's face. Mervyn, the driver of 55-4, commented a few days later that his "heart had been in his mouth" several times. Mary 273 replaced 253 when the wind blew half of one of the latter's skylights away and it started raining upstairs.

Coming back on the 12.48 journey from Saltdean, 273 very nearly went up on two wheels as she emerged in Ovingdean Gap – we felt the whole vehicle heave over; fortunately she heaved back again. Soon after we caught up with 422 running in from Eastbourne on the 12 and presented an awesome sight for cars as the two PD3s swayed, swerved and rocked in an unsynchronised way, all over the road. Some cars still overtook though. An additional inconvenience on 273 was that her rear-view mirrors were a bit loose and at each encounter with the gale were blown flat against the bus sides: Ron and I reset one each at Black Rock on each westbound trip.

Incidentally, most stops were 'Compulsory': the onus was on us to decide whether we could safely forgo them, rather than on the passengers to indicate any intention of getting on or off. This was common in Southern England.

Photo: Sue Osborne

Photo: Gary French

Thu 19 Sep 74: Eric Dore interposes himself amongst the incoming passengers as 264 is full – 6-4's rush-hour trip (1706 through Churchill square) – and 'rings' her off with a shout of "OK Jim!"

For the sorts of reasons identified by JMW on p.21 in service pictures of bus interiors facing backwards are rare and indeed all the interior shots on this page come from 1990s rallies – even if the top one is of the author conducting (see p.111). The picture **LEFT** does however come from 1974 and shows the conductor interposing himself amongst the passengers on 6-4's 17:06 through Churchill Square. 264 is full and Eric carefully truncates the boarding stream and rings off with a shout of "OK Jim!" to the driver.

RIGHT: This interesting 1974 picture of 924 at Newhaven shows her having another, pre-withdrawal, go at the route she and her batchmates had found so difficult in their youth—she negotiates the mess connected with the replacement of the channel port's historic swing bridge. This valedictory attempt at the 12 had been made easier for her by the hiving off the hilly West Dene operations at the western end of the route but towards the end the semi-automatics got generally more adventurous, even working Brighton local routes. *(Jim Jones)*

In staircasing terms the crew of 266 have slipped up rather here and seem to be towing half of Brighton's buses along Western Road in this April 1974 view; note the parallel Corporation 49 risking breaking cover from hiding behind the FLF now that 266 is leaving the stop. What we have here is a sixpack of Brighton buses at Norfolk Square and the multi-coloured livery spectacle prevalent at the time

Staircasing

There was an extra incentive for meeting the joint responsibility of keeping the bus to time. We have seen that the conductor's job got harder the busier the bus was: not only was there more platform supervision to do and more fare collection to effect, there was also more need to balance the two and more crowded conditions in which to do it. Busy conditions got worse the shorter the riders, for the higher the turnover the more passengers overall to be processed and the shorter the time for each one; the more crowded and chaotic the bus, with lots of people getting on and off all the time, the more chance there was of an expensive mistake or a culpable shortfall in courtesy or conscientiousness. The driver's job also got harder: the bus was heavier to drive and had to stop more often.

Thus both conductor's and driver's jobs were easier, the emptier the bus and the longer the passenger journeys. A crew endeavour to minimise loads and passenger turnover might seem to be contrary to the interests of the passengers and the objectives of the company but its first manifestation was not: it encouraged the maintenance of the schedule; not running late ensured that the bus only collected its own passengers – particularly its own short-riders – and not those of the bus behind as well.

So far so good. But of course if the crew's pursuit of the easy life was pushed further it fell out of line with passenger interests and company objectives. Crews periodically had to remind themselves that the object of the exercise was to carry lots of people and collect lots of fares whilst running to schedule ... and not to get the bus from one end of the route to the other picking up as few people as possible – and they preferably long-riders – on the way.

It is now necessary to make a small confession. Sometimes we did not remind ourselves loudly enough and found ourselves trying to take an empty bus around Brighton. The most common means of effecting this was 'staircasing': attention switched from the sensible objective of not having the bus behind's passengers on board, to the less laudable one of getting one's passengers on the bus in front – this involved following another bus in the hope that the passengers would get on it rather than you, which in backloader days had meant following its staircase.

The practice was most prevalent on Western Road because of its large numbers of short-riders. The fact that nearly all the routes went along Western Road was also a factor and it made the practice quite easy. That there were various entry points to the core route between the Steine and Hove Town Hall made for a fair amount of strategical manoeuvring amongst the participants. It was considered a bit *non-U* to follow one of your mates and at Conway Street there was a hierarchy of acceptable victims for staircasing; from the most down to the least acceptable, these were:

The Southdown 15 worked by Edward Street garage
The Corporation 49 (easy to spot, being bright blue)
Whitehawk vehicles not on your route
Conway vehicles not on your route
Whitehawk vehicles on your route
Conway vehicles on your route

Staircasing was most effective if operated at two stops remove from the victim, thus preventing him from sending passengers back to you. The more vehicles in front, of course, the better!

Staircasing could lead to some disagreements between crews, particularly when it went beyond the avoidance of central shortriders, and crews caught up a bus duplicating their route through town and out again or vice-versa thus avoiding long-riders and suburban short-riders as well! Thus crews on services 1 and 6 (west) sometimes had a stormy relationship, as did those on services 2 and 49 and 15, 26 and 55. Northbound saw 5 and 15 route crews not always on the best of terms, while to the east one occasionally found route 1 and 3 crews in conflict. This is something of a simplification as far as the 15 routemen are concerned: everyone had a stormy relationship with them!

Like passenger over-riding, crew staircasing was as often unintentional as deliberate; one would enter Western Road, see another bus in the distance and realise that an easy trip was in store. Few of us set out with the deliberate aim of running on the heels of another bus all shift, but if the opportunity arose on a busy day it was very tempting. Even so, it was not always taken up and we would go 'stop for stop' with other buses (ie each bus overtaking the other at alternate stops) fraught though this was with the danger of one of the participants unavoidably or deliberately dropping out while at the back.

Of course staircasing was only prevalent because, in those days, Brighton's buses were still extremely busy; there were so many passengers that the chance of dropping a few on another crew was a temptation. There was an advertisement in some of the buses of a smiling Billy the Bus type character in Southdown livery exhorting passengers to 'avoid the peak'. Some of these had had the information '... which in Brighton lasts all day' added to them, and so it seemed! The total number of passengers carried in the course of a 45-minute journey at any time between 7.00 am and 7.00 pm could total double or even treble the bus's authorised capacity (*i.e.* we had emptied and filled the thing two or three times) and 1000 tickets a shift was not that unusual. The most extreme cases of being busy ('slaughtered' in Conway Street vernacular) were not solely attributable to heavy demand, however, but to the practice of staircasing or to cancellations through staff shortage.

BELOW: The tables turned: a Corporation 49 stumbles up to Churchill Square under a full load with a trio of BH&D Queen Marys mischievously clustered behind (261 on the 2A, 273 on the 2, 969 on the 55) on Easter Saturday, 13th April 1974.

ABOVE: The final grind up the second part of Bear Road. No 261 turns out to be a sheep; she became the service bus on 6-6 during 1973 and is seen here in the summer of that year on that duty.

The Late Shift

On the early shift one gradually ran out of energy in inverse relation to the build-up of work. This was always taken to extremes by the author on his first early turn of each session at Conway, as he readjusted painfully to crack-of-dawn starts, and reached a nadir on Wednesday 10th July 1974. By 11.00 am the demands of a quick turnround off the 1 at Portslade Station were almost too much for him and 284 set off for Race Hill with her front number blind unchanged and me covering by standing half-dead on the platform muttering 'We're a 2A really' to incoming passengers. Even in normal circumstances the sight of one's relieving crew was a welcome one. Because the late shift saw energy and work decreasing simultaneously it was generally less tiring and nearly all of us therefore relieved early conductors approximately 1½ hours before the official changeover time, a courtesy highly-valued by BH&D staff. Crews would enter the numbers on the ticket-machine counters as opening or closing waybill numbers as appropriate. The machine would then be handed over, the late person would leave in the bus and the early one would go and pay in.

Late turns then consisted of a few busy shopper and holidaymaker trips across town and then a few more when those people were joined by school and business commuters. This mixture made the afternoon rush-hour busier than the morning one but once again 'Swingers' assisted. The rush-hour ended after several journeys with London rail commuters who emerged from stations between 6 and 7.

I described earlier the various components of the conductor's job and the balance necessary between the two main ones: platform supervision and fare collection. Let's now try and draw all that together by describing the conducting of a Queen Mary on the 2 pulling off Churchill Square westbound at 5.15 pm with a standing load. All pre-Churchill Square passengers should have had their fares taken while the bus was crawling through the traffic morass in North Street. As the lower deck gangway was full of standees, fare collection commenced around the stairs on the upper deck. Three bells should have got us through Preston Street still upstairs but we would probably have needed to descend at Norfolk Square and catch a few lower-deck short-riders steaming doorwards hoping not to make the conductor's acquaintance – and control incomers: we would not therefore have strayed far from the stairs while aloft (disembarking upper-deck short-riders could otherwise have blocked our return). After Norfolk Square, the standees should have thinned out a bit and, with a bit of persuasion could be shepherded to the rear of the lower saloon to facilitate collection of fares in the front half. From Brunswick Square to First Avenue, platform collection was probably most efficacious but by Hove Town Hall all the lower deck should have been cleared, the standees having got off or sat down and the back half having become accessible. The journey up Tisbury Road permitted the completion of upper-deck collection. Then after the bus had left George Street the conductor would have to go in amongst them again because we picked up a few shoppers there on all journeys before about 6.00 pm. After that we could start bagging up and chatting to the driver: they might have been interested in some details of the heavy load they had been

carrying or they may have had some items of information about the bus or the traffic that they wanted to share.

Here is perhaps an appropriate point to draw attention to yet more expertises of the conductor. All the above obviously required a capacity for mental arithmetic . . . and a fine sense of balance: the degree of stanchion support for our balancing act depended on whether we had a 'Lodekka' which had lots or a 'Mary' which had few, the note of the engine which was continuously subconsciously monitored to detect any imminent changes in the ride characteristics, and whether we were at Palmeira Square. One always hung on round Palmeira Square. Occasionally, very occasionally, our drivers would surprise us: I sat down on a passenger once when my crew mate overtook a car on Portland Road with two right-angled turns!

The late shift was not much different from the early one until six. After that things changed a bit. Thinner schedules (with longer layovers), emptier roads and fewer baggage-laden, questioning short-riders all made for easier maintenance of timings. There was a higher proportion of leisure travellers and, as the evening wore on, a greater likelihood of 'overtired and emotional' passengers.

Early evening saw us depositing revellers about our network – in summer we brought large numbers of foreign students into town to pick each other up at the Tower Clock. These journeys were great fun and I learnt a lot of useful phrases in other languages. Of course most of the 'perverse' behaviour of foreign students listed earlier resulted from their familiarity with the much more flexible systems of ticketing common on the continent. Throughout the year we took locals as well on these early evening journeys to town or to such places as the Dog Track. Once everyone was at their place of entertainment there was the quietest part of the day-the mid-evening lull. Then came the day's final

BELOW: Queen Marys on the 5 and CUFs at Conway Street were not common until 1975. No. 953 doing the slower eastbound Palmeira Square manoeuvre under a good load is seen in the summer of 1976. *(Authors' collection)*

ABOVE LEFT: After the conversion of route 26 there were no more one-man conversions at BH&D for a long time, but route reshufflings did reduce crew activity in the mid-seventies; this affected Lodekka mileage more than that of Marys. In the 1975 reshuffle, routes 1 and 2 ceased interworking and certain Portslade Station journeys of the 2 were renumbered 22 and extended to Mill House. This was to cover for the 11 which had merged with the 8 and become unable to meet its Mill House commitment. Mary 974 was clattering down Foredown Drive away from this newterminus on 19th February 1977, shortly before her withdrawal. *(Chris Warren)*
ABOVE RIGHT: In the 1976 reshuffle the 55 disappeared and certain journeys on the 1 were diverted at the edge of Whitehawk to proceed to Saltdean: 970 was involved in this new arrangement in early 1977. The 1976 changes also saw the extension of the 6 – not for the first time in its career -to Southwick and the introduction of a number of Limited Stop services, some of which were worked with Queen Marys. *(Paul Gainsbury)*

challenge – the only point on the late turn where conductor energy and work to do were not matched: the last journey!

In summer, vast crowds of foreign students, all hoping to board the last few buses, congregated in Churchill Square. Locals quickly calculated their chances in this scrum and started to head the buses off in the Steine and at New Road. Often this meant that one was full and able to go straight past Churchill Square. If one had seats available, one witnessed some amazing scrums as people tore eachother apart trying to get on – the both-sides-of-the-bar problem disappeared in these circumstances!

On the night of Sunday 28th July 1974 after a pleasant shift on 264 working 5-9L we were 'slaughtered' on our 10.06 pm journey from Mackie Avenue by enormous crowds in town. At Churchill Square, I took up a position at the top of the stairs as she filled up; this was out of a desire to be fair and fill the whole bus – if one was on the platform, the press of people there often made it difficult to check whether the upper-deck was completely full. My method carried with it problems of course: I was not on the platform to control things and, as we know, at the best of times – let alone at that hour – overloading was thus possible. Indeed it did occur that night but when I came down from my full upper deck and asked the twelve surplus standees to leave, they did. Danny, my driver, confided later that he had been beginning to lose faith in me whilst they were all piling aboard, apparently unheeded. At Norfolk Square, the Hardwick Road kids took advantage of our stopping to unload a few late-night short-riders to rush the bus. I took four and then had to push the rest off, yelling, "Shut 'em Dan", by way of a starting signal. The doors slammed shut before they had time to regroup and 264 ground away from the stop with the clientele "falling out of the windows". I should add that this was all a very good-natured affair.

Unless they headed the buses off in the Steine, the only way passengers could avoid these scrums was to take advantage of the stunned confusion produced by a numberless 'HOVE Coleridge Street' working or wait until things died down a bit at the end of August. Actually, the busier things were at this late hour, the less likely we were to encounter 'trouble' ... but if one did encounter aggression, one endeavoured to diffuse it with friendliness; it invariably worked: in this respect a late bus provided a crash course in behavioural science. In August 1974, working the 11.50 pm from Brighton Station with 293, most of the aggression was coming from the boisterous Scottish gentleman in the driving cab who appeared to be letting a random number of customers off at each stop and then closing the doors and driving flat out to the next one. I increased my standard NBC Late-Bus-Conductor-Affability-Toward-Passengers and we managed to avoid being lynched.

Readers may have noticed that last buses tend to go somewhat faster than other journeys: it was indeed heartening to discover just

how fast some of the Marys could go. One of the last buses out to the suburbs used, for instance, to operate an unadvertised Limited Stop Express service from Palmeira Square to the terminus. Car drivers coming to side-road junctions would look, see a bus, go to come out and then stop again suddenly as they realised just how fast it was going: the Queen Mary concerned would bound playfully about the Old Shoreham Road as she tore along, with the regular driver responsible for all this, sitting in his cab shouting *"I'm Ron Come fly with me."*

Another angle on late buses also occurred while working with Ron. This time we had 286. A girl got on with her boyfriend whilst we were laying over at Hollingbury and eventually went two stops. Ron cast aspersions on her sanity but I surmised that she came for the fifteen minutes upstairs with the lights out. We did once operate half a journey with dimmed upper lights for the solitary couple on the back seat but that was an FLF so I can't put it here.

The day ended with a long line of buses – the odd one possibly containing a foreign student who had not believed that the last trip did not run to the normal terminus – making its way through the washer and past the fuel pumps; the conductor completed his waybill, checked that it tallied with the money he had collected, tied it all up in his paying-in bag, slung it in the night safe, returned his box, and went home.

BELOW: 284 takes the short layover timetabled in Whitehawk in the shadow of the racecourse before working 1-17's 15:24 journey back to Portslade one afternoon in August 1974. The Racecourse was of course the scene of the crime rackets immortalised in Graham Greene's Brighton Rock. See the film of it starring Richard Attenborough for a graphic portrayal of Brighton's once co-ordinated transport: a BH&D Bristol turns into a Corporation AEC during its descent of Queens Road!

Livery Changes

Full NBC meant this. Grey fleetnumbers and standard white fleetnames. There were no grey fleetnumbers on traditional livery but some grey wheels did appear on green and cream Marys. The othe stuff was not standard but symptomatic of 270's continued attempts to meet the challenge of the seventies. Discarding her white livery in April 1975, she next sought to come to terms with the times by offering herself in this manner. The photo was taken in Palmeira Square on Saturday 28th June 1975. 270 spurned the BH&D option, only working there in her last operational months but few Marys could claim such short acquaintance. The main reason for this, as we have hinted, was that there was increasingly little work for them elsewhere. The map on page 66 shows the amount of crew (i.e PD3 give or take the odd Lodekka) mileage left in the Southdown network in 1976. *(Roy Simmons)*

Observant readers will have noticed an insidious change in the livery of our heroines during the last few pages. The flamboyant four apart, some pretty fundamental livery change appears to have overtaken the Queen Marys and this had been brought about, of course, by the National Bus Company's interest in having a Corporate Image. This interest started to have an effect at the time the Marys were beginning to congregate at Conway Street and involved them in various livery modifications during the gradual transformation from a grass green and cream fleet to a leaf green one.

Immediate Livery Tinkering

One or two NBC fleets endeavoured to modify and simplify their pre-NBC liveries in the early years of the National Bus Company's existence. City of Oxford, for instance, reduced its splendid old three-tone livery of scarlet, maroon and duck egg green to a rather less wonderful combination of scarlet and duck egg green. Southdown, however, did not do anything like this and stuck to their traditional grass green and cream to the extent of repainting BH&D Lodekkas in it. Southdown's only apparent manoeuvre in the livery simplification area in those early NBC days was the continuation of a process of rationalising the fleetname applied to service buses. This traditionally took the form of a set of huge gold block capital letters marching proudly across the bodywork to proclaim 'SOUTHDOWN'. In the early sixties, single-deckers had foregone this magnificence in favour of the script-style gold fleetname applied to coaches, and one or two 'deckers, had also tried it. In 1969 Portsmouth's 347 and 849 appeared with such script fleetnames. They were followed in 1971 by 828 sporting a fleetname composed of small gold capitals.

Queen Marys 830, 833, 836, 837 and 838 acquired similar style fleetnames proclaiming 'SOUTHDOWN-BH&D' when they became the first Marys to work from Conway Street and Whitehawk. Further Marys followed them to BH&D with this style of fleetname – the short stay CUF-registered ones lost the BH&D bit on their return and were thus rendered the same as 828. The small gold block fleetname became standard on repaints in September 1971.

A second livery simplification began in August 1971 when it became general practice to paint entrance doors all green rather than half-green and half-cream.

The Advent of Full Corporate Image

Such simplifications were however soon overrun by the concept of full corporate image which emerged in 1972 with the NBC delivering the edict that all its buses would henceforth have to be either leaf green or poppy red: Southdown's were to be leaf green. At the time, the company was busily painting the red and cream BH&D fleet grass green and cream. The switch left the allocation at Conway Street and Whitehawk in a delightfully multi-coloured state. In October 1972, the first PD3s (285, 287, 289, 290, 291, 292) emerged from Portslade in leaf green. The switch to this came halfway through the FCD-D batch's mid-life overhauls, with the result that members of this batch were some of the first and last to receive NBC livery. Mary 313 was, in September 1972, the last PD3 repainted in traditional colours.

Full Corporate Image—Later Marys

For most of the later Marys, Corporate Image meant initially the application of NBC Standard Fleetnames onto grass green and cream – a few in a sensitive cream but most in standard clashing white. Many also appeared with extensive advertising to the effect that Southdown was proud to be part of the National Bus Company with whom it could really go places. Later Queen Marys in the 'BH&D' fleet received an NBC Standard Fleetname of 'SOUTHDOWN-BH&D'. This all happened early in 1973. Repainting into leaf green followed at some point in the following three years. Sometimes this was preceded by the removal of the Southdown scroll plate from the grille: such removal was de rigeur on transformation into leaf green.

Full Corporate Image—Earlier Marys

For the older PD3s (the first 140) Corporate Image meant very little other than the occasional addition of an NBC-style fleetname to the PD3/4s and the systematic addition of same to the semi-automatics. Most had been sold by 1975, having sported basically traditional livery to the end.

added beneath the 'SOUTHDOWN' on both sides. In May 1974 the Conway/Whitehawk allocation lost its 'BH&D' fleetname appendage: now it was the latecomers who benefited as their offside letters could be removed without trace whilst the originals were left with a funny gap between 'SOUTHDOWN' and the symbol. The disappearance of 'BH&D' was to give a unified appearance to the public, but the erstwhile Tilling company continued to exist as a legal entity . . . and, as you may have gathered, in the hearts and minds of its former employees.

Programme Completion

Repainting of the later Queen Marys into leaf green continued until the last few emerged in 1976: the last two were 286 and 405 in July of that year. By that time the tricoloured NBC symbol on a white base had replaced the earlier version: the last few repaints received it as part of the repaint exercise and most of the rest of the fleet were attended to at garages. This new symbol permitted the re-adornment of radiator grilles—bare since Corporate Image banished Southdown scroll plates. Of the later batches, the only Marys never to receive NBC Standard Livery were 964 and 972 which were both sold in 1977 in rather a tatty old state after a period in store, and 427 which became a permanent open-topper in 1975 and left the fleet in 1977.

BH&D Complications

The BH&D variation of the standard fleetname was all very well for vehicles already at the requisite garages on application. It did not work so well for subsequent draftees already carrying NBC insignia. The policy was to run the fleetname away from the National symbol on the nearside and towards it on the offside. This made addition of 'BH&D' relatively easy on the nearside and impossible on the off. In these later cases it was rather messily

TOP OF PAGE: Stage 1, NBC in SMS: At first it was the leaf greens that stood out. In August 1973 the corporate Mary is the only bus not in traditional colours in this shot of the Old Steine.

ABOVE: Stage 2. SMS in NBC: Eighteen months later Churchill Square tells a different story; grass green VR 540 skulking behind 974 is the anomaly.

LEFT: October 1973 and 260 newly reallocated to BH&D, illustrates all-green doors, National Bus Company advertising and unmessily added BH&D fleetname; note however that in all this she has managed to hang on to her Southdown scroll grille plate. See picture p. 54 for messily-added BH&D and 264 on p.48 for messily-removed BH&D. *(Alan Snatt)*

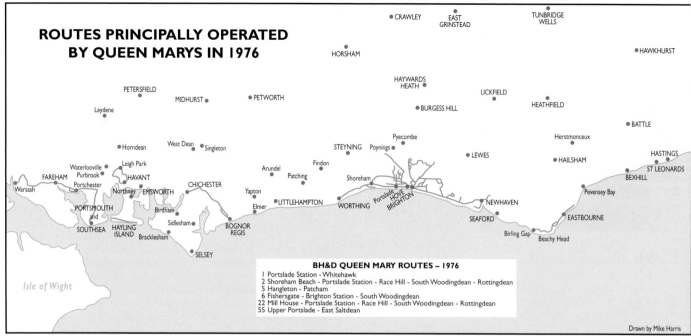

ROUTES PRINCIPALLY OPERATED BY QUEEN MARYS IN 1976

BH&D QUEEN MARY ROUTES – 1976
1 Portslade Station - Whitehawk
2 Shoreham Beach - Portslade Station - Race Hill - South Woodingdean - Rottingdean
5 Hangleton - Patcham
6 Fishersgate - Brighton Station - South Woodingdean
22 Mill House - Portslade Station - Race Hill - South Woodingdean - Rottingdean
55 Upper Portslade - East Saltdean

Drawn by Mike Harris

A sad comparison with the map on page 39 – the Queen Marys have gone from most of their old strongholds! Briefly casting aside our emotional attachment to Marys however, we should note that what happened in the seventies was all sound business management by Southdown as ever: it preserved its comprehensive network despite the restructuring applied to it -regular headways and connections were also kept, wherever possible. In the seventies' economic situation this would not have been possible without one-man operation.

Seventies: General

Throughout the seventies, route restructurings were adhering to a numbering masterplan designed to have all 3XX routes in the Portsmouth area, 2XX ones in the Chichester – Worthing sector and lXX ones in the Brighton–Eastbourne region, with numbers below 100 on Brighton local services. This was somewhat more logical than the original arrangement.

There were no major rebuilds of Queen Marys or accidents to them in the seventies. Worthing's 961 was involved in a nasty accident at Slinfold in May 1972 but it only resulted in a small rebuild and the disappearance of her dome ventilator. The only other incidents involved low bridges: 350 found one in Southampton while on a Private Hire in 1971, whilst 421 and 427 tackled two old favourites – Queen Street, Horsham and Emsworth respectively. 350 was repaired.

The five nodes of Southdown operation changed in nature during the seventies but only really – with the exception of Portsmouth – by degree. Brighton, for instance, became more bizarre and extreme as the decade wore on . . . some saw in this her long prophesied decline, but they didn't know Brighton! Where else could have turned a tatty old shipwreck into a major tourist attraction in the depths of January? Worthing and Eastbourne continued to be genteel seaside and retirement towns. Chichester remained a market town and administrative centre. All adapted to increased car traffic, Eastbourne rather cleverly.

It is at this point that our emotional attachment to Queen Marys re-appears. What we are going to do now is sorrowfully examine the gradual decline of Southdown Queen Mary activity beyond BH&D as a result of one-manning and restructuring and reduction of service. The strategies outlined earlier had been successful for the later Marys, but overall the 1970s Queen Mary story had been very depressing. Astute readers will have deduced that the Marys' best chance of survival in Sussex during the seventies was to seek out 'busy' services – those least susceptible to one-man conversion or restructuring. These might be defined by companywide criteria (eg. number of passengers per mile) or local criteria (eg. busiest service at the garage). At either level, definition depended on management and/or staff opinion on what constituted a busy service.

However defined, busy services held the key to continued Queen Mary activity. Therefore the Marys' decline will be characterised by a gradual concentration on to the busiest services – instead of sliding down a hierarchy they will actually be pushed further and further back up it.

To study this, we will reverse our sixties journey and go back across the patch from Eastbourne to Portsmouth. As we return west across the territory we will use the old sixties operational areas even though various changes to these took place during the seventies. Early on, Worthing/Chichester became Central Division and Portsmouth became Western Division in much the same way that Brighton/Eastbourne were renamed Eastern Division in 1966. This tied up with the route number masterplan. Later there was a disappearance of the sub-depot concept and nearly every garage operated as a unit – except those in the Portsmouth area and the Brighton town ones. By that time, nearly all dormitory sheds had been closed as had some quite large garages like Littlehampton.

Seventies: Eastbourne and Brighton

Attrition of Mary activity was slow and steady at Eastbourne.The abolition of Corporation protective fares in 1971 did little to stem Mary decline.

Services east and locally went first. Locals 93 and 96 had been converted to one-man operation at the turn of the decade. They were followed by the 15, the 99 (which continued in its summer crew operation, at least on Southdown's side, for a bit longer but was fully one-manned before the decade was very old) and the 94 (which clung on for a little longer but finally went over to one-man at the time of Eastbourne's restructuring and acquisition of masterplan numbering in April 1975; the Queen Marys disappeared four months earlier and the replacing VRs were worked crewed in the interim). That left east and locally only the open-top schedules, which remained crewed throughout the decade, and odd crew duties that had reappeared in one-man diagrams. Eastbourne's hinterland was one of the centres for one-man Queen Mary activity. See pictures on the right-hand side opposite for westward developments.

ABOVE: That elusive QM in Hastings picture! Actually taken at a running day in 1992, 409 shows blinds that Queen Marys continued to display in summer in the early seventies when the 99 kept its summer crew operation, at least on Southdown's side. (Alan Snatt)

BELOW: The 94 was the last crewed local service at Eastbourne – 294 in Willingdon Village in February 1974. (Alan Snatt)

Photo: Alan Snatt

Photo: John Bishop

TOP: Every half-an-hour for sixteen years a Queen Mary made this climb ... Western Queen Mary activity survived longest at Eastbourne and Marys continued to clamber over the hills between the town and Brighton for most of the seventies. Mary 960 had just ground up out of Eastbourne on 17th February 1974 when this photo was taken and 301 was at work on the route a few weeks later.

ABOVE: In 1975, the 12 was renumbered 112 as part of the route number masterplan but it remained crewed. This is illustrated by 962 here; observant readers may wonder how 962 can illustrate such a thing and need to know that she had stopped being a one-man bus some time previously. OMO use of Marys had gradually petered out. Westward PD3 activity was reduced to Seaford garage duties on Newhaven–Brighton services in October 1976 when the 112 went over to limited-stop OMO. (Paul Gainsbury)

LEFT: Open-top work continued throughout the seventies. (John Bishop)

RIGHT: At Ovingdean in early 1971, entering the famous gap of the same name, comes 259 still in full traditional livery and with a traditional downland windmill behind. *(Alan Snatt)*

CENTRE RIGHT and BOTTOM LEFT : Early OMO casualties at Brighton were the West Dene services and sub-depot 34: 814 and 976 are seen just before the respective axes fell at Tongdean Lane arch and Hurstpierpoint . Note the small gold fleetname on 976. *(both Jim Jones)*

BELOW RIGHT: Route renumbering had turned the 12B/12C into the 110/111 by the time this picture of 976 was taken at Rottingdean in 1977. *(Paul Gainsbury)*

With most Brighton area service pruning taking place on already one-manned country routes and little extension of OMO in the BATS area, attrition of Mary activity was less marked at company HQ than elsewhere. After the one-manning of such things as the sub-depot routes (last survivor was the 34, converted 10/72) and the more pointless BATS activities (38; 48; Peacehaven Annexe; West Dene; Bevendean) at the beginning of the seventies, Brighton settled down to a continued amount of PD3 operation. Mid-seventies restructuring and renumbering in the Brighton area carried with it few Queen Mary reductions and few full one-man conversions, and the Mary scene at Brighton was of course enhanced by their use on the former BH&D services.

As well as the Eastbourne service itself, the other Eastbourne Road services at Brighton remained crewed for most of the decade, with the exception of the 12A and West Dene limbs which, as already noted, were separated, and converted to one-man-operation early on. The trunk facility between Brighton and Seaford – cut back to Newhaven – remained in the hands of the Marys. Route renumbering had turned the 12B/12C into the 110/111 by the time the picture of 976 was taken at Rottingdean on Wednesday 25th May 1977;

also by that time double-manning on these short workings had outlived that on the main Eastbourne–Brighton route, and they no longer interworked with it. Absorption of Newhaven local services into the 110/111 route brought Queen Marys to Gibbon Road and Denton for the second time in their life.

Photo: Jim Jones

Photo: Paul Gainsbury

Photo: Chris Warren

A feature of BATS introduced in 1975 were the 'Timesaver' Limited Stop services which ran in the peak, and sometimes in the off-peak as well; most were operated by BH&D garages but not all. Marys often appeared on them and 268 was so engaged on Thursday 17th March 1977. It was found appropriate to recrew the Peacehaven Annexe service and include it in the Timesaver Network, where it became the 777; it interworked with the 110/111 during this phase – later some 777s became one-man operated and this renewed interworking ceased. Queen Marys occasionally returned to that other limb of the Eastbourne Road services lost in the early seventies – West Dene: usually they did this as Conway Street specials – 259 is seen at Mill Rise on Monday 12th January 1976.

Photo: Chris Warren

Trunk non-BH&D Brighton local services also continued to see Mary operation for most of the decade: until 1976 this meant the 13 and the 15. Queen Marys of the BUF-C batch had been staple stock on them almost since delivery and at one time the only Marys on Western Road. By the mid-seventies, however, they had been submerged amongst their sisters on BH&D service. The genuine Southdowns remained distinguishable, though, by virtue of their full blinds, their closed water filler-cap flaps, their fleetnames (until May 1974) and their crew uniforms (until late 1974). In 1976 the 15 route disappeared to be replaced by new service 25 and a periodic circularisation of the 13 service. The new 25 route covered the Portslade end of the 15 and then went up the Lewes Road to the University, penetrating the campus and at last relieving would-be academic patrons of the trek down to the main road. The 25 was the last major new Southdown service on which the Marys worked: shortly after it was introduced a still crewed 962 was observed on it and negotiating road-widening in Portslade on Saturday 16th October 1976. The hourly transformation of the 13 into a circular service covered the 15's London Road activity and, by looping via Seven Dials, gave Patcham and the Lewes Road estates a link with the station for the first time; at work on this new development on that same October day was 300, seen here at Preston Circus – note that extra boards had become institutionalised to the extent of adopting BH&D practice and having permanent holders for them grafted onto vehicle fronts. These changes involving routes 13, 15 and 25 further increased through services between the Lewes Road and the Clock Tower.

Photo: Chris Warren

Information about the pictures on this page is in the text.

Photo: Calvin Churchill

BATS open-top services were restructured during the decade, merging Southdown and BH&D routes: Queen Marys appeared on these but open-toppers were also a regular feature on ordinary BATS services during the seventies—the weather was definitely co-operating with this appearance of 425 on service 13 during May 1977. I was a little concerned for the conductors when these things stayed out after dark- how did they see the colour of people's money?

Photo: Roy Simmons

West from Brighton still saw Queen Mary working on the 31 but from 1971 they no longer operated through to Pompey: QM requirements and crew mileage were reduced by splitting the route at Bognor; and the western half was renumbered 131. Alternate 31s from Brighton still short-turned, but no longer at Littlehampton: they were originally intended to turn at Worthing Pier but well-organised lobbying from Goring residents, who had been simultaneously deprived of route 3, managed to keep the service extended to Aldsworth Avenue. On Saturday 25th March 1972, Mary 269 was setting out from Brighton for that terminus – this indicated by the board in the window: devices such as this were common before the exterior ones in special holders appeared. Use of this hard-won extension was not great. No. 269 had lost her upstairs quarter-lights some time in the late sixties.

Seventies: Worthing and Chichester

On arrival at Worthing one encountered a very sadly and suddenly depleted Mary scene. In March 1971, in the decade's first major restructuring exercise, the Town Services and the already-OMO 5/6 were replaced by a new network of OMO routes which represented a big reduction in service and Queen Mary activity in favour of ten frantic one-man Fleetlines. Later, Leyland Nationals appeared on the services, and at last gave Worthing's patrons lowish-floor-entry buses. This December 1972 picture of 915 Bognor-bound on the truncated 31 shows, however, an RELL at work on one of the new town services – note the masterplan route number. The Lancing services and the 9/10 also underwent revision during 1971: these reduced the Mary requirement at Worthing still further but both operations emerged still crewed: hence the rear of 357 here. The 7/17 were revised to concentrate on their North Lancing activities and renumbered as masterplan 207/217. The 9/10 diagram lost the 10 which was cut back to Swandean Hospital – before the two routes' parting of the ways – and renumbered 9A. A few one-man journeys were initially provided on the sector near Arundel. The 10 had been singled out for cancellations throughout 1970. On the positive side, Horsham was a centre of OMO Queen Mary activity in the early seventies.

Photo: Jim Jones

Further reductions in Mary activity followed soon after. The 207/217 service went OMO (with Fleetlines) in the summer of 1972 and in 1973 route 9 finally succumbed. The designation 9A had rarely been displayed on Swandean Hospital journeys, as evidenced by this view of 420 on the very last day of crew operation, Saturday 5th May 1973, in Hammy Lane, Shoreham – familiar board-in-the-window arrangements covered the destination. Leyland Nationals took over the following day and, even working a shortened service between Angmering Green and Brighton (as route 109), proved well-founded the crews' 1967 worries about good timekeeping if the route were one-man operated. It was soon after cut back to Broadwater, a part of Worthing. 420 has one of the cream NBC fleetnames.

Photo: Chris Warren

So, by 1973 Worthing Mary activity was down to little more than the 31 route. In 1975 even that was reduced when the route was cut back still further – no journeys then ventured west of Worthing Pier and the resulting Worthing–Brighton service was renumbered 230. In May 1976, 277 was on the service. The Worthing–Bognor road was subsequently serviced by OMO routes 231 and 232. The Marys used on Service 230 were initially provided by both Library Place and Edward Street garages. By April 1st 1975 Worthing's Mary allocation totalled a mere seven.

Photo: John Bishop

Much the same sorry story of decline could be told at Chichester. In 1971 the Selsey Bill routes went one-man (although Mary participation remained for a while with OMO conversions 955 and 971 working Limited Stop journeys in the revised 52/53 schedules). The 60 route also became one-man-operated in 1971, and the route changes to the 31/131 reduced PD3 requirements. In 1973 the Bognor local routes went over to one-man operation: 283 is seen just before the change with insidious NBC influence throughout her traditional livery – the Southdown plate has gone from the grille, and she now has all-green doors and an NBC-style fleetname. In 1975 most crew mileage on the old 31 route disappeared when a major restructuring with masterplan numbers occurred. The 31 retreated to Worthing and became the 230. The 131 retreated to Emsworth and became the OPO 331. Other OPO routes appeared to cover most of the space left vacant and PD3 activity in that space was confined to a few journeys on new routes 249 (Chichester–Bognor) and 250 (Selsey–Emsworth) – this latter did however re-introduce Marys to Selsey Bill; there were also PD3s about on the 245 between Bognor and South Bersted and as everywhere on miscellaneous school and works duties. Mixed OPO and crew mileage, as found on the 249, 250 and 245, was a common phenomenon initially in both the Worthing and Chichester rationalisations: usually it meant the odd crew working in an essentially OPO schedule but the 249 had a lot of Marys and reverted to them completely in 1976.

Photo: SEC

The rest of the pictures depict a 249 – 424 at Bognor Bus Station on July 30th 1977; a 245 – 402 at Chalcraft Lane, South Bersted on Saturday 5th March 1977; and a miscellaneous school duty – 257 in the last of her harmless allocations as the Midhurst school bus. Only in her mid-career spell on the 31 did she ever do anything very exciting.

Photo: Richard J. Cossey

Photo: Chris Warren

Photo: Calvin Churchill

Portsmouth too, the original home of the Marys, found their services dispensable in the seventies as the dreary Victorian city living in the shadow of the Navy, changed rapidly. The top picture, taken on Friday 15th December 1972, does indeed show Naval Dockyard workers cycling home in a two storey Victorian landscape and across a thirty-year-old bomb site but it also shows a building crane at work behind a hoarding and new tidal-flow overhead traffic lights on Commercial Road – symptomatic of the new white-hot technological Portsmouth that emerged during the decade, as were the continued highway improvements near Hilsea illustrated in the middle picture. The associated, somewhat belated, rise in living standards and the continued dispersal of the area's population into a vast new exurbia, had a rather dramatic effect on bus services – need for convoys of Queen Marys seemed to vanish overnight. Thus came the usual OMO conversions, route restructurings and difficult times for Queen Marys. The first operation to go was that on the London Road which gave way to initially-crew VRs in 1972. By that time, of course, Havant Road route 31 had turned into truncated 131 and Mary 285 shows the new designation in 1973. This change was only an interim measure for the Havant Road was soon to follow the London Road into OMO: the Hayling services went in 1973 and the 131 followed in January 1975 at the time of the major restructuring of the Portsmouth services and the introduction of master-plan numbers. As part of this, the 131 was fragmented into a 331 between Southsea and Emsworth, the 250/1 between Emsworth and Chichester and the 249 between Chichester and Bognor. The Portsmouth area 331 was OMO. Thus, a dedicated traveller wishing to journey from Portsmouth to Brighton by ordinary stage carriage bus, then had to use five routes – 331, 250/1, 249, 232 and 230 – where once he had needed only the 31. However, at the same time, Southdown, responsive to the changing nature of demand along this axis re-introduced the through Portsmouth–Brighton link with its very successful Limited Stop 700 service. Other features of the Portsmouth area restructuring were several other Limited Stop services with masterplan 700-series numbers (*e.g* 742 Southsea–Petersfield) and

the restoration of some links severed in the sixties *(e.g* through buses from Southsea to Westbourne – service 357). Generally though from 1975, frequencies were reduced and crew mileage restricted – to the Fareham Road; note how the OMO conversions had actually followed the familiar old hierarchy instead of the reverse – although of course, this meant that they had followed the Queen Mary expansion at Pompey in reverse. In 1976, Mary activity became even more restricted when a lot of crew work on the Fareham Road was replaced by the new one-man-operated Limited Stop X71 to Southampton.

Photo: Alan Snatt

Things in Southdownland had not been good for the Marys in the seventies but after 1977 they got worse.

Photo: Calvin Churchill

Queen Mary Sussex Twilight

Until 1978 there had been enough PD3s around to make them, despite the traumas of service reductions and OMO conversions, fairly ordinary: the Twilight Years saw them gradually becoming unusual. I was alerted to the beginning of this period by the Marys' sudden and seemingly almost total disappearance from their last bastion, BH&D, and the simultaneous arrival of widespread crew operation of OMO vehicles at Conway/Whitehawk. Actually their peak strength with BH&D had been reached in 1976 and a relicensing of some Lodekkas late that year had re-dissipated the PD3s slightly (the majority of those displaced went back to Portsmouth). But it was the appearance of Fleetlines and VRs on 1s, 2s and 6s, carrying orange-on-black-boards proclaiming 'Conductor Operated Bus' that really made me sit up and take notice that the Marys' Sussex phase was reaching its final chapter.

The Twilight Period was not signified by the one-man conversion of their remaining routes – the later Marys gradually left the fleet whilst management and staff still discussed whether the remaining crew routes were slack enough for OMO conversion. The Marys had had a less precipitous decline than might have been expected; they had survived their full twelve-year lives. In other words they had met the challenge of the seventies! Having done this, from late 1977 they gradually departed and left their remaining strongholds in the hands of one-man vehicles working with conductors. This was most obvious at 'BH&D' of course but also characterised those small pockets of Mary activity at other garages. The big reductions at Conway/Whitehawk had the effect of removing the Queen Mary spotlight from BH&D however. As they departed, the game became 'Find the PD3' – the latest round in that perennial bus enthusiast pastime 'Locate the Old Banger'. Only now the Queen Marys were the old bangers.

By 1977 there were two areas of PD3 activity left at Portsmouth: the 347, which was the remains of the Fareham Road (and staffed of course by the oldest vehicles) and the Havant–Leigh Park operations, of which the renumbered 46 survived. **ABOVE:** Panoramic 367 was in Leigh Park on Saturday 18th March 1978: the preponderance of Building Society ads is an interesting sign of the times in which the Marys now found themselves operating – where did all the cigarette and pools ones go? **BELOW:** At the end of 1978 nearly all Portsmouth's Marys were delicensed, leaving the 316 and the 347 almost entirely in the hands of crew-operated OMO vehicles. This was the sort of scene to be found in the weeks before – 312 experiencing a crew change at Hilsea on Friday 1st September 1978; note the VR on a Limited Stop London Road service, not to mention the almost vintage Corporation Panther Cub.

LEFT: Non-BH&D BATS services and Eastbourne Road duties continued to exhibit Marys amongst the crew-operated OMO vehicles until the middle of 1978. This is 355 on Good Friday 24th March 1978. *(Calvin Churchill)*

BELOW LEFT: There was a sorry scene in the west garage at Conway Street after the April 1978 fire. VR TNJ997S, only a few weeks old, and probably the seat of the fire, melted; Fleetline 2117, Queen Mary 303 and earlier VRs 531 and 502 fared little better. The hulks lingered for nearly a year whilst insurance formalities were completed. They were finally cut up and sold in March 1979 and 301, 351 and 348 are seen shortly before.

'Brighton Hove & District' continued to use some Marys during 1978 and 1979 with some FCD-Ds' lives extended because of the fire.

BELOW RIGHT: 297 shows the advantage of the QM windscreen on hot days during May 1978 whilst **BOTTOM LEFT** passengers on 415 enjoy even better ventilation the same day. 415 was officially 3215 by the time this picture was taken in Braybon Avenue but continued to ignore the fact until well into 1979.
BOTTOM RIGHT& OPPOSITE PAGE TOP LEFT Readers attention is drawn to the upstairs ventilation of 285, seen here leading a convoy of Bristol VRs up North Street on Friday 7th July 1978, and they are referred further to p.83 & p.85. The destination shown on 285 is correct because in June 1978 Service 2 took over the section of the 49 route west of Portslade Station: the Corporation were further ahead with agreements on one-manning and this allowed almost complete one-man operation of their route. In doing so, the 2 was unable to service Mill House as a 22 any more and, accordingly, this section of route was attached to the Portslade end of Service 1 and the 22 disappeared. Mary 308 still did not seem awfully certain of her new destination when seen on the Old Shoreham Road on Friday 28th July 1978.

Photo: Authors' collection

ABOVE RIGHT: One Timesaver service, the 776, ran throughout much of the day for some years: it provided a twenty-minutely service between Patcham and Mile Oak. It was crew-operated and often saw Marys such as 295 here: she was climbing up past the Clock Tower on Tuesday 30th May 1978. Having missed out in the programme to fit external board holders, she was unable to excite passengers with the information that she was Limited Stop.

The chronology of the withdrawals was as follows. 1977 saw the departure of the 1964 Hardtops, 964 and 972 still sporting proper livery and 970 in slightly incapacitated form having collided with VR 552 in May of that year. The turn of the year saw the main exodus of BUF-Cs. There was then a temporary hiccough in the withdrawal programme, due to the Conway Street garage fire in the early hours of Friday 14th April 1978. Marys 301, 303, 306, 346, 348 and 351 were written off slightly prematurely as a result of it and 304 and 310 proved too badly damaged to see service again but other FCD-D registered buses, already earmarked for disposal, had their Southdown lives briefly extended to cover for the fire victims. Nonetheless by the middle of 1979, there were no FCD-Ds in service. In June 1978, Mary 354 was also destroyed by fire – this conflagration was at Worthing garage, one Saturday night.

In 1978 the convertibles became fully depreciated vehicles and were accordingly renumbered in the appropriate 3XXX series: 400–420 and 422–429 became 3200–3228 respectively (421 had left the PSV fleet in 1976 to become tree-lopper 0421). The process of physically renumbering the vehicles was not carried out particularly thoroughly – while most external markings were swiftly attended to, interior numbers – particularly the vintage gold pre-National Bus Company ones upstairs – remained largely untouched for much longer; Brighton Hove and District garages were rather lax about external ones too. When interior numbers were attended to a variety of new styles – some rather makeshift – appeared.

The convertible open-top buses were the only Southdown double-deckers to have interior upper-deck numbers; this was to ensure the fitting of the correct roof to each bus. One switch did occur though: following damage to her own roof and the decision to make some of the convertibles permanent open-toppers, 402 received 410's roof during 1979 and more swaps were to follow. Some convertibles also acquired their new numbers outside on their roofs.

As you will see, I never really got used to these new numbers and apologise for random use of the old 4xx ones henceforth.

Throughout all the withdrawals of the Marys in the CUF, BUF-C and FCD-D batches the convertibles continued in service with the exceptions of 427, 428 and 429. Our Twilight story contains, therefore, mainly convertible pictures.

It was in late 1977 that I first felt the wave of nostalgia that eventually led me to produce the first book. The initial trigger was the chastening realisation that the 'CUFs' – whose delivery I could remember – had just been withdrawn: travelling up the A23 on Monday 14th November 1977 I passed just sold 960, 965 and 971, their Southdown fleetnames newly obliterated, pausing in a lay-by while their collecting drivers had a cup of tea. Unlike the one hundred and forty earlier Queen Marys, the later PD3s were disposed of through various Barnsley dealers.

Nostalgia, of course, focused on the heady days of the sixties, and drew sad comparison with 1978. In that year there was still a little Mary mileage being run from most garages but not much. Vehicles which had once been new and abundant, surrounding time-expired back-loaders, were now themselves the curious antiquities at the back of the garage, brought out occasionally to assist the all-conquering one-man-operated fibreglassware. More sadly still, a full bus was, by 1978, a fairly unusual sight, and the Marys looked rather pathetic running along only a quarter full. Somehow one was used to a Leyland National so laden but not a Queen Mary. Couldn't one remember them with standing loads grinding in and out of Pompey in convoy or carrying the heavy demand for travel on the Brighton–Peacehaven axis or even taking 69 passengers out of Chichester down Selsey Bill? Even around the turn of the decade full buses were not uncommon really ... especially on BH&D.

Nostalgia would not bring back that lost world; it would however, give a new piquancy to one's appreciation of the surviving Queen Marys ... I set about having some tearjerking nostalgic rides on them as their days in regular PSV service became numbered, partly as book research but mainly for the sheer pleasure of it. Most of these were on the 230 but not all, and two classic days involved intensive travels around the BATS network.

I came to realise that nostalgia draws on many things and that whilst, at one level, it was the fact that I was travelling on a Queen Mary, a vehicle from a bygone era making its way through familiar streets in less welcoming times, that was misting the eyes, with busy journeys particular fun, the full effect was made up of lots of little things such as: **noises** (engines gurgling, or roaring under a good load, sneezing brakes, coin-tap starting signals, droning saloon heaters, chattering conductors ...), **conductors** (do you remember how conductors used to make bus travel interesting and often amusing? – the late seventies were their last days too. There were the real characters like George Pore, doyen of Worthing conductors and delightful local personality, who was known by name even to his less regular passengers and could always be relied upon for a merry quip or comment; he deservedly got the BEM in 1976 for being a nice person. George saw out his last years before retirement on the Queen Marys chugging between Worthing and Brighton, dispensing advice like, "Buy a return ... you'll never regret it" and,

LEFT: 3209 returning to the Christmas 1980 lights of central Brighton from Rottingdean during the Marys' very last BH&D/BATS fling.

CENTRE: Inside on 3209 we see that, 2½ years after her renumbering, she still thought she was 409 upstairs. From the array of stickers, eagle-eyed readers will be able to deduce that musical instruments were doubly forbidden when roofs were on the convertibles and some passengers must have wondered why a disclaimer notice was needed about injuries from overhanging trees.

"I reckon all children under 14 should wear handcuffs". But there were others. The conductor made a busy trip on the Brighton 2 on a rainy February night interesting by being a bit of a novice. I knew it was going to be an entertaining journey as I boarded 3206 for I had seen that the 2 and the 49 in front were both missing. At Churchill Square, the waiting crowd broke and charged the bus. As we proceeded, the excess of demand was exacerbated by the conductor often not being in the right place at the right time: the driver took to pulling up at stops with the doors shut and waiting for him to go to the platform and sort out the crowds on either side of them (which he did quite well) and at one stop, surrounded by newly-disgorged football supporters, the driver decided driving straight past was his best option, somewhat to the irritation of the people planning to get off! The conductor would often be in noisy conversation with the driver on a Mary and one might thus hear interesting views about one's bus, especially if one sat over the very thin cab ceiling. "This don't sound much cop either" and "at least she hauls better than the other one" were the opinions of the gentleman propelling 3212 on a December 1980 trip, for instance. 3212's conductor incidentally sought my fare with the words "Yes please sweetheart" . . . very Brighton!), **hill-climbing** (straining engines and finely-judged – or less so – gear changes: star trip here was 3204's laborious ascent of Bear Road which featured a stop half-way up whilst the crew discussed where first gear might be) **and, in a way, driver unfamiliarity with Queen Marys** (by 1979, few drivers had had much practice on PD3s since leaving the training school and I had several other rather peculiar gearchanges during these rides plus some running of red lights as such changes loomed and various odd turning manoeuvres as well. On the 3206 trip, we slipped through Ship Street lights as they turned red and were going to do likewise at the Clock Tower, demurring owing to the presence of a policeman on the pavement and eventually crunching noisily through the low gearchange on our way upward).

A ride on 3209 was a summary of these nostalgic twilight rides. I boarded it Rottingdean-bound on the No 2 in Hove, just after lunch on a murky December day in 1980. It was very popular and by Palmeira Square was full; the conductor looked round, enquired

LEFT: Convertibles were the last type of Mary to reach Conway Street, not doing so until 1977. During 1978 and 1979, one of the most frequent performers on Brighton Hove and District services was 3206 and, as seen in the photograph, she included a few days in October 1978 operating with her radiator grille upside down. *(Nigel Lukowski)*

RIGHT: At Portsmouth for reasons outlined earlier, Queen Mary sightings during 1979 were rare, except for those of local celebrity 3222 which combined being Portsmouth's sole remaining Queen Mary with having been allocated there all her life. On 29th August 1979 she was disappointing holidaymakers on Hayling Island by operating the open-top service with her roof on.

CENTRE RIGHT: At Chichester, Marys still worked journeys on route 249 during 1978 and 1979; No. 3207 is seen at Bersted in October 1979. *(Calvin Churchill)*

The reader may note that it is the 'genuine' Southdowns here that are displaying single-track displays while the 'BH&D' buses are giving via details (in vintage upper case what's more). Both phenomena were common by the end of the seventies. (See 367 p.73 for another Southdown one-liner. Most of the later transfers to BH&D did not have their destination boxes masked, thus permitting this development or displays such as those of 295 on p.75). Note also that the lettering of the Southdown blinds has been getting smaller: decrease in the use of intermediate displays and reduction of type face size led in 1981 to some surviving PD3s receiving masking which was more restrictive than anything early Conway cars had received (See 3202 p.81). Single blinds were re-introduced in the 80s.

"Anybody off?" in true Conway Street throwaway fashion and, on receiving no response, tapped a coin three times on the bulkhead window to initiate an express run to the centre of Brighton. Having lost most of its passengers in Churchill Square and charged a businesslike column of jaywalkers at the Clock Tower, 3209 set off for a rather undignified clamber over the hills to Rottingdean, finding some inclines surprisingly taxing and with a driver who seemed very unhappy with his antique charge: most hill-starts started backwards and turning manoeuvres seemed more suited to buses with driving positions ahead of the front axle.

RIGHT: Queen Marys had been very few at Worthing since the early seventies but, having held constant at their small strength, were in a position to become proportionally more significant again at the end of the decade. In 1979 they could still be found there in groups – here on Saturday 6th October two show school blinds in the garage alongside a Daimler Fleetline and a Leyland National.

The delicensing of the Portsmouth Marys at the end of 1978 concentrated most remaining PD3 activity in the Worthing–Brighton area. Subsequent delicensing of all BH&D FCD-Ds except 307 in spring 1979 threw the Queen Mary spotlight onto the 230 route. The 230 continued to be the key Mary area for the following 16 months – into the 1980s – despite a few workings from BH&D and other garages, including the odd relicensing, during that period; on many days, it was worked entirely by our heroines.

Phasing out of Panoramics began in summer 1979. Soon after, final agreement to eventual complete one-man operation at Conway Street and Whitehawk garages was achieved, a new understanding having been reached as to what constituted a busy service: nothing. As a first step nearly all conductor-operated duties became middle shifts, buses on such duties working with a two-man crew between 8 am and 6 pm and being one-man operated at other times. There was also some peak-hour crew operation of essentially OPO duties.

Colour-coded stickers were introduced on the fronts of the buses to indicate what form of fare-collection was in operation: white 'PLEASE PAY CONDUCTOR' ones were displayed on boards during periods of

crew operation . . . yellow 'PLEASE PAY AS YOU ENTER' ones stuck on the panelling were immediately more widespread. Passengers were familiar with this general concept through the boards warning that a Fleetline or VR was not OMO as they might expect, which appeared with the advent of widespread crew operation of such buses in 1977, but now all buses had some sort of sticker. Although they could not really be one-man operated, the remaining PD3s at BH&D garages received appropriate stickers. They were then more or less confined to various special workings and two all-day duties each on the 2 and the 6.

The last Panoramics were withdrawn in March 1980 and most of the batch had been dispatched to dealers by October of that year. That should, of course, have eliminated the Mary from Southdown and concluded the Twilight Period. The convertibles however, survived. They continued the trend of leaving crew routes – now down to the 230, the 347 and the BH&D and open-top remnants – to crewed one-man vehicles but they did not leave the fleet. Until 31st August 1980, it was still easy to find them on stage service (mainly on the 230) but after that they went into semi-retirement and their performance on miscellaneous duties – increasingly highlighted as the years had passed – became the centre of attention.

TOP LEFT: On a nostalgia ride day in February 1979 I photographed, but missed sampling, 307 as she ran in early, having no late crew. This was compensated by, inter alia, the marvellous ride on 3206 in which she was 'slaughtered' all the way to Southwick.

TOP RIGHT: One of the PD3s that spent her last fully operational months chugging from Worthing to Brighton and back was 3224; she is seen here heading home along Hove Kingsway beside a wild sea on 16th December 1979.

ABOVE: 359 has a "Please Pay Conductor" sticker applied directly to the panelling in December 1979. The last Panoramics went soon after concluding somewhat troubled Southdown lives with ventilation and leakage problems throughout and, at the beginning, a high early failure rate on the bearing surfaces of their main shafts, caused it was believed by a metallurgical fault.

RIGHT: The photo shows one of the Queen Marys' last appearances on stage service – 3200 on 30th August 1980; she had just entered a Dutch Elm Disease Control Area at the time.

By 1981, the Southdown Queen Mary fleet consisted of the remaining convertibles and the rolling tide of nostalgia was making even 1978 look like a year of Queen Mary abundance. Southdown's services became totally one-man operated during 1981 and the semi-retired convertible Marys contented themselves with various special duties which did not require fare collection, like school and works contracts and pensioner specials for Worthing Council, and a general cultivation of eccentricity.

Queen Marys came to be used more and more as a sort of 'Fun Bus' fleet, hired out for all sorts of bizarre activities. No. 270 had given up her bizarre attempts to challenge the seventies but the convertibles, born survivors, got sillier and sillier. They had actually tested the concept during the sixties with the odd football homecoming and continental visit; they then developed it during the early seventies, with such things as 425's publicity work for Walt Disney's 'Robin Hood' and 416's mysterious 'Flower Show Special'. By 1975, the Southdown Enthusiasts Club news sheet was including notes such as "Car 428 was noted at Bognor with a large number of balloons and what appeared to be a piano on the upper deck". As the Twilight darkened they started turning up all over the place, doing all sorts of silly things.

LEFT: In 1978 a new twist on football homecomings appeared to come when Arsenal chartered Mary 420 and, so the story goes, decorated her with slogans congratulating the team on winning the FA Cup; unfortunately they then lost it. Rumour has it that rapid redecoration then took place! It is much more likely that two sets of banners were prepared to cover either contingency. Our picture shows 418 parading newly-promoted Brighton and Hove Albion through the streets the following year. (Brighton Evening Argus)

ABOVE: In 1979 a new silliness, but in a good cause: charity towing. On Sunday 9th September tug-of-war teams from West Worthing Working Men's Club pulled 3219 the length of Worthing sea front to raise funds for St Barnabas Home. On paper, 3219 was also being rather silly about her allocation, being simultaneously allocated to three different garages. *(Worthing Herald)*

A 1980 example of Fun Bus activity was 3217's trip to Aarhus in Denmark, which revived the idea of the continental visit, pioneered by 429 and 954. *"Hilsen til Aarhus Fra Alle I Brighton England"*. In 1981 Fun Bus Activity really took off and all sorts of new activities began to be undertaken: one convertible, for instance, was used as a publicity vehicle by one of the parties in the Croydon North-West by-election. She featured in a rather amusing TV sequence where interviewer and interviewee kept having to abandon political analysis to duck overhanging foliage as the PD3 made her way round the constituency. In the 1987 General Election, 412 and 423, by then in Provincial ownership, fulfilled similar roles in Portsmouth.

During the rail strike of summer 1982, 3204, 3208, 3211 and 3224 appeared on National Express coach services, including the Victoria–Gatwick Flightline; later in the year, a mass gathering of our heroines attended the Tall Ships Spectacular in Southampton.

Anti-crook special

SUSSEX Chief Constable Sir George Terry with the force's new double-decker crime-buster, which hit the road against rogues today.

Each bearing anti-crime posters,—200 similar buses form the spearhead of the 12-week campaign, officially unveiled at Sussex police headquarters at Lewes.

Costing "several thousand pounds," it is aimed directly at obtaining more help from the public and Sir George said: "The small cost of the exercise is nothing compared with the huge loss caused by crime. In 1981, the total was over £10 million in Sussex alone."

Grief

"But it isn't only a matter of money. Crime is a story of grief, injury, shock, terror and inconvenience."

Sussex had 48,928 recorded crimes last year and the figure for the first four months this year is already 19,072.

During the campaign, police will select a "crime theme" for each week, including burglary, vandalism, and offences against children.

First theme is robbery, running from May 24-30.

ARGUS 14 MAY 82

BOTTOM LEFT: By 1982 it seemed that one never turned a corner without coming upon a Convertible doing something silly. In August 1982, a Lancing Schoolmaster and his family undertook a sponsored cycle from Land's End to John O'Groats to raise funds for their school; in connection with this, a local estate agent chartered 3210, put a band and numerous waving children upstairs and had her jive through Worthing trailing streamers. Earlier in the year, 3217 had been commandeered by the chief constable of Sussex to spearhead a new onslaught on the county's rising crime rate. Both 3210 and 3217 also looked into the possibility of becoming advertising billboards. **BOTTOM RIGHT:** 411 pretending to be a National Express coach at Victoria during the 1982 rail strike. *(David G Savage)*

ABOVE LEFT: In 1982, 3209 decided to become a ship and appeared as MV Southdown, the Maritime England bus, in connection with Maritime England Year and was so successful with this bit of silliness that 3202 was persuaded to join her. 3202 was photographed whilst working one of the free services laid on to a display of Accident and Emergency vehicles in Worthing in August 1982. The horsebus was a seasonal tourist attraction. *(Nigel Lukowski)* **ABOVE RIGHT:** Convertible silliness continued through the rest of 1982 and beyond. 3203's appearance on a Limited Stop Portsmouth to Brighton 700 journey in June 1984.*(Bob Mackenzie)*

The following year found large groups attending the FA Cup semi-final and the two finals, full of hopeful Seagulls' supporters, and 3215 reappeared in traditional livery, ostensibly in connection with 'Beautiful Britain Year', starting work on a totally unpublicised irregular open-top service between Bognor and Littlehampton. A major rail replacement operation at weekends at the turn of the year produced packed Marys running between Havant and Bognor, and they covered several similar situations at other points of the rail network at different times. Later in 1984, No. 3217 turned up working a special service providing free transport – for holidaymakers only – to the Dog Stadium in Hove and 3215 (but more often 3209) reappeared on the secret service between Bognor and Littlehampton. No. 3202 had a busy year: she attended the Edinburgh Festival with the Mary Rose Theatre Company, was pulled from Hilsea to Southsea by Southdown staff to raise money for Southampton Hospital's heartbeat project and then went off to London to join other buses protesting about the government's proposals for the privatisation of services (this latter does not necessarily indicate political inconsistency for, as a convertible, 402 would not have carried any adverts protesting about nationalisation in 1967!). Marys had also become regular "novelty" transport

for outings provided for delegates attending conferences in Brighton.

By 1984, I was so inured to the eccentric behaviour of Southdown's remaining PD3s that when, on August Bank Holiday Monday, No.3209 passed by my window, festooned with streamers and with a bunch of loonies waving from the upper-deck, I hardly gave her a second glance! I imagine she had been taking part in Worthing Carnival. Apart from all these frivolities, the convertibles continued to make appearances on schools and other contract services and even began making isolated appearances on normal stage service again – this reached a high point with 3203's appearance on a Limited Stop Portsmouth to Brighton 700 journey in June 1984. Another gem occurred on the Friday after Derby Day 1984 when 3209 worked the Chichester–Worthing Shopperbus service (as an open-topper). These last Southdown PD3s were certainly showing no inclination to be pensioned off: this Twilight was becoming somewhat Scandinavian and perhaps reflective of this, 3213, having acquired 3217's Danish blind, appeared on some of the PD3 stage journeys displaying 'Aarhus Centrum'. The Twilight was to continue for a few more years but, to make sense of the rest of it, we should consider other Queen Marys again first.

BELOW LEFT: A key place for Queen Mary fans in the Sussex of 1982 was Steyning, where Brighton, Worthing and Henfield PD3s congregated on school work. When I went to watch the show on Thursday 2nd September the performers were 3200, 3201, 3204 and 3208; here 3208 and 3200 arrive at the second main pick-up point. 400 DCD was allocated to Worthing for her entire Southdown career and was thus a particular favourite with the author. Only she and 423 DCD could claim such garage loyalty after twenty years of service. **BOTTOM:** 3215 reappeared in traditional livery, ostensibly in connection with 'Beautiful Britain Year'. **BELOW RIGHT:** A major rail replacement operation at weekends at the turn of the 1983 produced packed Marys running between Havant and Bognor.

Of course a key reason Southdown retained the convertibles was their usefulness – even after 30-odd years – on the first Wednesday of June each year when they would all troop off to Epsom Downs for the day. Here are scenes from three such merry occasions:

June 1972: In the good old days, Southdown – with its customary touch of class – had a blind saying 'The Derby'; Queen Mary 408 above was one of those displaying it at the 1972 Derby. That same day one of her sisters was suffering rather from unequal distribution of punters: she was thus overladen in Southdown's private enclosure (another touch of class) at Tattenham Corner. Note all the coaches – Southdown once had the largest coach fleet in Britain.

June 1979: The 1979 Derby found Mary 423, newly 3222, collecting her crowd of racegoers to watch the first race.

June 1982: At this Derby, 3206 and 3224 made these raucous departures. Note that by now advertisements were being applied to convertibles...and also the upturned V instead of the usual gymnastic N next to the fleetname. This was to draw attention to the fact that Southdown had received the first NBC Chairman's Award for Innovation (for computerising faretable production). The entire fleet acquired them.

Photo: Authors'

RIGHT: Many thanks to Conway Street Garage management for their acquiescence and to Ray Darby for shunting most of the garage around to produce this line-up of PD3s in the Service fleet. Left to right: temporary driver trainer 364, Market Analysis Project mobile office 292, driver trainer 871, temporary driver trainer 362, treelopper 421. This latter and the VR in front of it were both static exhibits on the day in question, Saturday 8th January 1983, hence their positioning. The later PD3s (except 421) joined this fleet when their sisters were being withdrawn from the passenger fleet but the CDs outlived their batchmates as service buses by some margin working well into 1974; 880 was not withdrawn for conversion until March 1975. 421 became the treelopper in early 1977, having been deroofed by Queen Street bridge in Horsham the previous year. She replaced PD2/12 783 which had in turn replaced a pair of Guy Utilities, one of which can be seen with 827 on p.7. The Market Analysis Project was a National Bus Company-wide market research exercise.

CENTRE RIGHT: 421's haul being unloaded on a farm near Chichester, presumably with the farmer's agreement. *(Andy Izatt)*

BELOW: The MAP bus found a new role in 1984 as the booking office which became the sole remaining Southdown presence on the site when Hyde Park Road garage in Portsmouth was closed. Despite a sign by the door, visitors like the gentleman approaching had some difficulty working out whether it was worth getting in 0292 during her spell as an office and, if so, how to go about it – cheerful shouts from the staff within assisted. It was replaced by a leased office nearby in August 1984; this picture was taken the previous June. She then returned to census work in 1985 aided by a refurbished 880 which stayed in Sussex when 871/ 2/77 set off for the Barnsley scrapyards.

It is not quite true to say that the convertibles were the only Queen Marys in the Southdown fleet by 1981 as since 1974 a small number had found their way into the service fleet. Queen Marys 871, 872, 877, 880, 293, 294, 295, 296, 360, 362, 364 and 365 were driver trainers, the Panoramics having joined on a temporary basis and subsequently been delicensed; Mary 421 was now a treelopper, 292 was the mobile Market Analysis Project office and 347 joined the Apprentice School at Portslade for most of 1980. Most of the permanent members of the service fleet were painted yellow; 292 was painted green and grey. Temporary additions retained fleet livery.

Nos. 871, 872, 877 and 880 were withdrawn in 1983 and the four 'temporary' trainers were relicensed and accorded full yellow status.

Preparation of Marys 292–296 had resulted in a certain amount of window-swapping to rid them of upper-deck draughts and Rotovents, worn examples of which tended to open of their own accord. The exchanges resulted in at least 264 and 268 being sold with swapped Rotovents in them, and a mistake whereby 285 lost all her Rotovents and ended up with a curious configuration of sliding windows instead (p.74). Several Rotovents stayed on 292–6.

The 1983 fleet lasted until the division of the company in 1986 which saw the sale of most of the trainers – mostly to carry on training

Secondhand Marys in the UK 1971–1985

So much for the Marys staying to meet the challenge of the Sussex seventies. What alternatives were there for those vehicles which were withdrawn? By 1985, of course, many PD3s had taken this option and adopted alternative lifestyles. What had they been doing? Very few of the Marys did not see further service. Obviously accident and fire victims sold locally for scrap, did not: 839, 884, 939, 301, 303, 306, 346, 348, 351 and 354, nor did those cannibalised: 923, 927, 929 and 304. A few others never emerged from the dealers' yards: 953, 970, 271, 310, 312, 314, 352, 353 and 359. Attentive readers will be able to suggest why 970, 271 and 310 never saw the light of day again. Queen Mary 312 had fallen victim to either vandalism or suboptimal shunting at Conway Street before dispatch, and 314 spent $4^{1}/_{2}$ idle years in Barnsley before being scrapped in 1983. 428 went to oblivion in the non-active fleet of Keenan of Coalhall. But the rest of the Marys were snapped up and went on to lead complicated second, third and even fourth hand lives in many different colours: until 1977 most Marys had been green – but no longer.

So what were they all doing?

Driver Trainers

Many Queen Marys were to be found in later years being used to teach people bus driving, the majority being transferred by Southdown to other NBC fleets to fulfil the role. Presumably the combination of front engine, manual gearbox and internal access to the cab made the Queen Marys particularly suitable for this role. Marys 250, 251, 252, 253, 254, 255, 256, 259, 262, 269, 289, 309 and 313 joined Northern General and these did remain in green, this distinguishing them satisfactorily from the red of the passenger fleet. Queen Marys 357, 363 and 369 were a bit luckier than those sent to NGT livery-wise and ended up in Yorkshire Traction's colourful blue, white and red trainer colours. The NGT fleet (with the exception of 253) and 357/69 were phased out during 1981. No. 269 continued as a trainer with the Ayrshire Road Transport Training Group Association in white. No. 357 was purchased as a

source of spare parts by the Doncaster Omnibus and Light Railway Society, after a failed attempt to become a mobile cinema. No. 369 was parked in the axed compound at Wombwell Garage and sold in November 1983. The others also went for scrap. Private schools using Marys are detailed in the caption below; Hibberd of Coventry added 973 in 1983.

Other types of NBC transfers are listed on page 123.

Factory Staff Buses

Some other Marys became staff buses at factories. By far the most significant user of Marys in this way – and indeed one of the most significant users of them overall – was the British Shoe Corporation in Leicester.

The BSC's enormous factory on the western outskirts of Leicester was opened in 1964. In 1966 it was decided to buy a fleet of staff buses to ferry employees to and from the rather remote site. The Motor Transport foreman at the time, Dennis Bradshaw, was an ex-Southdown employee and recommended the purchase of withdrawn buses from the excellently-maintained fleet of his former employer. PD2/12 KUF715 became the BSC's first staff bus and a fleet of ex-Southdowns was rapidly built up.

As time went by, the original vehicles were replaced by later Southdown cast-offs, and the first Marys joined the fleet in 1972. These were 852, 853, 854 and 857. By the mid-1970s an all-Mary fleet was operated, consisting of the above four, 863, 882, 885, 892, 909, 911, 918, 925, 948 and 952. Towards the end of the decade these, in turn, were phased out in favour of later Queen Marys and in 1982 the fleet comprised four of the CUF batch (960, 961, 965 and 974) and eleven of the FCD-D batch (285, 287, 288, 290, 291, 297, 299, 302, 305, 307 and 308).

The Queen Marys were bought 'as seen' from the dealers but required very little subsequent attention. As far as chassis and engines were concerned, the story was the usual one of unexciting reliability and some needed no attention at all after acquisition. The only small

LEFT: On Sunday 11th March 1979, Marys 259, 250 and 262 were sunning themselves outside South Shields garage in the company of various NGT single deckers, one of which had also started out as a southern bus. **BELOW RIGHT:** Queen Marys 357, 363 and 369 and two other members of the Yorkshire Traction training fleet were parked for the Bank Holiday at Barnsley on Saturday 23rd August 1980. **BOTTOM LEFT:** The Wallace School of Transport in London bought two of the one-man Queen Marys with their useful reversing windows and used them for six years or so. At what seemed like the crack of dawn, but was probably somewhat later, on Saturday 16th June 1979 they were both parked amongst the uninspiring surroundings of Purley Way Freight Terminal. The anomalous 257 joined the fleet of Southern Motor Schools of Croydon to perform driver training activities; she was accorded the privilege of a framed life history in their office and became a frequent attender at rallies and similar events. She was now white; Hibberd 973 was cream.

ABOVE and RIGHT: Queen Marys in use as staff buses at the British Shoe Corporation's factory at Leicester. In 1982 the immaculate blue and white fleet carried 8,000 passengers a week over 21 different routes, assisted by three coaches (two of which were also ex-Southdown). Individual journeys took place at certain times of the day but at major shift change times, spectacular convoys were the norm. At 1982 prices, the BSC bus fleet cost £250,000 to operate per annum, an expenditure of 60p per employee per week. The BSC final Mary fleet was phased out after 1982, most going for scrap as had the earlier ones.

area of difficulty experienced by the British Shoe Corporation was (surprise! surprise!) heating and ventilation. The Rotovents on the FCD-D buses were found to let in the rain and were replaced where possible by sliders removed from the earlier Marys that they were superseding. Perhaps BSC got the idea from what Southdown had done to 285. Also the FCD-D buses – and possibly some others – received new saloon radiators to remedy complaints that they were too cold in the winter and too hot in the summer. A minor problem was sweating window rubbers, marking the clothing of passengers, and this was solved by treating the rubber with fluid.

On a much smaller scale was another factory Mary activity: Queen Mary 964 was a staff bus for Shaw Pallets of Diggle near Oldham. As mentioned earlier, she, 972 and 427 were the only later Marys not to be painted leaf green. 972 was a seasonally used berry-picker bus and 427 was repainted by her new owners, but 964 emerged from the Barnsley yards to properly carry the green and cream tradition into the eighties. By 1982, she was ten years past her last repaint but still displaying her ancestral colours on her daily circuit through Ashton-under-Lyne and Oldham. Southdown's repainting of 3215 in 1983 removed 964's distinction of course, but for five years she had kept the tradition more or less alone.

The only other Marys to become factory buses were 298 of the FCD-D batch, which revived an old tradition for ex-Southdown buses by working for Silentnight, the bed manufacturers of Barnoldswick in Yorkshire for a short period, and Panoramic 368 which was used by Turners Foods of Tunbridge Wells.

Sort of generically the same as factory buses were those various fleets of old buses stirred into life for a few weeks of the year to carry seasonal farm workers to fields and hedges for the berry-pick; 954,972 and third hand 274 performed in these Scottish fleets. A picture overleaf.

298 was withdrawn at the end of 1980 and 964 in 1983.

RIGHT: No. 964 was also sold for staff bus use, this vehicle going to Shaw Pallets near Oldham.

ABOVE and OPPOSITE: In June 1981 the regular driver of 268 informed the author that 276 was a plodder that got there in the end, but that his own machine was a "canny bus": this was neatly illustrated that day (with 268 where 266 is here on the school run from Wolsingham whilst 276 was on the distant horizon) but by the time this picture was taken, 268 had become less canny and been cannibalised for spares. 266 is thus first into Tow Law in April 1988. Opposite are four of the Weardale fleet at Wolsingham School in November 1981, 266 running home up the valley on stage service in June the next year and 259 from Northern General being broken up for spares

Queen Marys with Independents

Quite a few Marys joined the fleets of small independent operators, who used them mainly on contract work and schools and works runs – but some did see stage service.

One of the largest users of Queen Marys was Weardale Motor Services in the beautiful Wear Valley of up-country County Durham. They repainted 266, 267, 268, 276 and 350 in their splendid scarlet, white and maroon livery and kept them in immaculate condition. Apart from school runs to and from the big comprehensive at Wolsingham, they also appeared fairly frequently on the Company's stage service from Bishop Auckland and Crook to Stanhope – OMO. Weardale also purchased 259 from Northern General and broke her up for spares.

Another large user of Marys with a territory overlapping that of Weardale was the famous firm of OK of Bishop Auckland. Seven Marys wore their distinctive scarlet, cream and maroon livery. Four of these were Brighton Hove & District XUF-registered

LEFT: In use to convey farmworkers for berry picking from a farm in Errol is 274 (BUF274C), still in the livery of previous owner, H&M Coaches of Chasetown, near Walsall. 274 was part of a large fleet of 1960s nostalgia which included lowbridge PD3s from Alexander Northern and a Lancashire United Guy. The other picture **BELOW LEFT** shows it at Chasetown in 1981. **BELOW:** 848, still in OK colours but working for Moffat & Williamson of Gauldry, climbs back to its home village after working a wedding contract in Leuchars in June 1981. Dundee and the Tay are behind.

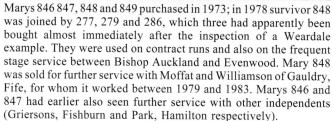

Marys 846 847, 848 and 849 purchased in 1973; in 1978 survivor 848 was joined by 277, 279 and 286, which three had apparently been bought almost immediately after the inspection of a Weardale example. They were used on contract runs and also on the frequent stage service between Bishop Auckland and Evenwood. Mary 848 was sold for further service with Moffat and Williamson of Gauldry, Fife, for whom it worked between 1979 and 1983. Marys 846 and 847 had earlier also seen further service with other independents (Griersons, Fishburn and Park, Hamilton respectively).

These two independents (Weardale and OK) combined with the NGT fleet to produce in the North-East one of the largest concentrations of secondhand Marys in Britain.

Leicester, home of the British Shoe Corporation, was another nucleus of Queen Mary operation. Independents in the area with Marys were Confidence of Oadby – a long-time user of ex-Southdowns – and Astill & Jordan of Ratby. The first Mary bought by Confidence was 845, and 272 and 356 followed later. All wore the black and grey livery. Astill & Jordan bought 355 to be a reliable – *i.e* front-engined – OPO bus but found passenger unfamiliarity, cab noises and heat and leaking windows pushing them to scrap after engine failure in 1983. Until then she had at least been reliable regularly performing a difficult school journey and once being the only bus to get through a blizzard to the school. After scrapping, many of her parts went to Confidence to help keep theirs on the road. Elsewhere in the Midlands, one could find 273 and 274 with H&M Coaches of Chasetown in the coalfield behind Walsall: they were painted 'sort of mustard' according to one of the people I spoke to there – "we tried to get 'em the same colour as the coaches" (orange) "but it didn't work out quite right". Also in the area was Mary 261 which first worked for G&G of Leamington Spa and then for Brittain's of Northampton, painted basically blue throughout. Marys 845, 273 and 274 were sold out of the area by 1982. No. 261 was withdrawn in 1983 and only 960 of the BSC's castoffs was known to remain in the Midlands (at De Courcey's yard in Coventry). No. 973 arrived to redress the outflow slightly.

No other parts of the country saw such concentrations of active secondhand Marys as the North-East and the Midlands. 'The North' (traffic areas B & C) for instance, only had nine: YTC's,964, 298 and four independent examples: 270 (red, cream and black with Stott's of Oldham), 278 (NBC green with Finch, Higher Ince – used for

TOP RIGHT and BELOW: Two views of QMs in interesting multiply-sourced fleets –279 with sundry ex-Newcastle Atlanteans at OK in 1988 and 272 with an Atlantean of similar ancestry and other secondhand goodies with keen ex-Southdown user, Confidence of Leicester the previous day; Confidence also used 845 & 356 and 356 works a school contract in Evington in April 1988 in the bottom picture. Parts from 355 sustained 272 and 356 after her short career with Astill & Jordan during which she was worked both crewed and OPO.

carrying Morris Dancers among other things), 281 (white and navy blue with Thistle, Doncaster) and 963 (thirdhand with Alpha of Bootle, fourthhand with Beauside of the same town and fifth hand with the Fernhill Morris Dancers). 963 had started off as a Welsh Mary: she and 973 worked for Lloyd, Bagillt in cream but were sold in 1983, 963 sporting a novel rebuilt front after an incident involving a lorry. Once on Merseyside,963 was silver and blue. Other than these, Wales only saw a few of the XUF-registered

LEFT: 286 heads through West Auckland Evenwood-bound with OK in August 1980.

MIDDLE: 311 climbing out of Sligachan on June 8th 1981.

WEST HIGHLAND FREE PRESS

Old School, Breakish, Isle of Skye IV42 8PY

Telephone:
Broadford (04712) 464
Telex: 75425

No. 434

FRIDAY
22 AUGUST
1980

15p

Double trouble over Skye school

now-infamous double-ker bus was introduced week on the school sport route from Broad- t to Portree.

t instead of the 73 pupils n education department offi- estimate should be trans- ed on the bus only a maximum children were on it when it ed outside the High School on nesday morning. And some dford pupils missed their first

day at school in Portree. For at a meeting in Broadford the night before the parents of many of the pupils involved decided ... their childr despite assu officials tha mode of tra At last m Highland Re mittee it was 4 that the, Nicolson, Bor allowed to repl

decker coaches which conveyed th

AT bus arrives in Broadford on Wednesday morning, as a gro

buses sold in 1973: 844 was the last of a long line of ex-Southdown deckers with Cream Line, Tonmawr, 850 worked for Roberts, Cefn, painted yellow, and 851 was in Morris of Swansea's fleet. 429 and third hand 278 worked later as driver-trainers in the Valleys. Sole East Anglian settler was red and cream 260, with Jennings of Arrington. Of the above, 844, 850, 851 and 281 had been withdrawn for scrap by 1982.

Scotland had just the berrypickers, the two thirdhand members of the XUF batch and similarly well-used 269, 300 which worked for Shennan of Drongan in the early eighties (she retained NBC green, apparently because she did a Catholic school run and "they like a green bus") and 311 on the Isle of Skye. Her purchase (to operate a school contract in place of two single-deckers and become the first double-decker in regular use on the island) was not without incident. By Friday 22nd August 1980, two days after her introduction at the beginning of the autumn term, the West Highland Free Press was describing her as the 'now infamous double-decker bus'. Parents were concerned that 311 could not cope with the road and weather conditions on Skye, and that supervision of the children would be a problem. Feelings ran so high that some children missed school for a few days at the beginning of the term as parents refused to let them travel on the big green bus. To allay such fears, the owner Calum Nicholson provided supervision on her and by the time the picture was taken of her climbing out of Sligachan on Monday 8th June 1981, during her morning run from Broadford to Portree, the whole business had died down. Having served reliably throughout the winter, 311 had been accepted into the community and the story of the introduction of a double-decker had run its familiar course yet again! No. 311 was later repainted blue, but she was withdrawn and parked out of use in 1983.

One or two Marys were not so keen on the adventurous life and returned to the south of England. We have already made reference to trainers 257, 955 and 977 (although here it should be noted that 955 was sometimes seen in Wallace's HQ, Nottingham) and Food Bus 368. There was also 936 with the Islington Bus Company (until a collision with a bridge in 1981) and two PD3s that actually came all the way home to Sussex and ICC Coaches of Worthing. One of these was 347 and she is seen on this page still wearing the green livery of Don's of Dunmow in whose fleet she briefly sojourned after reluctant departure from Sussex via the Apprentice School at Portslade, before being swapped with ICC for ex-London Transport DMS 556. In 1982, she was joined by third hand Mary 273, painted white.

BOTTOM: 347 with ICC Coaches of Worthing, amongst spring flowers on the Downs on Monday 17th May 1982 during her regular school run between Findon and Angmering. In 1983 the bus was repainted from green (Don's of Dunmow livery) to scarlet and black. This was at the request of Southdown to make the bus look less like one of theirs and reduce complaints about buses ignoring stops!

Unorthodox Uses

I have employed a spot of artistic licence in presenting this geographical summary so soon: this is not yet the half of the secondhand Queen Mary story. We have yet, for instance, to deal with the contingent of Queen Marys that fell out of mainstream bus type use after sale. Here we find the hospitality units, the exhibition units, the hospitality & exhibition units ...in all three instances with a combined publicity role, the playbuses and caravans, and the exotic staff buses that couldn't quite be squeezed into earlier categories.

PLAYBUSES

TOP RIGHT: 315 was the first Mary to become a Playbus and was used by local play groups, mother and toddler, youth and old peoples' groups, play schemes, community associations and other voluntary bodies around Nottingham. Startling yellow with rainbow stripes, she featured an upstairs play area and a lower deck with seats, cooking and heating(sic from newspaper article) facilities. Nottinghamshire County Council voted £3,500 for the playbus scheme in 1980–1 and Nottingham City Council supported the urban aid grant which met the cost of buying Mary 315 and the necessary overhaul work. Islington's 936 is believed to have also served as a Playbus eventually and thirdhand 974 performed a similar role in the Daventry area: it is seen here amongst the bins at Weedon Primary School.

Photo: Peter Raw

> **Exotic staff buses included:**
> **Jazz Band Conveyance**
> 845   Third-hand with West Auckland Grenadiers Juvenile Jazz Band, 1981-1983. See also 427 overleaf.
> **Scout Troop Vehicle**
> 358   Sold by Tilleys (a Burgess Hill garage) without use to the local scout troop in 1983. Clever 'Scout uniform' livery. (NBC green with a blue and yellow waistband dipping into cravat shape at the back)

EXHIBITION UNITS

ABOVE RIGHT: Mary 366 got up to all sorts of unusual things after purchase by Pearson's of Stockbridge and conversion to semi-open-top. This picture supplied to us by the estate agents carries the self-explanatory caption, "Fleet Half-Marathon, Sunday 4th April 1982. The Pearson's bus followed the runners to collect the dead bodies". **RIGHT:** She also attended the 1981 Derby and various other events including a number of property auctions in connection with Pearson's business. Later she worked for AMF Humber Bowling and was then often seen back in Southdownland as here in Portslade.

Photo: G. Smith

BOTTOM RIGHT: Third hand from the British Shoe Corporation, 961 joined the Medical Campaign Against Nuclear Weapons to fulfil this role in 1983. She was based in Torquay and during her first winter sojourn there assumed a new registration identity and was repainted in a shade of blue darker than the one she wore when with the British Shoe Corporation. The change in the regulations governing vehicle registration in November 1983 led to a rush of transfers of non-year-suffix marks onto coaches, many using handy elderly buses. Thus, 960 and 961CUF became coaches in Young's of Romsley's fleet, whilst our old friends that used to answer to these identities became HOO343B and YCV28B respectively. Meanwhile, Southdown Nos 3206–3208 became WRU 702/3/1B when a desire to use coaches Nos 1276–8 on National Holiday work in 1985 clashed with their having corporately unacceptable R-registrations and they became 406–408 DCD. 961 was photographed in Brighton in September 1986 whilst attending the Brighton Corporation 75th Anniversary Rally.

EXHIBITION UNITS – continued

BELOW: Another of this band, 275, spent longer as a non-PSV than a PSV: used initially by the London Borough of Lambeth as a consumer advice centre (and portrayed by the usual myopic London mediafolk as a Routemaster on the publicity leaflet: have you noticed how the television and the papers still refer to bus conductors, apparently unaware that such things virtually ceased to exist outside London manyyears ago?) she later became a campaign vehicle. 275's first Lambeth role involved travelling around schools, helping to make lessons more relevant to the world without...and she was so engaged here in Tyers Street SE11 in April 1979. Like most of the other Marys discussed on these two pages, her interior was extensively modified for her new role. 287 became a community service vehicle in Gloucestershire after five months in a scrapyard post-British Shoe. She was sponsored by the county council and the Cheltenham & Gloucester Building Society.

LEFT: Mary 427 joined West Kent Car Sales, Biggin Hill, after an abortive attempt to become a roadster for a pop group (itself a pretty unorthodox pastime). With WKCS her lower deck was carpeted and the seats recovered in green velour and rearranged around tables. Fridge, bar and small kitchen were added, as was piped music. After two more owners, she later performed in another hospitality role for Airfayre of Bristol – this picture comes from their publicity. *(Airfayre)*

CARAVANS

LEFT: Queen Mary 361's new career involved taking adventurous young people across Europe on holiday. She was modified fairly substantially, as may be gathered from the view of her in the Praca do Comercio in Lisbon, during the summer of 1981. Although purporting to be based in Zurich, she still claimed to be HCD 361E. It is believed that convertible 3218 was loaned to Suntrekkers by Southdown during 1979 – possibly for evaluation before the concept was developed with 361. 273 was purchased from ICC by a private buyer; based initially near Winchester, this Mary attended all the major UK pop festivals in 1984, painted green.

Photo: John Shearman

Nor is that yet half of the secondhand Queen Mary story. You will probably have noticed that nearly all the foregoing was talk of later Queen Marys. Whatever happened to all those early PD3s? The TCDs? The VUFs? the XUFs? The CDs? The answer to that is very simple: the vast majority of them went to Hong Kong where they assisted the China Motor Bus Company with its major expansion and double-decking programme.

Overseas Queen Marys – Far East 1972–1985

Hong Kong

From 1933 to 1998, the China Motor Bus Company Ltd (CMB) held a franchise to operate bus services on Hong Kong Island – one of the pieces of south China administered by Britain for most of the 20th century . Until the sixties, these services – many over steep mountainous roads with overhanging rockface projections – were the province of short wheelbase 25–30 seat single-deck buses. Pressure of population led to the appearance of double deckers – first on the flat, more densely-populated coastal routes and then, with short wheelbase models on the more hilly runs; this double-decking happened at a fairly slow rate however – China Motor Bus did not seem to respond very positively to the rapid increase in Hong Kong's population, apparently content to run infrequent very full buses. It was also concerned about using bigger buses on the more tortuous hilly routes. Much of the demand for public transport started, therefore, to desert it in favour of the then illegal minibuses operating as communal taxis on semi-fixed routes.

Determined moves to regain its share of the market found CMB frantically expanding and double-decking in the early seventies. Secondhand buses began to play an important role in this after the first ones – Southdown PUF-registered Guy Arab IVs – sailed in in 1970.

The population continued to grow as CMB battled to catch up, and in 1972 the pressure increased when the Cross Harbour Tunnel began to near completion. All harbour crossings up to then had been by boat and no bus routes had used the vehicular ferry. But with the tunnel imminent the Government Transport Department indicated that it would require CMB and the Kowloon Motor Bus Company (1933) Ltd (KMB) to jointly operate an entirely new network of cross-harbour routes. Various schemes were drawn up for this and agreement on the exact style of service to be offeredwas reached only days before the tunnel opened : the final estimates required each operator to provide 33 buses to service three routes – 101, 102 and 103 – and carry a projected total of 19,000 passengers a day.

In order to keep pace with the expansion represented by its repenetration of the still growing island market and by the projected cross-harbour tunnel routes, CMB was forced to increase its intake of secondhand vehicles. By this time, with its collection of single and double-deck models, CMB had become the operator of the largest fleet of Guy buses in the world and, in the interests of standardisation, it sought more of the marque – preferably now examples suitable for one-man operation: CMB was introducing this as the best way to collect fares on large-capacity vehicles that were frequently full. A small group of 30ft long Lancashire United Arab IV backloaders were obtained and converted to front platform/staircase, but no further secondhand examples were available. Neither were new ones, for at that time Guy, rather unsportingly, ceased production of the Arab.

This was the Queen Marys' big chance!

Forced to look to other makes, CMB was fortunate enough to purchase four of our heroines – 858, 860, 862 and 856: they joined their erstwhile Guy Arab shedmates early in 1972. A direct quote from Mike Davis is appropriate here to give a Hong Kong perspective: "They presented a most impressive sight with their Southdown specification coachbuilt bodies, complete with fully-upholstered moquette-covered seats and striking pre-NBC livery of green and cream. Until this time, with one exception, all Hong Kong double-deckers were of pre-fabricated aluminium kit-built construction with loose rattly full sliding windows and hardboard-backed seats."

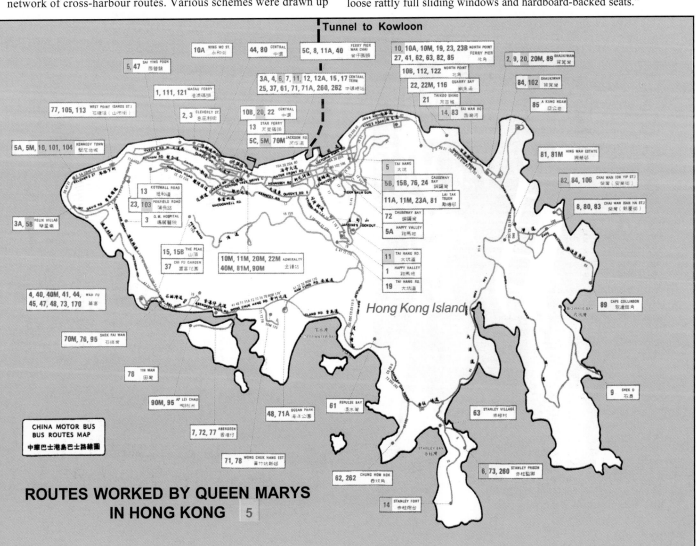

ROUTES WORKED BY QUEEN MARYS IN HONG KONG   5

With some adjustments to suit local conditions, these first Hong Kong Marys entered CMB service on Thursday 9th March 1972. Because of their chassis type, CMB designated them their PD class and 858, 860, 862 and 856 became PDs 1-4. Queen Mary 862 thus became PD 3 which seemed particularly appropriate. They were followed into service between June and October 1972 by a further 15 Marys plus two northern cousins from Ribble. These were PD3s with Burlingham bodies of similar design to the Southdowns and were purchased for use as driver trainers for our heroines. However these Ribbles were pressed into passenger service, becoming PDs 18 and 19 in the Queen Mary series.

On Thursday 3rd August 1972 the Cross-Harbour Tunnel was opened, linking the road systems of Hong Kong Island and Kowloon for the first time. Soon after the introduction of the attendant tunnel-bus services, it became apparent that the Government predictions of 19,000 passenger journeys a day requiring 66 buses were a little bit out, as traffic quickly developed to 120,000 passenger journeys a day – or 500% above prediction.

The need to meet this almost overwhelming demand placed an enormous strain on the two bus operators. China Motor Bus was, as we have seen, already undertaking unprecedented expansion within its hitherto traditional operating area and KMB was up to much the same sort of thing across the water. Orders were placed for new vehicles, but this could not be the short-term answer and a further increase in the use of secondhand buses was decided upon. Another 13 Queen Marys entered the CMB fleet in early 1973.

CMB's Traffic Manager, Lyndon Rees, set off to the UK on a mission to purchase additional suitable vehicles, with a particular brief to try and secure the Scottish Bus Group Bristol VRs. For a number of reasons these were not considered suitable and the hunt was extended. The entire London Transport Atlantean fleet – the XAs – was acquired but a mere 50 buses did not solve CMB's problem. Among other purchases, CMB decided to buy 42 more Queen Marys, having been satisfied with those that it already had. At this time, most of the remainder of the first 100 were leaving Sussex. Lyndon liked Southdowns because they were well looked after and not excessively over-worked; they also operated in a balmy climate which did not require much corrosive salt and grit in the winter. By the time he had finished, the CMB fleet of Southdown PD3/4s numbered 76, representing all of the first 100 – bar those scrapped, sold late (BH&D XUFs) retained by Southdown, or bought by the British Shoe Corporation. This was perhaps slightly more than would have been purchased in a perfect world – their non-automatic gearboxes being anomalous in the CMB fleet – and the evidence suggests that the original plan was to stop at PD 34. But with enormous queues for Tunnel Buses, things were not perfect... or perhaps, a bit too perfect. CMB was now, in contrast to a few years before, running *frequent* very full buses.

The Queen Marys were shipped in an assorted fleet of container vessels. The early ones went from Hull (eg, 822 and 825 on the Ben Lawes, sailed July 1972); the last 42 went from Southampton – some of the ships involved were the Benalder (sailed Thursday 1st March 1973), Bremen Express (Monday 19th March 1973), Liverpool Bay (Tuesday 27th March 1973) and the Kurama Maru (Wednesday 4th April 1973). The journey took about 23 days, port to port, thus removing any chance of a trite slow-boat-to-China reference.

ABOVE: PD1 (858) was rushed into service in March 1972 without much more than a coat of paint to prepare her for duly in Hong Kong. She is seen here soon after on a special Sunday service to Repulse Bay beach. The UK size opening windows must have been insufficient even in March! The radiator grille was soon enlarged following overheating problems. *(Lyndon Rees)*

China Motor Bus to Southdown Fleet Number Conversion List

CMB Queen Mary numbers: PD1–17, 20–76, PD501–528, followed below by Southdown numbers

1	858	25	840	47	833	69	881	513	937
2	860	26	834	48	837	70	891	514	942
3	862	27	842	49	838	71	905	515	914
4	856	28	827	50	874	72	907	516	921
5	843	29	828	51	897	73	908	517	924
6	855	30	824	52	869	74	865	518	926
7	859	31	835	53	879	75	887	519	931
8	813	32	832	54	886	76	902	520	944
9	814	33	826	55	894	77	903	521	946
10	819	34	831	56	896	78	906	522	951
11	816	35	836	57	898	501	938	523	915
12	818	36	904	58	864	502	940	524	919
13	815	37	870	59	867	503	941	525	930
14	823	38	875	60	876	504	950	526	943
15	817	39	889	61	883	505	913	527	920
16	820	40	900	62	890	506	928	528	934
17	861	41	901	63	895	507	917*		
20	822	42	868	64	899	508	932	*917– PD527 from 1984	
21	825	43	873	65	910	509	945		
22	829	44	912	66	830	510	947	**NOTE:** Missing PD18 & 19 were similar ex-Ribble PD3/4s	
23	821	45	888	67	866	511	922		
24	841	46	893	68	878	512	916		

BELOW: Mary 873 (PD 43) eyes three former London Atlanteans in Wong Chuk Hang garage during 1973 in an endeavour to size up what she has let herself in for. The XAs had been repainted in CMB livery but not yet tropicalised by substitution of full-depth sliding windows, etc. *(Lyndon Rees)*

The Queen Marys were modified quite a lot before they were put on the road in Hong Kong. They were given a full mechanical overhaul – some of these being undertaken in Manchester before shipment – and were 'tropicalised' to cope with Hong Kong's heat and humidity and altered in one or two other ways to make them suitable for local conditions. This work included repainting.

All modifications not connected with tropicalisation were made before the PD3s were put into traffic. Full tropicalisation did not however necessarily precede entry into service and some such adjustments were made to some Marys later in their CMB careers. Indeed PDs 1–4 initially entered service more or less unaltered in this respect: their small external radiator grilles and unchanged UK window arrangements soon led to overheating – the former of the engines and the latter of the passengers ... and both of them of the drivers, who were in inadequately ventilated cabs on top of inadequately ventilated engines, grappling with unfamiliar manual gearboxes in heavy traffic. Even so, subsequent PD3s – though better ventilated when they first took the road – did not always meet the standards of the 'tropical ventilation master plan' initially and other, less obvious, tropicalisations took even longer to characterise the whole fleet.

The master plan for tropicalising Queen Mary ventilation was as follows. For engine comfort the radiator grille was replaced by a large rectangular opening which was protected by vertical bars on early conversions and expanded metal mesh on later ones. In order to further improve cooling, additional vanes were fitted to the radiators themselves while openings cut into the lower sections of the nearside cab doors facilitated the extraction of hot air from the engine compartment, and replaced the little louvres there on most QMs.

For driver comfort, in addition to the work on the engine, the nearside screen opening portion was enlarged or, in the case of the TCD and VUF registered Marys, introduced.

For passenger comfort additional areas of opening window were provided. This was achieved on each side of the later batches by replacing all fixed glasses in passenger areas, except the upper-deck first and last windows, by sliding panes in aluminium channel section frames. To effect this with the lower-deck last side windows, they were divided in two by a new pillar and equipped with a square sliding section and a fixed quarter-light. The TCD batch were modified to conform with this pattern, which meant that they lost the 'sliders' in their last downstairs side windows and in their short middle ones. All other sliding windows were retained. Some of the original TCD middle windows were used as temporary middles in their sisters. The upper-deck front windows of the Marys were replaced with sliding glasses in aluminium frames. There was a bit of a problem here with the TCDs and VUFs because of the shape of their front uppers. They received therefore an arrangement involving cumbersome wooden frames. Eventually it was discovered how to bend the rectangular aluminium frames and thereafter some were refurbished with units like those fitted to the other Marys. The rear emergency door windows on both decks of the PD3s were also provided with sliding panes. Generally engine cooling was more successful than saloon cooling.

There were various other desirable changes connected with tropicalisation that were less immediately obvious than the cooling ones. Moquette seat covers were in some cases, and particularly on the cushions, replaced by more tropically sensible PVC or leather-cloth. The ambient high humidity in Hong Kong produced problems for electrically-operated equipment as insulating materials deteriorated rapidly in the moist conditions: the Marys' windscreen wipers and doors were converted to air operation. The doors on the ex-Ribble Queen Marys were air-operated but they too had to be modified

BELOW LEFT: Early conversions entered service with various compromises about tropicalisation. Mary 821 (PD23) entered service with UK front upper-deck windows and original upper middles. She was still so equipped in April 1974 when seen in Wanchai. TCDs kept their upper-deck rear sliders throughout.*(Mike Davis)*
BELOW RIGHT: 855 had few concessions to climate here and still needed the emergency exit open for adequate ventilation! Even fully tropicalised ones sometimes operated thus. *(F. W. York)*

ABOVE: Mary 836 (PD35) in experimental livery in King's Road depot on 1st August 1974. The lower panels were red but we are not illustrating that so that we can take the opportunity to show one of the very rare pictures of a Queen Mary without her clothes on. *(Mike Davis)* **ABOVE RIGHT:** Queen Mary 898 (PD57) in November 1977, trying to look happy with a different paint scheme to help disguise the 'sad eyes' disliked by the local drivers. *(David Withers)*

because they were of the sliding variety and it was found that they would not open against the normal braking moment of a CMB bus! The original alkaline batteries of some of the Queen Marys gave off unpleasant fumes in temperatures above 80°F and were replaced with lead acid ones after complaints from passengers.

So much for tropicalisation; the Queen Marys had a number of other modifications to make them suitable for Hong Kong operating conditions.

Blind apertures were reduced in a variety of ways so as to suit CMB displays. The rear skirt panels were cut away, as indeed they had been on the later Southdown Marys from new. CMB had a particular interest in increasing ground clearance in North Point depot and at the turn into Tai Hang Road on route 11 (which the PDs eventually took over from the PUF Guy Arabs). Rear light assemblies were changed and raised. The translucent panels in the roofs were panelled over to reduce heat and rainwater leaks.

The Marys were converted for one-man operation. They lost the glass from their bulkhead windows and received a Bell Punch Autofare farebox, without ticket machine, on the front bulkhead. The one-man operated system then becoming universal on CMB used a farebox and flat fares with no change and no ticket. This reduced the drivers' interaction with the passengers to watching them put coins in a receptacle: this minimised the difficulties of swivel-round and engine noise inherent in the conversion of a Mary for one-man operation. The system ideally required a separate entrance and exit and some confusion was inevitable on vehicles of one-door layout like the PDs. Purpose-built China Motor Bus one-man buses had narrow entrances to ensure that everyone passed the farebox but such constriction was not possible where the entrance was also being used as an exit: buses so laid out, like the PDs, were fitted with a one-way (out) turnstile guarding the rear half of the doorway from boarding passengers evading the

BELOW: Glistening with new paint on her first day in CMB service, Friday 18th April 1975, is PD507 (Mary 917). Her tropicalisation has involved what appear to be TCD rear side windows upstairs – presumably from the lower deck of one of that earlier batch. PD 508 (932) also entered CMB service so equipped. Note how the mesh grilles vanish into the scenery in these pictures – unlike the vertical bars of the earlier conversion as on 821 on p.93. *(Mike Davis)*

farebox. This ensured the correct pattern for people getting on, but with no equivalent turnstile on the other side there was no prevention of those getting off spoiling the system by seeking to leave via the front half of the doorway. Unlike the Southdown OMO conversions, CMB's were not given reversing windows, there being few reversals at termini in its network: PDs 22 and 34 (829 and 831) kept theirs though. No CMB conversions featured periscopes.

The last CMB 3/4 PD, 78 alias Mary 906, entered service in April 1974. CMB was pleased with the Queen Marys. Lyndon Rees wrote to the Southdown Enthusiasts' Club saying that they were "outstanding vehicles and extremely popular with drivers, passengers and workshop staff (the latter since they rarely see them)" and when their semi-automatic sisters came on the market in 1975, he was particularly keen to secure some of them. These were the only Marys with Hong Kong-style gearboxes and 28 of the PD3/5s were purchased, the first four entering service in February 1975. They were modified in the same way as the PD3/4s except that they did not get turnstiles (visible farebox evasion had been found to be rare) or, in some cases, a big push-out in the nearside windscreen. The only major external difference from the PD3/4s – the offside illuminated advertisement panel – was painted over; at night the fluorescent tubes could easily be seen shining through the cream paint – eventually they were repanelled flat. Because of their mechanical differences from the PD3/4s, which prevented full interchangeability, the PD3/5s were distinguished by a new series of fleet numbers within the PD series: they became PD 501–528 (5 signifying PD3/5).

At the time of the Queen Marys' arrival in Hong Kong, all of the OMO double-deckers of CMB and KMB were being painted into a half-and-half, cream over red livery with black beading and the Marys went straight into this. Variety was introduced by the operation of some specimens in an orange variant of the red, during evaluation of alternative paint supplies, and by the appearance of PD35 in a non-standard application of the livery with cream surrounds to the lower-deck windows, in addition to the cream upper-deck.

In the mid-seventies CMB decided to change its livery so that its buses could be differentiated from those of KMB on Tunnel Services. PD57 appeared in unusual shades in the resulting evaluation of trial liveries and with the colour division cut straight across the front dash panel Panoramic-style: this was believed to have been in an effort to make her look 'happy' – it was said that some drivers disliked the Queen Marys not only for their gearboxes but because their downward curving windscreens gave the appearance of 'sad eyes'. All the Marys, except 5 and 9, were repainted in the final choice of new colours, in which blue replaced red. PD 5 (843) was involved in a very serious head-on collision with former LUT Guy LW114 in 1976 and was withdrawn and scrapped as a result. PD 9 (814) was scrapped in 1977 when she was found to have a cracked chassis.

Until 1973 the only fleetname carried was the company crest – a circular device placed centrally on the lower deck side panelling. There then followed a period of experimentation during which PD 57 (898) became the only CMB bus in modern times to carry the fleetname in Chinese characters. The outcome of this experimentation was the 'China Motor Bus' legend in English above the lower-deck windows supplementing the crest: all surviving Queen Marys eventually carried it.

So much for preparing them for service: what did they do when they got out there on the streets of Hong Kong? Routes on which the PD-class were used, prior to the commencement of the Tunnel Services, were mainly those such as the 2 and the 5 along the flatter north shore of Hong Kong Island (the Island Corridor). PDs 1–4 did however see early service on Repulse Bay journeys across the mountainous middle.

From August 1972, Queen Marys became the main-stay of the Tunnel Routes the first three of which were: 101 (Central–Kwun Tong), 102 (Shaukiwan–Lai Chi Kok), 103 (Pokfield Road–Wang Tau Hom). As a result, years later, they were still affectionately referred to by CMB's Chairman and Managing Director, Mr. Ngan Shing Kwan, as the Tunnel Buses which saved the day for CMB in their time of need.

With the gradual arrival of more suitable new and secondhand buses from 1974, the PDs were progressively cascaded onto island routes, including the newly-introduced express route 20 which hurtled to Shaukiwan via the dual-carriageway waterfront road, built as part of the network of feeder roads to the Tunnel. The last PD3/4s and the PD3/5s did not operate regularly through the Tunnel, if at all, and as the PD3/5s went into service in 1975 the Marys were allocated to routes as follows:

ROUTE		PD ALLOCATION
5	Kennedy Town–Tai Hang	20
5B	Felix Villas–Causeway Bay	9
6A	Central–Repulse Bay	*2
8	Wanchai Ferry–Chai Wan Estate	7
11	Central–Tai Hang Road	#14
20	Central–Shaukiwan (Limited Stop)	19
25	Central–Tin Hau Temple Road	7
80	Central–Chai Wan (Limited Stop)	1
	Chai Wan garage spares	9
	TOTAL	**88**

*PD3/5s
#Mainly PD3/5s. This was a change of plan; the PD3/5s were originally going to be kept on the flat.

ABOVE LEFT: Even in black-and-white, you can tell PD50 (874) is now blue whilst PD505 (913) remains red. A third, unidentified Queen Mary, also in blue, can be spotted between the back of 913 and the front of the approaching KMB Fleetline. (Lyndon Rees)

ABOVE RIGHT: Deep inside KMB territory at Lai Chi Kok. By 1974, Marys were being pushed into the background on Tunnel routes. LF11 was brand new and the sign of things to come.(Lyndon Rees)

ABOVE: Queen Mary 835 was one of a number to use a TCD-batch lower-middle window for an upper. She is seen here in June 1974 at work on the 25. Note the "cumbersome wooden frame" front uppers. A rather curious lazy blind arrangement with one end of the route displayed on a metal plate flapping noisily from the nearside cab door is also evident. Mary 835 was one of the VUFs never to have received a dome ventilator. (Mike Davis)

BELOW: By July 1974, Queen Marys were a familiar sight in Hong Kong. Here are three at the Central Bus Terminal about to set off for some snatch-change-ridden mountaineering behind North Point. Mary 905 (PD 71) is due to assail Tin Hau Temple Road whilst 904 and 813 (PDs 36 and 8) are going to scale Tai Hang Road. Incidentally, 813 was fitted with the later, trimmer TCD/VUF front upper window arrangements by the time of this photograph. She was also illustrating the increasingly prevalent off-centre destination aperture. The radiators of PDs used on the 11 and 25 received modifications additional to those described in the text to tackle extra boiling problems. (Mike Davis)

BELOW LEFT: Preparing a 3/5 for service. One of the Metal Sections-bodied Guy Arabs disparaged at various places in the text may be glimpsed alongside. (Mike Davis)

Although displaced from the prestigious Tunnel Routes, the PD3s still set a standard in luxury and comfort compared with the older Guys, and were thus next used in the suburban 'stockbroker belt' – the affluent, hilly suburbs in the middle of the island . The routes here had some nasty hill-starts and heavy loadings: there were problems with both types of Queen Mary.

With the 3/4s' lack of synchromesh between first and second and difficulties in maintaining uphill momentum during a double-declutch, to avoid failed changes or long, slow crawls in bottom gear, the drivers needed the snatch-change described earlier by Bruce MacPhee (p.42) and Stephen Morris (p.57). This, it will be recalled, involved bringing the gear lever sharply back to engage second with a single tap at the clutch: if judged right the teeth of the dog clutches engage before they have time to grate, engine revs do not fall off and uphill momentum is maintained. If judged wrong, much noise, less momentum. Such changes were necessary on Chai Wan Hill but one of the drivers' biggest challenges was where the 25 pulled off a stop in Tin Hau Temple Road and immediately made an uphill right turn across the traffic into Braemar Hill Road. This latter manoeuvre would have been almost impossible without the snatch change to maintain power for the climbing turn. When completed correctly this could be very smooth but, if it was misjudged, brute force took over to crash the gears home in the way described. The force of such changes resulted in many of the gear-levers eventually snapping off about six inches below the top, sometimes with attendant hurtling of the top half, complete with knob, into the lower saloon; as a result, repairs involved welding and reinforcement with metal rods.

Unfortunately, once perfected, the snatch change was sometimes employed on the flat in place of double-declutching: this, added to hurried synchromesh changes, led often to a rather jerky ride. If frequent braking was then a feature of the journey as well, somewhat porpoise-like progress developed.

The PD3/5s, with boxes similar to the Guys, made gear-changing easier but of course they had other issues and, as on Copse Hill, West Dene, thirteen years previously, there were problems on the gradients. Some of these were solved by increasing the engine power and the unusual expedient of swapping the LT Special O680 engines in the XAs with the PD3/5s' O600 units, was adopted. This was a successful move and all twenty-eight buses were so treated: it also, incidentally, solved problems of engine overheating on the XAs.

But the 3/5s also had downhill problems where absence of engine braking combined with the usual PD3 footbrake efficiency to worry drivers. Eventually, more MetSec Arabs were 6LX repowered to replace the PDs on these routes, reportedly much to the disgust of the customers who liked their more comfortable seats as well as their softer suspension.

The PDs did well on the Express Route 20 along the North Shore of Hong Kong Island between Shaukeiwan and Central via the Waterfront Road expressway. In its heyday, this route had an allocation of up to 30 PDs running a three-minute peak-period service, which was full from end to end. It was flat except for the westbound approach to the Waterfront Road. Provided they had a good run along King's Road and attacked the short but very steep Tsing Fung Street flyover at full power, drivers could usually creep over the top without changing down, followed by a gradual wind-up to 50mph or so along the fast route to Central. They needed care on the curves, though, since with anything up to 20 upper-deck standees the old PDs had an alarming tendency to roll around. The PDs were gradually cascaded to the flatter but very intensive and heavily loaded Island Corridor routes and it was on them that your intrepid author found these old friends in 1979.

If there was nostalgia in grinding along Western Road in a fully-loaded 406, it was nothing compared to the misty-eyed reunion with a lost youth possible on a CMB Queen Mary. Here was the once-familiar in unusual new surroundings, and the nostalgia would be produced by those remnants of Southdown ancestry seeping through the new role. Queen Marys would come roaring through the Island Corridor and the tropical humidity, sagging kerbwards under a glittering canopy of Chinese signs, stuffed full of humanity, surviving frequent snatch gear-changes, continual lane-changes and various near misses of other traffic… still containing the odd throwback to their Sussex past in the form of a panel or a seat or a sign or a belltone – or a stupid gwalo bus enthusiast, *i.e.* me. Circumstances were such that I was able to visit Hong Kong several times between 1979 and 1984 and fight my way on and off numerous Queen Marys.

My intended first journey on Wednesday 2nd May 1979 had to be aborted, though, when PD 517 (924) arrived with custom falling out of the windows such that the driver did not stop. Later that day I succeeded in getting on one – PD 15 (817) – and observed through the press of standees that she still had her brown Formica fascia panelling at the front of the upper deck. Disembarking was the soon-to-be-familiar battle, squeezing past standees on the stairs and through the press on the platform . The next journey was equally memorable: it was undertaken on PD 23 (821), during a torrential

LEFT: This is the tropical downpour referred to in the text taken minutes before I boarded 821; the two 2s in front of her were 856 and 944 and here the former lurches impatiently round the latter and very nearly eliminates a pedestrian. Visibility from the cab was never good when it was raining.

BELOW: Queen Mary 876 demonstrates the Yee Wo Street lunge on the afternoon of Sunday 4th May 1980. This picture should be studied in conjunction with the one of 856 and 944 which illustrates the nature of the bend. 876 is midway between stops and thus also illustrating that standard description of a Hong Kong QM journey – lurching from stop to stop via the outside lane. Sunday afternoon in Causeway Bay – people walking on each others' heads.

BELOW LEFT: Queen Mary 921 was altered little by CMB internally as may be gauged from this shot, taken while she was at work on the 2, on Friday 2nd May 1980.

tropical downpour in which I tried to find the balance between getting soaked and having the windows all completely shut, with attendant 600% humidity inside the vehicle. I also noted with pleasure surviving green window rubbers amongst the newly blue 821 and was greatly cheered to hear the once so familiar cracked note of a Queen Mary platform bell.

Over the next three years I enjoyed innumerable trips around Hong Kong on Queen Marys marvelling at the skill of their drivers in keeping their big charges up with the cut and thrust of the rest of the traffic. Interiors varied considerably. Although these were basically blue, nearly all PD3s seemed to retain pieces of brown Formica panelling and some green window rubberings. Some, moreover, retained their moquette-covered Southdown seats in some or all of the bodywork; others had blue PVC or leathercloth covered cushioned seats. Some had much

less acceptable hard plastic seats: the upper deck of PD 36 (904) was fitted out entirely with these sadistic devices. Any combination of seat-types was possible within a PD or even within a seat, *e.g*, there were some cushioned seats with hard plastic backs to lean on.

Backs to look at varied similarly and could be Southdown (it is had unlikely that the Portsmouth vandal who, for reasons best known to himself, carved 'Leeds Fulham' on one of 867's seatbacks envisaged its eventual study by numerous Chinese people), PVC leathercloth, hardboard or Formica. One or two had cushions or even an entire seat missing. Miscellaneous signs clinging on included PD 50 (874)'s 'Smoking in Upper Saloon Only' and the 'Landograph of Hove' warning signs on one of the semi-automatic's doors. PD 522 (951) still her Portsmouth allocation disc in the cab. CMB added few signs of their own.

TOP LEFT: Hong Kong Central looks like the business district of any big Western city, only more so, as land is at such a premium. Here, 876 clatters over a temporary road surface covering the final construction work for the Mass Transit Railway on Sunday 6th May 1979.950 behind is on the 10 which the PDs took over in 1975 from Guy UFs
TOP RIGHT: A typical queue, and 897 absorbs some of it at the Cleverly Street terminal of route 2 on the same day. Note in all these pictures the contrast in loads between Hong Kong and Sussex. Was this really retirement?
LEFT: In somewhat different surroundings to those on page 25, Queen Mary 928 takes her layover at the Sai Ying Poon end of route 10 on Monday 7th May 1979.
BOTTOM: 910 and 867 picking their way through the organised chaos of Hong Kong's Western district *en route* to Kennedy Town, in May 1979 and May 1980 respectively.

LEFT: After a period of Hong Kong's heavy loadings, the PDs had both a distinct nearside lean and a rear-end sag. CMB sorted this out by adding additional nearside spring leaves and, more defeatistly, trimming the rear panels but throughout my May 1979 stay 924 was operating with this alarming list to port - this was not the camber! Several journeys after the aborted one mentioned in the text, she was in North Point bound for Shaukiwan. **RIGHT:** This arrival of 914 in Yee Wo Street during the afternoon of Sunday 4th May 1980 was greeted with tremendous enthusiasm by the assembled punters.

Aural nostalgia welled up around such items as those platform bells (most still had them) or the rattle of the semi-automatics' centrifugal clutches and, of course, the familiar gurgle of a PD3 going about her business. No need to try and see the droning heater fans in a sympathetic nostalgic light however: they were not required in Hong Kong.

Although mostly synchromesh, the manual gearbox PD3/4s were not popular with CMB drivers who had the job of driving buses on some of the world's most crowded roads (218 vehicles for every kilometre of road in Hong Kong in 1979) and were used to some form of automatic transmission: this was apparent in some of the more inventive gear-changes that could be experienced on CMB Marys, as already mentioned. On one occasion though, there was possibly more to it: we set off from the Causeway Bay terminus of route 5B on PD 61 and the driver spent most of the initial journey round the one-way system grinding and crunching the gears in vain attempts to select one or other of them, or coasting along in an evasive neutral. I thought at first that this all reflected rather badly on him but then realised, as he eventually got some loose measure of control over the machine, that this might, in fact, be the finest proof possible that this was Mary 883. Southdown drivers used to dislike her for just the same gearbox perversities, and Edward Street appeared to allocate her to the 9/10 road so that Worthing and Littlehampton crews would end up driving her for most of the day. Was this really the same eccentricity twelve years on?

Apart from the general difficulties of handling an elderly, manually-geared bus in Hong Kong's teeming traffic, there was an additional problem for CMB's drivers—one that had been experienced by a few of their counterparts in Sussex. The layout of the cab presented some difficulties for short people in reaching the pedals and, in general, Chinese people were smaller than Europeans. On one journey on PD 36 (904) in 1979 I discovered that the driver had 'enlarged' the pedals with long pieces of wood.

The semi-automatics were more popular with the drivers and rides on them tended to be less eventful from the mechanical handling point of view. I did however have one journey on PD 506 enlivened by the sudden engagement of second at 30mph—928 seemed to stop dead, shuddering violently. On a trip on PD 520 (944) I was mildly disquieted to see what appeared to be smoke coming out of the gear gate.

I visited Hong Kong just in time because the period 1979 – 1982 saw the gradual decline of the Queen Marys in their adopted home. They had outlived nearly all the other secondhand purchases, the PD3/4s despite their gearboxes, but, by the turn of the decade, they were too small and one-doored for a fleet that was ordering very-long, three-axle, 200-passenger buses – and driver dislike of the PD3/4s was not diminishing. The PDs' relative inadequacy was very clear during route changeovers when they created severe bunching problems due to their much slower performance compared to, say, a two-door 6LXB Fleetline.

Already in 1979 several PD3s in addition to 843 and 814 were, to all intents and purposes, withdrawn: they were parked around North Point and Chai Wan as sources of spare parts, staff "living quarters" etc. Those still going were more or less confined to four routes:

2	Central –Shaukiwan
5	Kennedy Town –Tai Hang
5B	Felix Villas – Causeway Bay
10	Sai Ying Poon – North Point (3/5s)

where they were ending their days nicknamed 'hot dogs', saloon cooling having remained a problem throughout their CMB careers.

By 1980, Queen Marys had come off routes 5 and 10 and PD3/4s were getting thin on the ground – they still maintained the 5B but now shared the 2 with the later variety displaced from the 10.

BOTTOM LEFT: Queen Mary 946 in Central on Monday 9th February 1981 ... but the Year of the Rooster was not going to be a Kung Hei Fat Choi for the Hong Kong Marys. **BOTTOM RIGHT:** Also February 1981, and a Jumbo Metrobus speeds tunnelwards past the despondent huddle of Marys at Wanchai. The ten clearly visible are, from left to right, 838, 912, 860, 822, Ribble Intruder, 823, 855, 873, 868 and 842.

By 1981, there were no PD3/4s in service and the remaining semi-automatics were scheduled for route 5M, a feeder to the newly-opened Mass Transit Railway's Admiralty Station from Kennedy Town; additionally a few were still on the 2 but that was largely the preserve of Fleetlines. The PD3/4s were gathered in despondent huddles at Wanchai and Chai Wan (not to be confused with each other). Negotiations to sell them (to Djakarta or Colombo ... or possibly even to what was to become the enormous city of Shenzhen, over the border in China) which had begun in 1979 came to nothing and in September 1981 the reluctant decision to scrap them was put into effect. In that gloomy month, two contractors – Li Kwan and Chi Hing – wiped out all but six of the still extant PD3/4s. PD 11–13 and 33 (816, 818, 815, 826) were spared, partly because of Mr. Ngan's affection for his 'Tunnel Buses', PD 52 (869) disappeared mysteriously (her absence was only noted prior to offering the tender for scrapping) and PD 16 (820) continued as the Chai Wan scrapyard social club and mahjong parlour, a role she had filled for some time.

Of these survivors, PD 11 became the last PD3/4 to remain licensed with a Certificate of Fitness and on Saturday 31st October 1981, the day her licence expired, she ran a commemorative tour with Lyndon Rees at the wheel and a group of mostly British bus enthusiasts on board. She did not however enter into the spirit of things: her fuel line suffered a blockage and after a fitful performance she eventually ground to a halt on Chai Wan Hill during the return leg. She had to be temporarily abandoned but did return to the garage later with something that looked like an adapted biscuit tin as an emergency fuel tank.

This was not really an appropriate finale to the Hong Kong Queen Mary story, and fortunately there were two more. Following the demise of the PD3/4s in 1981, a programme was implemented to salvage up to twenty of the PD3/5s for one or two years' further service, there being little legitimate ground for complaint by the drivers in view of their gearboxes. PDs 511, 513 and 528 (922, 937 and 934) were scrapped with the PD3/4s; the remainder – by then off the road – were examined and a group which could be recertified to form a pool of buses for the 5M was identified. This little group would be enough to provide scheduled requirements and all spares. To it was added the sole Indian-built version of the PD3/5 in the fleet APD 1 (A for Ashok-Leyland). PD 510 (947) was the first Queen Mary to reappear under this new plan and did so just before Chinese New Year 1982 – perversely working a duty on route 2.

ABOVE: September 1981; even sadder times at Wanchai. No. 879 is reduced to a chassis and 900 (PD 40) is next to head for that great bus station in the sky. Excessive tropicalisation of 821 (PD 23) was also in progress. *(T. V. Runnacles)*

BELOW: Queen Mary 820 in use as the Chai Wan scrapyard social club. Like several long-term residents of one sort or another, the exact date of her demise is hard to define: she was still there in November 1984.

BOTTOM LEFT and RIGHT: Hong Kong 1983. Strange goings-on at North Point and Chai Wan are producing Queen Marys like the one on the right! Bits of 913 belt into Quarry Bay North Point-bound on the 4th November 1984. The vehicle under conversion was 915 (PD523) and was seen at North Point on Saturday 1st October 1983.

ABOVE LEFT : Chai Wan conversions were a little more eccentric than North Point's. Note, for instance, the bell-shaped front of PD33 which had resulted from this particular half-cab graft. This, erstwhile 826, was one of two TCDs that participated in these late developments, becoming semi-automatic in the process. *(Derek Nicholls)*

ABOVE RIGHT: The other was 816 (PD11) and it and 917 ('PD527') were even more substantially modified than the rest by the replacement of most of their side-windows with full MetSec equipment. No. 917 displays this at Chai Wan on 3rd November 1984 whilst laying-over off service 82A; some of 928 chugs past. Despite the substantial modifications, quite a lot of original Mary survived in most of these conversions and some items displayed impressive tenacity: for example, the experimental dome ventilator fitted to 943 in 1966 was still there in the twice re-registered half-cab that that PD3/5 became. The interiors of the buses changed little but they no longer made the right noises.

In April 1982, PDs 501, 502, 506, 510 and 516 (Queen Marys 938, 940, 928, 947 and 921) were scheduled for route 5M and PD 505 (913) was rostered as spare. Subsequently 503 (941) and 508 (932) joined the spares list but no others joined this happy band and the programme was presumed to have finished earlier than originally planned. Most of the rest of the PD3/5s thus remained out of use at Chai Wan along with the surviving 3/4s.

By the beginning of 1983 all the remaining PDs were back 'temporarily delicensed' at Chai Wan, driver dislike of them then centring on their brakes. However, the decision to refurbish a number of older buses for operation until the extension of the Mass Transit Railway in 1985 rendered many surplus, led to yet another reprieve for the remaining Queen Marys in the summer of 1983. PD 510 (947) was the first again and reappeared as a standard Mary with Leyland engine, full-front and original Westinghouse brakes. Others of the batch were much more drastically refurbished though, receiving Gardner engines and new brakes and transmission grafted on with the half-cab of a Metsec Guy Arab in replacement of the original full-front! This pleased the drivers but ageing gwalo enthusiasts found it hard to get used to growling, half-cab Queen Marys. Fortunately for them, another Mary, PD 516 (921), returned to service in original condition. By September 1984 the following half-

cab Marys were in service: 11, 33, 501, 502, 503, 505, 506, 507 (which for some reason had assumed the identity of PD 527), 508, 510, 518, 523, 525 and 526. PDs 11 and 33 had additionally been converted to semi-automatic. PDs 11, 33, 518, 523, 525, 526 and '527' had been re-registered because they had been off the road for more than two years. Most of the half-cab Marys were employed on short routes based on Chai Wan. Concurrent with these finales was PD12's sale for use as a site hut in North Kowloon and the rumoured reappearance of mysteriously vanished PD 52 in similar use on Tsing Yi Island during 1982.

CMB's was the largest scale use of OPO Queen Marys. The scale overcame the problem of passenger unfamilarity which could otherwise hinder successful operation. Astill & Jordan of Ratby and Brighton Corporation both had passengers ignoring their drivers: in 1974, when I was working in Brighton, there was a story going the rounds of a woman who had boarded one of the Corporation's OMO Titans – then in their eighth year of such operation – and refused to pay the driver, treating him as though he was running some sort of sideline, extorting money out of passengers before they got to the conductor. Hong Kong's flat fare no change scheme removed the problem of engine noise competing with fare transactions.

Japan

The other Far East Mary was my old friend 284 (the bus I conducted most often), which in May 1982, having spent four uneventful years in a Barnsley yard, slipped out of the country and went further than any other Mary. In October 1983, I found her parked outside a restaurant in Nara, one of the ancient capitals of Japan, where she was serving as a publicity device and gimmick; the reception desk at the restaurant had a huge board covered with photos of happy diners posed in front of her, She was turned out in 'London Transport' livery, complete with outsize fleetnames. This picture 1st November 1984.

Overseas Queen Marys – The Gulf 1978–1996

Nineteen more of the later Queen Marys sailed away to foreign parts – they ended up in The Gulf, transporting the workers building the various new structures in the oil-rich shiekdoms. Like the Hong Kong ones they followed other Southdowns – in this case, coaches – and numerous other secondhand British buses. They transported workers between sites, various residential camps and company HQs, spending most of their day festering at one or other location. It is believed that double-decker buses gained favour, at least in the U.A.E., after an open-truck carrying workers overturned with unfortunate loss of life.

December 1979 – Saudi Arabia Sand all round the big hotel car that met me at Dhahran Airport and Islamic music on its radio, so we were definitely somewhere in The Gulf . . . to be precise, in the vast sprawl of Dammam – Dhahran – Alkhobar, wherein the Arabian Mechanical and Engineering Company (AMEC) had six Queen Marys – 958, 959, 962, 967, 975 and 976. AMEC's Marys sported huge extra bumpers and cutaway skirts and their fuel tanks had been relocated under the stairs. At the time of my visit they were green but they were subsequently painted cream. Whilst initially involved on local staff bus work in Dhahran, the QMs were eventually seen in other parts of the country and 958 was converted to be a mobile living unit for thirty with bunk beds upstairs and aircon devices in the roof. In this guise and towing a loo/shower trailer and a generator, it completed a 1,500 mile round trip from Alkhobar to Taif and back without mishap. As you deduce, AMEC regarded them highly and told also of an occasion when one of a pair transporting staff to the ARAMCO refinery uncharacteristically broke down. Her load transferred to the other one and the Saudi police, detecting a spot of overloading, eventually stopped her and discovered that she was ably transporting 130 people. One assumes average weight per person not too great though – a similar attempt by European students boarding prior to crew arrival on the last High Salvington in Worthing in summer 1970 was less successful: 301 refused to move off. Research by the conductor led to the tightly-packed upper-deck standees being ejected.

ABOVE: Nos. 967, 976 and 975 sport huge bumpers and Saudi Arabian number plates in Dhahran on 2nd December 1979. **BELOW:** During my visit 958 was being converted into mobile living accommodation: she is seen here as converted and in the later cream livery.

Photo: Terence Jones

BELOW: AMEC also purchased 957 and 969 which they resold to Crescent Transport. This firm finished them in an attractive livery of scarlet, white and black. In December 1979, Mary 969 was out of service awaiting a spare part and gradually turning into a sand dune. I believe she never ran again, although 957 remained active.

QUEEN MARYS IN THE GULF

SAUDI ARABIA

AMEC—DHAHRAN

No	Local reg	Southdown No
617	SA 42894	976
618	SA 42895	958
619	SA 42896	959
620	SA 43086	975
621	SA 43087	967
622	SA 43085	962

CRESCENT—DHAHRAN

No	Local reg	Southdown No
6335	SA 43264	957
6336	SA 43265	969

UNITED ARAB EMIRATES

DUTCO—DUBAI

No	Local reg	Southdown No
T784	60896	971*
T785	60897	968*
T786	86809	956*
T787	86003	966*
T806	60358	263
T807	60357	265
T1027	32842	280

DUTCON—DUBAI

No	Local reg	Southdown No
B1	70867	258
B2	71295	282
B6	87894	367
EB1	71004	283
EB2	71578	264

* Originally with Qatar Construction Pauling in Qatar

AMEC passed two of their imports on to Crescent of Dammam; 969 soon became a source of spare parts but 957 was active for several years – with no modifications, she became battered but unbowed.

Other QMs were to be found in Qatar for a while and Dubai in the UAE for many years, where they worked for the Dubai Transport Company (DUTCO) and its subsidiaries. As in Saudi, these Marys transported workers to the various building developments that sprang up throughout the late seventies and the eighties. If you stay at any of Dubai's tourist hotels of that era you can be pretty certain that the people who built it turned up each day in a Queen Mary. The yellow and orange PD3s also ventured quite far afield – as well as all over urban Dubai, they went up into the mountains, near the Oman border to attend the construction of the Hatta Fort Hotel and over the Oman border to other projects.

RIGHT: Dutcon Queen Mary 283 in a suburb of Dubai which looks like part of the desert (I suppose it is really) on Thursday 10th September 1981. The buses' drivers and passengers – in the U.A.E., mostly migrant workers from the Indian subcontinent – were all most helpful to me, making various unscheduled stops and manoeuvres and often joined in deciphering the NCME bodyplate on the stairs. This tendency to be parked for long periods explains, I think, why the wretched things were always found in the photographically unhelpful back-to-sun position: it keeps the cabs a bit cooler. The fact that they normally moved at dawn and dusk, may also be pertinent to 367's purchase and survival.

ABOVE: As the sun goes down on Jumeirah, Dubai, on Monday 19th April 1982, Queen Mary 258 waits to take some Dutcon workers back to their camp.

ABOVE RIGHT: The DUTCO camp at Hatta was in a magnificent setting in the mountains, fifty miles inland near the Oman border. On December 4th 1979, Queen Mary 265 was there pretending to be a London Transport bus, the livery being a result of the Queen's visit to Dubai in February that year and attendant expatriate flag-waving.

BELOW: 263 with Dutco at their Rashiyida HQ in Dubai the same day.

ABOVE: The Doha Two had gone to ground and proved harder to find than the others. In response to a prior intimation of the purpose of my visit, John Emery the British Airways Manager in Qatar, had been very kindly trying to locate them; they had not been seen for three months prior to my visit – before that they had been commonplace. Their hiding-place still being a mystery on my arrival, we spent part of the afternoon searching vainly for them. At the time I thought we were looking for three Marys – 956, 966 and 971: I was unaware until I reached Dubai that 971 had transferred thither. We visited Um Said port, where the PD3s' arrival two years previously is said to have had quite a traumatic effect on the locals, but found only the derelict remains of a Southdown coach. Eventually we gave up and I left for Dubai. The people at the Dutco company however knew where they were and I prepared to return to Doha. Before I could notify John, I was whisked off to Hatta and then to 282. Meanwhile, one of John's many enquirees had called him back asking if the idiot looking for buses was still around – by the time I reached a phone, John had left word that he had found them. I flew back to Doha and, at 7am the following morning, finally pressed the shutter on 956 and 966 which were in store in a quarry discussing with each other their possible fate. They too later transferred to Dubai

Gradually their use declined and by 1989 only two were still active: 264, in a subsidiary company by then, and 258. Four had disappeared without trace and six more were parked out of use at Rashiyida. Of these, 367 was in a rather sorry old state having collided with a crane or something (probably at the instigation of heat-crazed inhabitants. The Panoramics had been a bit hot and stuffy in Brighton's summer, and temperatures in Sussex rarely reach Dubai's June July figures of 130°F!; she was not tropicalised in any way), but the other five –263, 265, 280, 956 and 971– looked in fine fettle. However, they were sold in a yard clearance and transferred to the premises of Abdul Wahab in Al Qusais near the Sharjah border. They looked too good to scrap and maybe were purchased with his other business of plant hire in mind. 264 continued to ply daily across Dubai to Jumeira where new beach hotels were going up but 258 also came to rest at Rashiyida – as a static mess room for staff rigged up to its own a/c plant.

ABOVE: Last QM active in Dubai was 264 latterly with Dutco subsidiary ANC – she is seen here at Rashiyida in February 1990.

ABOVE: Finally becalmed in the sand, 258 was a static mess room in Dutco's Rashiyida HQ in Dubai, rigged up to its own generator for aircon, for its last years: this picture August 1992. By 1990 Dutco had reabsorbed Dutcon but Dutcon's livery appeared to have prevailed as Corporate colours with most of the lorries etc in blue and orange. 258 was always a Dutcon bus; the Abdul Wahab five **BELOW** were still in Dutco yellow

Whilst building continued apace and building worker transport continued to be needed, things got trickier for ageing right-hand drive double deckers like 264 – not least the construction of numerous very low road signs; the municipality also developed a concern about such buses' centre of gravity. Abdul Wahab finally broke up his five in 1994. Eventually 264 and 367 went for scrap as well, although rumours of bits living on and even of the complete 264 reaching Karachi were heard. After, where large numbers needed to be transported, contractors used big articulated single deck units

Finally in 1996 scrap-dealers arrived at Rashiyida, cut up 258 on site and took away the last U.A.E. Mary

But in telling this Gulf story, we have run ahead of the rest of the world, not without purpose though for the complete extinction of the Queen Mary in Arabia serves to highlight by its very anomalousness the remarkable goings on in other parts of the QM world.

Survivors 1985–1997

To illuminate these remarkable goings-on, we must return to 1985 in all the other Queen Mary stories and see the build-up to the pivotal year of 1987. As detailed earlier, the 1985 situation was one of a small group of Marys still with Southdown and quite a few other survivors elsewhere. In addition to the convertibles (Nos 3200–3225), the Southdown remnants were nine driver-trainers, a treelopper and a mobile office in the service fleet. The office (once No 292) had started off in 1978 as the mobile unit for the Market Analysis Project and had subsequently been a temporary booking office at Portsmouth. In 1985 it reverted to survey mode to carry out a sort of 'son-of-MAP' exercise before becoming a mobile training unit in all but name, taking tuition in the use of the new high-tech Timtronic ticket machines around the Southdown area, whilst still claiming to be a 'Passenger Survey Bus'. As for the convertibles, after 100% OPO in 1981, they had had to content themselves mainly with various special duties which did not require fare collection like school and works contracts, Pensioners' Specials for Worthing Council and a whole range of bizarre and eccentric activities.

During 1985 and most of 1986 these arrangements – very acceptable to Queen Mary enthusiasts – continued more or less unchallenged, although the Pensioners' Specials had been discontinued by then. The PD3s were to be found all over Southdown's area trooping off, at specific times of the day and often in convoy, to some school or works contract, frequently attended by miscellaneous enthusiasts admiring the spectacle. If British Rail had need of a substitute service for any reason, a parade of Marys would invariably turn up whilst a good proportion of their time continued to be spent on promotional eccentricities and other more specialised uses: on Sunday 7th September 1986, for instance, No 3220 was chuntering between Brighton and Worthing, draped in banners, as a live outside broadcast studio for Radio Sussex whilst No 3210 was up at Haywards Heath doing a special service thence to a vintage bus day at the Bluebell Railway. Other noteworthy events in a very long list were No 3217's slightly incongruous appearance amongst all the flash modern glitterware at a Club 18-30 promotional jamboree in Brighton when the main contractor (not Southdown) found itself a coach short (November 1985) and No 3201's taking part in Worthing Carnival – it was one of four vehicles offered free by Southdown in August 1985; charity-towing also remained a popular pursuit with No 3223 so hauled on 8th September 1985 and 17th August 1986 to name but two days. In addition to all this, PD3s performed on a number of open-top services and, very occasionally turned up on ordinary stage-carriage duties covering for a defective modern vehicle (*e.g.* 3209 on the 729 Brighton–Tunbridge Wells on 9th September 1986).

Two minor tremors shook our confidence in the Marys' future slightly. The first was Southdown's 1985 division into four units: East and Mid-Sussex, Brighton & Hove, West Sussex and Hampshire. The Brighton & Hove unit (soon after to become a separate fleet) decided that it did not want any PD3s. This was particularly bad news for the training fleet, most of

Information about the pictures on this page is in the text.

Photo: Nigel Lukowski

which was based on its premises and six of its number left, five to find similar employment elsewhere and one (the oldest, No 880) after store, for scrap. Not that by then, No 880 wasn't a real blast-from-the-past anyway, having been reprieved from the Barnsley scrapyards, to which sisters Nos 871/2/7 had gone in early 1985, to join No 292 as a Passenger Survey Bus in the 'son-of-MAP' exercise. The allocation of the rest of the PD3s to one or other of the new divisions, or the coaching sub-division, and the appearance of the new divisional fleetnames, with stylised 'S' logos in lieu of National double-Ns, on most of them suggested that their future remained, however, secure as did the appearance of No 3209 back in the traditional Southdown colours that were being readopted as fleet standard.

Actually it reappeared in these colours in stages. First of all the lower three-quarters were done, for open-top operation; then, after a while looking rather silly with its Maritime England special livery white and blue roof atop the green and cream, it acquired a green roof as per the 1980s Southdown double-deck livery; and then finally in early 1988 it reverted to the livery it had worn when new by gaining a cream roof (see p.67).

Tremor number two was the re-registration of most of the pre-year suffix buses, a process that began everywhere in the mid-1980s after freer transfer of plates became legal. The first three Southdown Marys to lose their identities were, of course, Nos 3206–3208. Subsequently other plates were appropriated to disguise the age of coaches with Nos 880 and 3203, which were languishing out of use at Horsham, the next to donate. In the summer of 1986 Hampshire Division descended on its Marys and whipped all their registrations, leaving most of them with what would have been 1964 Hampshire numbers had they been issued then; No 3222 acquired, for no reason known to anyone, the plate WOW 993T! Nearly every time one of these exercises took place a story surfaced of two vehicles with the same number being espied on the road on the same day: 16th July 1986 saw a coach and a PD3 numbered 423 DCD for instance. However, re-registered, the PD3s soldiered on.

Photo: Nigel Lukowski

Photo: Richard Marvan

SEQUENCE RIGHT: Newly repainted in traditional livery in 1986, 3209 making a rather fruitless journey to Beachy Head. It displays Southdown East and Mid Sussex as a fleetname but with no accompanying doubleNs nor yet replacement Ss; an N still skulks on the grille and NBC grey numbers on the apple green give a combination not seen during the reverse livery transformation of the seventies. In November 3209 had acquired Ss in all the right places whilst still showing East and Mid Sussex but 3206 was about at this time with just Ss. 3209 gradually then returned to original colours. The next two pictures from 1986 and 1987 respectively show the next two phases.

LEFT: 416 reduced to a board on the grille for destination advice. Worthing June 1986.

commented that it would not be long before the doors were sealed over and the PD3s were thrown away. It turned out to be less of a joke than I thought.

Nonetheless, having become so used to these anachronistic old bangers surviving in the fleet by fulfilling all these special duties, their demise during 1987 came as a shock. Deregulation seemed to be the cause as still NBC Southdown did not do too well in the new, rather crowded, market and quickly found itself with a surplus of vehicles, garages and staff. Contract work was significantly hit and Marys began to aggregate in withdrawn clusters at various garages until by July 1987 there was only one left in PSV use. This was No 3209, which continued on school duties at Haywards Heath longer than intended due to the indisposition of a VR and even went on to turn up pretending to be a Route 41 minibus on Eastbourne Carnival Night. Whilst the other Marys were thus becalmed, the opportunity was taken to procure the rest of their plates for coaches and, by late 1987, all but No 3209 had been nominally allocated new marks. 3209 was allowed to remain 409 DCD as it was to become a company preserved vehicle and join the small PD3 team that was to remain with Southdown after 1988.

No 3209's 'active preservation' meant performing much the same duties as in the previous few years but in complete 1964 format (traditional livery plus old-style fleetnames, Southdown script grille badge, two push-out windows at the front upstairs etc). No 3223 had also reappeared in traditional colours and in recognition of its almost 3209-like status it regained its original registration in 1989 during one of the periodic reshuffles of the non-suffix marks; every time the vehicles carrying them were to be sold, they obtained their third mark and the DCD numbers went somewhere else. Trainer 294 was also turned out in green and cream – but eighties-style. No 292 became an office and crew accommodation at Bexhill for the joint Eastbourne/Southdown Topline company in 1989.

Mind you, we should have suspected that a fairly short life was envisaged for them as more and more bits of them were being irretrievably painted over or nailed up. Rear number boxes started to fall out of use and disappear beneath paint all over Southdown in 1985 but only QMs began to lose front apertures; most just lost their destination boxes but No 3220 lost its number one as well! Grille-boards substituted where necessary. Discreet plating over of dome ventilators also began. Then, in December 1986, No 3200 was noticed with a huge silver plate hammered over where its dome ventilator had been. Seeing all subtlety thus abandoned, I jokingly

By the end of 1989 Southdown had become part of Stagecoach but we'll pick that story up in a minute after considering how the Marys withdrawn in 1987 had fared. For most of 1987, Southdown's last ones sat around in despondent huddles at various garages as a prelude to setting off, in early 1988, mainly for Ensign's yard, many still claiming to belong to the divisional units which had been discontinued almost as soon as they had appeared and carrying their old DCD plates . . . tired, shabby (especially those that had been parked in the open for over a year), 24 years old and hard work to drive, they seemed destined only for the scrap yard. Yet surprisingly nearly all of them were snapped up to carry on as trainers or 'Fun Buses' all over the UK, joining survivors from earlier batches that they had outlasted for so long at Southdown.

ABOVE: Still bearing its old registration, 414 DCD, and Southdown West Sussex fleetname 3214 awaits a buyer at Ensigns on 16th April 1988. Some sales were not via Ensigns.

The surprising life continuance of the convertibles highlighted an interesting change of circumstance in the late eighties as withdrawals and scrappings of QMs slowed to a trickle – most Marys extant in 1985 still existed ten years later, having merely changed owners along the way – and sometimes occupations if the situation had developed to their disadvantage.

Those for instance that were trainers in the late eighties – and more joined this band as the decade proceeded even as others left – found themselves a little while later at a potentially loose end thanks I believe to some new speed requirement that many of the old dears were apparently unable to meet (which surprised this ex-Brighton conductor, survivor of many extremely rapid last journeys to garage!) but nearly all of them survived into other uses. By 1997, only 292, 404 and 418 remained in use as trainers. Could they go faster than the others?

ABOVE: In 1988, I found 365 at Northern Scottish's Stonehaven garage. Their Marys were kept here because they were too tall for Aberdeen garage: the unusual front dome featuring, I think, the rear end of an Alexander Y-type, resulted from someone physically proving their incompatibility with that garage. I was told that sister 362 was 'away to Dundee'; having seen a picture of 362 which showed its badges – two Leyland and one Daimler – I was rather sorry to miss it (but see page 123). 362 was scrapped in 1993 but 365 was sold for local use as a vintage engine transporter and was not finally broken up until 2002.

No	Owner, location, period in use
	Secondhand QMs in Use as Driver Trainers in the UK
	1985 onwards. All Marys in Trainer use in 1985 and after. Those continuing in Trainer use with an owner through 1985 show original start date, those changing Trainer owners in 1985 show only new owner.
960	de Courcey, Coventry 1983-1989; Enterprise, Coventry 1989-1994
963	Fareway, Kirkby 1990-1994
973	Heart of England, Coventry 1983-1985 (out-of-use from 1985)
401	Lancaster City Transport 1989-1991 (Training for Boroline Maidstone)P
404	Stagecoach United Counties, Bedford 1989-1997*
405	Brighton & Hove, Hove 1988-1991*
407	Brighton & Hove, Hove 1988-1991
408	Grummett, Mansfield 1989-1991*
413	Brighton & Hove, Hove 1988-1991*
414	Grummett, Mansfield 1988-1991*
418	Stagecoach United Counties, Kettering 1988-1998 P
419	Trent, Derby 1988-1997 (trainer until 1996)P
423	People's Provincial, Gosport 1987-1993 P
429	Thomas,Tonypandy 1987;Powell, MerthyrTydfil 1988-1992*
253	Go-Ahead Northern, Gateshead 1978-1992
269	Ayrshire Road Transport Group Training Association, Prestwick 1983-c1990
270	ACL, Kirkby 1989-1992
277	Northumbria, Ashington 1989-1991P
278	Thomas, Tonypandy 1987; Boroline, Maidstone 1987-1993 (part-time PCV later)P
286	Northumbria, Ashington 1989-1991 P
292	Stagecoach South & United Counties 1989-1998P
293	RTA London SE6 (Catford) 1986-1991 (open-top;low bridge by garage)
294	Stagecoach South & antecedents 1978-1995 P
295	Shamrock & Rambler, Bournemouth 1985-1989; North-Western 1989-1995
296	Stagecoach South & antecedents 1979-1991*
302	Carlton, Gillingham 1986-1989; NTT Yeadon 1989-1991
347	Claus,Peacehaven 1985-1986; Coles,Southend 1986-1987;Bender,Laindon 1987-1992P
358	RTL, Eastbourne 1988-1989; Rennie,Dunfermline 1990-1994
360	Stagecoach South & antecedents 1979-1993(P)
362	Northern Scottish, Stonehaven 1985-1992
363	Yorkshire Traction, Barnsley 1979-1993 P
364	Alder Valley, Aldershot 1985-1992
365	Northern Scottish, Stonehaven 1985-1991*

No 269 was the only sold NGT one to survive to thirdhand use. Harris, Grays used 416 as a trainer for a while in 1988.
*Further use; P: Passed directly into preservation.

BELOW: The Trainer 253 story begins in 1977 when Northern General purchased 13 Marys for driver training work; it used them for five years before selling all but one for, as it turned out for most of them, scrap. No 253, having escaped this purge, went on to train for another ten years. On 15th April 1988 it was having a very long lunch-break at Gateshead Metro, proudly displaying its new Go-Ahead Northern fleetnames. In 1992 it was sold and, after donating spares to preserved buses, was scrapped in 1994.

As part of the dissolution of the National Bus Company, NBC Southdown became two companies again—'Brighton & Hove' and 'Southdown', but with the former taking with it some of the once-Southdown interurbans based on Brighton. Southdown joined the Stagecoach Group in 1989 but with its heart having been taken out by the dissolution arrangements it was no surprise to see Stagecoach soon after reconstitute operations into two companies—'Sussex Coastline', based on Chichester, and 'South Coast Buses', based at Eastbourne and including the once Maidstone & District operation at Hastings. This was not really of great moment to the Queen Marys as by 1989 there were few of them left in Southdown ownership.

Southdown 'Queen Marys', 1989		
3209	409DCD	Active preservation, convertible open-top Trad livery
3211/21	AOR160/57B	Stored NBC Green
3223	424DCD	Active preservation, permanent open-top Trad livery
0421	421DCD	Tree lopper Yellow/white
0292	FCD292D	Office Green/Grey
T294/6	FCD294/6D	Driver trainer 80s SMS(294) Yellow/white (296)
T360	HCD360E	Driver trainer Yellow/white

Subsequent transfers within Stagecoach and purchases by the group found Marys also in the ownership of other stripey companies viz: Hampshire Bus, United Counties and Cleveland Transit. Stagecoach also had 3200, 3204 and 3218 in Cumberland territory in the late

eighties where the first two formed part of its blockade of Keswick Bus Station. The Stagecoach purchase ended the revival of traditional Southdown livery but 409 and 424 retained it thereafter.

So far there have only been two QMs in Stagecoach colours – Stagecoach South trainers HCD 360E and FCD 292D..... here together at Basingstoke in November 1992.

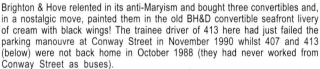

Brighton & Hove relented in its anti-Maryism and bought three convertibles and, in a nostalgic move, painted them in the old BH&D convertible seafront livery of cream with black wings! The trainee driver of 413 here had just failed the parking manouvre at Conway Street in November 1990 whilst 407 and 413 (below) were not back home in October 1988 (they had never worked from Conway Street as buses).

ABOVE: When not letting her on short loans (*e.g* to Polar Motor Company in 1980), Paul Sykes used 429 in a somewhat unorthodox manner themselves prior to sale. This included her having a key publicity role in the 1980 Barnsley Marathon for example. Eventually she went to South Wales where she worked as a driver trainer for two firms although here she was in classic convertible funbus use in her adopted Merthyr home. (*Gareth Powell*)

BELOW: 311 about to be rescued. June 1985. (*Tameside Social Services*)

Use of Queen Marys as playbuses also ended, (unless 315 resurfaces from the 'Whatever Happened To?' box on p.124) but with at least one survivor: 974, once so employed in Northants became a source of spare parts for preserved 954 in 1991 and hung on into the next century so used. Sadly 311, the famous *Tilly Tameside*, had to go for scrap after some mindless vandalism. The playbus part of 311's story is one of those heartening snatched-from-a-scrapyard-at-the-eleventh-hour ones. In June 1988, I spent a most enjoyable afternoon in Tameside at the invitation of Clem Boultbee-Scott, a great PD3 fan who ran the playbuses. FCD 311D of Skye fame had been put to one side and eventually sold in the early 1980s just at the time that Tameside's first playbus, an ex-Wigan and GM Titan known as *Tommy Tameside*, was proving such a huge success that a sister vehicle seemed necessary. As No 311 was making its way to the Barnsley graveyards, Clem was setting out in search of another bus; her path crossed 311's apparently the day before it was due to become razorblades (in June 1985) and it was rescued and brought back to Manchester to become *Tilly Tameside*.

Clem offered me the chance to drive No 311 which I accepted ... slightly reluctantly. Having never driven a QM before, I could not miss the chance but, as a very occasional bus driver I am always apprehensive as I climb into the cab. I have the impression that buses are big and heavy and need strange gear manoeuvres. Moreover, Dukinfield, where we were at the time, is rather hilly, I had been the lazy owner of an automatic car for three years and the streets were full of school kids: I could see the headlines already. Nonetheless, 311 was a delight to drive; surprisingly light and responsive with much better visibility than I expected and very easy gears. All that notwithstanding, I decided to forego the right turn on to the winding main road at the bottom of the hill; vanity would not let me risk writing off a Queen Mary!

Later we set off 'on business' to a school, also in Dukinfield, No 311 now carrying a group of volunteers. The 22-year-old bus did not baulk at the steep hill up from the Tame but neither did it zoom up it at a jaunty speed; we soon had a long tail of cars strung out aft as we ground slowly upward. At the summit, as we started heading, with relief, for top gear at last, we rounded a bend to see a light go red just too soon for our going through it to have been any way excusable. The driver said a word my colleagues in Brighton used to say in similar circumstances in another hilly town and we pulled to a halt. At the school, *Tilly*'s arrival was greeted by hordes of enthusiastic kids who gathered around in a bobbing mass as the various games were unloaded and the slide that comes out of the upstairs emergency exit then organised; a continuous procession of kids using this device then made its way through No 311.

Another use that petered out was berry picker transport but once again some of the Marys moved to other uses.

So, notwithstanding changes, the story from 1985 was one of survival and we still had most of 1985's QMs to enjoy ten years later! A 29-year-old example made it to a 1993 'Buses' cover, whilst working on service!

BELOW: Former 311 (FCD 311 D), named Tilly Tameside, in use with Tameside Social Services as a playbus. *(Tameside Social Services)*

Photo: Nigel Lukowski

TOP, ABOVE and BELOW: Some Queen Marys in revenue service in the late eighties. It was rather a shame that 3222 became a trainer with People's Provincial as, along with sister 3212, it started with higher aspirations when purchased in 1987 (after a trial with 3215): they spent their first summer on an open-top circular service (on which I had the pleasure to travel on a superbly driven 3222) and there was talk of winter working on the Fareham–Gosport trunk route. But it was not to be and 3222 was demoted whilst 3212's use was more intermittent and special than perhaps was originally intended – although she did compete against former fleetmate 424 in Southsea in 1990. She was named Queen Mary in April 1988. In the mid-eighties, 278 started swimming against the tide: after two stints as a trainer, it reverted to full PSV status with the erstwhile municipal operator in Maidstone and whilst QMs elsewhere donated their non-suffix registrations to ageing age-conscious coaches, 278 swapped a suffixed one for a non, becoming 217UKL. On September 29th 1988 278 operated in the morning, did a school run mid-afternoon and then this rush hour Senacre Wood journey. Her first training stint had been in South Wales and the second with Maidstone, training drivers for all their London tenders.

Still buses

Throughout the survivors phase we had, in pride of place, that elite band of Marys still in revenue-earning service, still buses and in the early 90s the band was still quite big. The cover star was 415 in its last days of working for Lancaster City Transport, the new owner of its original operator having already loomed over the horizon to absorb the municipality but not the Mary; 415 saw further service with an Ormskirk operator (who purchased arsonised 270 for spares) before passing into continued revenue-earning service outside the U.K.

Not that there weren't other Marys in revenue-earning service in the U.K. Not that Stagecoach didn't have Marys in revenue-earning service come to that. Stagecoach South, as the heir to Southdown, had two in proper livery – 409 at Eastbourne (South Coast Buses) and 424 at Worthing (Sussex Coastline) – and, whilst essentially 'special events' vehicles, they regularly appeared on stage service covering for indisposed Leyland Nationals. On 24 January 1992, for instance, 424 appeared thus between Brighton and Worthing, open-top; the Southdown Enthusiasts Club noted "..there were no passengers on the upper-deck despite the frost having been less severe than the previous day"; what wimps these passengers are nowadays. 422, one of an additional pair retained by Southdown in the big 1987 sell-off of convertibles, spent several years on various services for Abacus Leisurelink: summer 1992 found her on the Gatwick Zoo–Bluebell Railway route, for instance, and from 1994 she was really back home, working various services in Brighton mostly on a celebrity appearance basis. 410, meanwhile, remained in PSV use, with London Hop-on Hop-off sightseeing, amongst whose DMSs it appeared, especially at

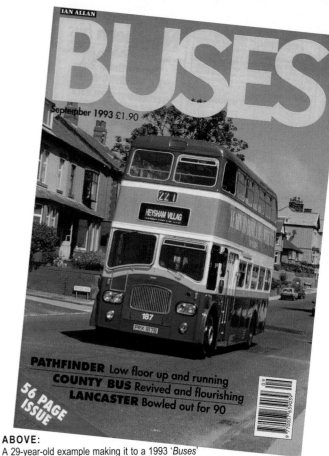

ABOVE:
A 29-year-old example making it to a 1993 *'Buses'* cover, whilst working on service! 415 in its last days with Lancaster City Transport. *(Ian Allan)*

ABOVE: 424 arrives back in central Worthing on 21st August 93 having worked a journey on local service 4 covering for a sick Leyland National. Such journeys briefly returned crew operation to Sussex's streets. I believe, though that some QM buses of the 90s ran effectively OPO.

ABOVE: 422 back on home ground. Leisurelink occasionally used its QM on its ordinary stage services east from Brighton and when it branched into cross centre routes, 422 occasionally showed up on those too as here in December 1996, complete with festive holly. *(Richard Maryan)*

BELOW: August 1994 on Madeira Drive in Brighton: 422 giving Guide Friday a run for their money; photography of this phenomenon was somewhat frustrated by real and hoax bombs, the Palace Pier area having been cordoned off before the sun came round on the eventual day of my visit.

Stephen Morris driving QMs in 1996 ..from p.57

At the end of the day I thought that was that. I had revelled in the opportunity to renew my acquaintance with the Queen Mary after all those years, and wasn't particularly expecting to do it again in a hurry. However present at the Shoreham event was one Clifford Jones, supremo of Leisurelink, by then running local bus services in the Brighton area in a bid to bring in some income over the whole year rather than just the summer. Amongst his fleet was another convertible Queen Mary, 422, and it was decided that Messrs Morris and Osborne should perform their double act for real, on route 12 between Newhaven and Brighton a couple of months later.

422 was a much-loved member of his fleet which didn't often see action along the coast road service, normally the preserve of rather more mundane Fleetlines. Luckily it was a warm, sunny September day so passengers wouldn't mind too much the opportunity to sample the sea breezes from its open top deck. There was added spice, in that he was a comparative newcomer to roads served primarily by Brighton & Hove, hence those very striking-looking and powerful East Lancs Cityzen-bodied Scanias running against Leisurelink's rather older stock.

Driving a PD3 in service, against the clock, can be quite an exciting if tiring experience. Though in fine fettle the Leisurelink vehicle was not quite so lively as 294, nor was it quite so light. It shared with 294 a tricky change from first to second, and was rather sluggish to start in second. Thus for any stop on a slight upgrade at least first was required for restarting. On a tight schedule, and with a certain obligation to try and keep ahead of Brighton & Hove, there was no time to go down the double-declutch road; a snatch change was really needed, and nearly every one was accompanied by an awful lot of noise. I understand from my conductor that this was the source of much ribald comment from passengers! However it did at least get us under way with a degree of speed, and despite the noise it did condescend to go into gear each time.

Naturally everyone was keen to sample the delights of this fine veteran? Well one might expect so. However let no-one kid you that a nice new bus is not a draw to passengers. This was amply demonstrated when we pulled round the corner out of Old Steine on to the stop on Brighton sea front, one of the busiest on the route. A large crowd surged for 422's platform; but before more than one or two had boarded the following B&H Scania appeared. Immediately most passengers changed their minds and went for the newer bus instead. Maybe they thought they would get home quicker on that, but we had the advantage of a conductor and could make much better time. Nonetheless it was hard work to keep up to schedule.

I have to say that while the drive was tremendous fun, I was very aware of how antiquated the Queen Mary was for a driver. Given that it was built 12 years after the first Routemaster had shown what could be done with power steering, automatic transmission and independent suspension, and 10 years after the first Atlantean had shown how the driver's lot could be improved by moving the engine out of his left ear, it was all terribly hard work. The engine is deafening in the cab, especially on full song on the earlier trip, climbing to Woodingdean, you have only one chance to get those gearchanges right, I had to crouch to see out of the windscreen and I ached for days in my back, thighs, shoulders and arm muscles. Yes, by 1966, when 294 was built, the Queen Mary was becoming dated – even if they still looked handsome enough and gave the passengers a good ride. By 1996 there was little comparison with say a modern Dennis Dart – or a B&H Scania.

But there is no doubt that there is a much greater sense of achievement driving something like a Queen Mary, and while you can get away with driving a modern bus as badly as you like, with something like a Queen Mary, the bus will quickly bite back if you don't give it its due respect. It must be very embarrassing getting your passengers to walk up the hill just because you missed first gear. . .

..and Julian Osborne goes back conducting

1996 found me for the first time in 22 years taking up the conductorial arts . For the first occasion I collected for charity and distributed souvenir tickets on one of the buses out and about on the splendid 7th July 1996, with the only real conducting authenticities being chatting to driver and passengers and not having a clue what was ahead and behind – always a feature of the complex 2 timetable;

apparently five of us went round clockwise and one anticlockwise. But on the second occasion I did it for real issuing real tickets, collecting money, giving change and accounting for it all on a waybill. On both these occasions my driver was Stephen Morris, editor of *Buses* and you read about his experiences above. What he has omitted to say is that he is a very fine driver indeed: a conductor's delight in his combination of steadiness and expedition but then he's a modest chap if given to exaggeration about other people's ageing processes.

What struck me first of all after all this time was how easy it was to fall into the old routines again (helped of course by the fact that both events took place in Brighton) with only one real important difference – not knowing the fares. On my afternoon working the Leisurelink Mary I was reminded more than once of my first afternoon on my own back in 1973. BH&D always started you on a Saturday afternoon and preferably with a backloader – as Lodekka RPN 9 made her way along New Church Road I forgot most of the fares I'd learnt on my training week and charged what seemed likely until challenged! On 422 I had the regular driver (Geoff and then Kevin) as a talking fare table but I still felt a little at sea. I also had great difficulty in getting the ticket machine fitted comfortably (Morris is wrong here – I wore it round my waist and that took some customisation of the belt I remembered too late !!) and it was also much more complicated than the wonderful old bash-'em out BH&D Setrights. So what psychologists call 'hygiene factors' impinged a surprising amount at first.

But all that apart the rest came back like it had been yesterday: watching people on and off, ringing off from where one was (Kevin thought I'd packed up once when I went and sat on the bench seat and was surprised to hear the bell go as he went for it! Hey! We used to sit and read the paper and conduct from there on a Sunday morning!!), keeping payment in your hand until you gave change (although one didn't get many "I gave you a fiver" jokers on the Coast Road). They were always a nice bunch and they still were in 1996 with again time for some chats. These were possible 20 years ago but not so often! Even on the Sundays that started so leisurelily we'd be carrying standing loads throughout the afternoon and evening in summer.

Some 90s concerns also impinged. I felt more for passengers distressed at the entrance step heights. Indeed after an hour or so of running up and down stairs and leaning over the engine (noisier I'm sure), I felt more physically challenged than I did in 1973. I also wondered if phrases such as "love", "dear", "mate" and "Squire" were as acceptable as they used to be let alone lending a helping hand aboard, but I didn't really put this to significant test. The other difference was the keenness of other buses to uplift passengers. Unlike the famous Southdown 15 skulking along two stops behind us, we had B&H Scanias glued to our rear end before strategic stops so they could offer an instant alternative to waiting customers.

I also had a serious customer service doubt. One or two passengers remarked that it was nice to see a conductor but was it? Conductors make buses move faster which is nice once you're on but they also imply a lot more rush & bustle. On an OPO bus it's usually (not always!) only the last aboard who has to 'hold tight' as the bus moves off whilst they make for a seat but in the good old days in Brighton it was both sides of the bar please, last person clear of the doors and we were away, the conductors arm behind those last to stop 'em falling off again. Theoretically we could help with luggage and pushchairs and sometimes did but often we were just too busy managing the flows on and off and collecting the money to be much use there. On quieter runs sure we would give real customer service – help with stuff, travel advice, a general natter even but too many quiet runs and we weren't economic. Gosh! Is a half empty OPO Dennis Dart giving better service than a crewed QM stuffed to the gunwales, crowds battling on and off and three bells dinging at every other stop?? Yeah probably but not so much fun.

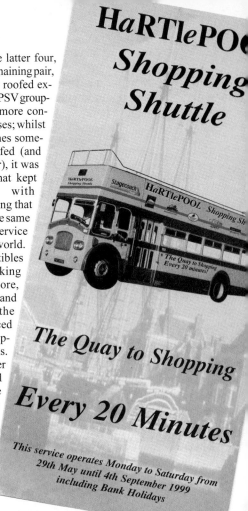

ABOVE & BELOW RIGHT: 410 joined the interesting collection engaged on London sightseeing work after a spell with The Kings Ferry: a remarkably quiet recruit to the ranks, its engine barely audible as it trundled around the sights – and *Bertie* when with London Ho-Ho, named by the owner's nephew, a Thomas the Tank Engine fan.

weekends, trundling around the sights. The Osborne family were kindly invited to spend some time at the Hop-on Hop-off garage where 410 sojourned with some old Brighton PD3s, an ex-Barrow PD2 and the aforementioned DMS hordes and had a very enjoyable Thursday morning, the high point of which was our personal trip on the QM from the garage to Tower Bridge to pick up a tour. Hop-on Hop-off passed into London Pride ownership but 410 remained at work before passing into preservation.

Other Marys still in PSV use by then were 425 at work for Wallace Arnold on Torquay Sea Front (and earlier with another owner in Scarborough), 417 with Cleveland Transit, 279 with OK, 260 with a new East Anglian owner and the two remaining Weardale examples

awaiting sale. These latter four, and Confidence's remaining pair, were the only really roofed examples still in the full PSV grouping and they were more contract than service buses; whilst the "Southdown" ones sometimes appeared roofed (and 415 did at Lancaster), it was the convertibility that kept the 4xx batch with Southdown for so long that was now allowing the same buses to be the last service Marys in the wider world. Not that all convertibles were strictly speaking convertible any more, various low bridges and roof-swaps over the years having produced some permanent toplessness in the ranks. Incidentally, the other 1987 retainee, 411 was not as fortunate as 422 and after five years festering in Worthing garage, donated its roof to make 424 convertible anew and left on the proverbial one-way trip to Barnsley.

Photo: F. Lawrance

ABOVE: Here is 411 inside Worthing garage in May 1988, beginning its ultimately fruitless period of retention, with the new 411DCD behind.

ABOVE and BOTTOM LEFT: 425, whilst nominally owned by Harris of Grays, worked in Scarborough on hire to Applebys of Conisholme for most of its time in Essex ownership. Wallace Arnold used 425 on a variety of duties in Torquay from 1994 and so successful was it that 267 was purchased from Weardale and converted to open-top for similar use in Leeds. 426 and 416 were bought and used by Harris. 416 later passed to a Scout Troop in Ipswich.

Photo: Alan Snatt

Roofs notwithstanding, some might argue that some or all of the foregoing were in active preservation rather than being really buses and by the mid-nineties there was certainly a rather grey area between the two classifications here – especially when we consider such as the Peakbus operation, which I understand used Marys, and the appearance of other examples on special (not always non-revenue) services. At the 1993 Southsea Spectacular, Mike Payne's 401 made a fine sight (and sound) leaving the Common for Broad Street Museum under a full load and at the 1995 event conveyed me and many others on a most enjoyable tour of Pompey which had as its high point (ho! ho!) an exhilirating (if ultimately somewhat suspense-laden – would it make it?) ascent of Southwick Hill Road onto Portsdown Hill behind the city.

Certainly the biggest growth sector in the Queen Mary world between 1985 and 1997 was in preserved examples. At about the time 409 became a company preserved vehicle, 406 was sold by Southdown directly into private preservation. From then the numbers grew steadily such that by 1997 scarcely a rally passed without an example putting in an appearance.

408, 414 and 405 at Lydney in September 1992. 428 at Coalhall June 1988

Standing around in yards

A number survived standing around in yards. These inhabited another somewhat grey area as some dealers are scrappers as well and vice-versa. By this time few Marys were instantly scrapped but whilst

ABOVE: Spectators and 356 look on at the Schools Polo Tournament, Windsor Great Park June 1994

BELOW: 420 surrounded by action at some 'Hunter Trials' at Bletchingdon June 1994.

hearteningly, many seemed initially to be tagged for resale, demise could gradually sneak up on them. 963 for instance, which went to Norths at Sherburn-in-Elmet in 1994, was still extant enough to donate her staircase to 419 two years later (see p.120) but after that and having already lost her engine and front lower deck corner, her resale possibilities had diminished somewhat. And not only in dealers yards did possibilities gradually evaporate: 973 was put to one side by its owners, Heart of England Transport Training in 1985. They planned to give it to Tile Hill College for apprentice use, but had to abandon that after vandalism and sell it at the turn of the decade to a buyer in Birmingham who eventually scrapped it after further vandalism. 428 stood at Keenan's in Coalhall unused for 16 years before being sold for scrap in 1995 – here there had been plans to sell it as a trainer.

426, on the other hand left Ensigns triumphantly bound for preservation in 1996, after a five year sojourn . Another that seemed safe but more settled was 408; after working as a trainer alongside 414 with Grummett, Mansfield this was serving as the gatepost at London Bus Export's Lydney yard and when I visited in 1992, just constraining one of those completely deranged Alsatians that enthusiasts so look forward to meeting when visiting such places. It subsequently became a shed there. And others left Lydney to take up new occupations.

Ever more unorthorthodox uses

Some QMs remained in interesting non-PSV use into the nineties. 420 and 356 were wired for sound as commentary boxes and to be found at one equestrian event or another, established with a good view of the action from which their occupants could reach every corner of the site with their observations. At 'Hunter Trials' it seems that the best such spot is right in the middle of the course, such that when your intrepid author visited 420 at Bletchingdon in the summer of 1994, he needed all his years of traffic-island hopping skills to identify a good photographic standpoint that could be reached and used without being flattened by a horse in the process! The following week 356 was parked slightly more safely at the 10-yard spillover line beside the Schools Polo Tournament matches in Windsor Great Park but the 18-line disclaimer in the programme warned me that (and I summarise) 'polo is a dangerous sport, be careful, no-one but you is responsible if six horses, riders, etc. land on top of you whilst you're photographing the commentary box'. Owner Laurie Strangman, a great QM fan, had bought 420 in 1987 and monitored the Panoramic herd assiduously until the opportunity to buy 356 from Confidence appeared; shortly after he sold 403, which he had not converted, into preservation.

Meanwhile, back at the 1995 Southsea Spectacular, preserved (since 1991) 412 created its own personal grey area for this paragraph by being drafted in to replace a silly white hut as the public address point for the prize-giving ceremony, interviews with winners being broadcast from its top deck

In 1989, the Medical Campaign Against Nuclear Weapons sold 961 to Scottish CND and it set off north from its home in Devon. Unfortunately, by the time it reached its new abode, it had left most of its roof on a bridge in Manchester. As a result, its new owners forebore from using it and it lay idle until spotted by Clown Jewels, a roving band of entertainers based beside Cromarty Firth, in that part of Britain where after 800 miles of arctic progression the signs still point to 'the North'. 961 joined a fleet of Bristols that took various educational entertainments around the Highlands and was converted into a mobile stage, such that in most pictures of activities it disappeared behind backdrops and frontdrops – the nearside hinged open to create the stage.

Thirdhand, 307 is interesting and needs setting in context. The British Shoe Corporation jettisoned the large fleet of Mary staff buses in the mid-1980s in favour of ex-Nottingham Atlanteans; three, including 307, lingered amongst the newcomers for a while but soon only one (308) remained. British Shoe hoped to preserve it but unfortunately had to abandon the project and send it for scrap. Ironically some other BSC Marys survived in third or fourthhand use: 960, 961, Playbus 974 and 302 were all ex-BSC buses as was C&G 287, a scrapyard escaper like 311; and so was 307 which was used by the Leicester Mercury as a display bus. 287 entered a new phase when she became a publicity unit for The Little Pub Company in the Midlands.

In summer 1986, a convoy of vehicles owned by people who had rejected the values of contemporary society hit the headlines as it made rather forlorn progress around the highways and by-ways of Southern England in search of a campsite, surrounded by police and TV cameras and in this raggle-taggle band was No 273, sold into fourthhand use in 1984. Many of the vehicles involved in this hoo-ha were impounded by the police and later ordered off the road but No 273 survived and still appeared at pop festivals, midsummer debacles and the like ..for several more years. It was seen more than once in France.

In 1986, as noted, it was a TV star, albeit only as a crowd extra. It thus holds no candles to the London Borough of Lambeth's No 275 which starred on the television news earlier that year; it had been converted into a campaign vehicle for its council's efforts to resist rate-capping and surcharging and, having taken them to the Law Courts on 5 March, appeared U-turning before the whole country on the TV news bulletins. It was sold in 1988... it later became a display unit for a furniture maker in Cornwall and then went to America.

I dithered for a while about including a 'Queen Marys and the media' section. Such long serving and ubiquitous buses must, inevitably, feature as background – or more – every so often. Thus 295 appeared in 'Bread' when a North Western trainer, 358 drowned out Anneka Rice when inconveniently passing during a Scottish 'Challenge', a CMB Queen Mary diverted Inspector Clouseau into a parked car in 'Revenge of the Pink Panther...' the thespian predilection for Brighton means that Marys appear regularly on arts programmes profiling performers. They appeared in newsreels, and beyond the broadcast media in newspapers, magazines and books – like this one and many others including another DTS Publishing tome (on CMB)! Where does one draw the line on the media aspect?

427 remained in use as a corporate hospitality unit now restaurant-based. 402 became an Exhibition Unit for Kenwood, the kitchen appliance manufacturer, based at Havant. 366 was used by the St John's Ambulance in Cleveland. Launched in some style by its new owners, it was a recruiting device, plans to use it as a travelling first aid unit having been stymied by weekday non-availability of drivers. It subsequently passed to a band in Newcastle before being advertised for sale in 2000. After its sale by Bluebird Northern, 365 was used by an Aberdeen owner for the transport of vintage tractor and stationary engines to and from vintage vehicle rallies and 405 had a new role as a training unit (not a driver one) with Dixons, the electrical people who entered into the spirit and sent it to the 1996 Coastline rally.

Finally, No 349 was an inspiration to all of us who believed that a long silence, especially after sale to a dealer, meant that a Mary was no more. In 1988, after six years of no news, up it popped in Castleford, working, it appeared, as a display bus for a firm listed in the telephone directory as an 'under carriage parts repairer'. But what exactly did it do? – it's now back in the WEHT list on page124 but still inspiring us to wonder what other long silent Marys still exist? Even not so inspired, QM fans still, as you see, enjoyed the 90s.

ABOVE: 961 at work with Clown Jewels and fellow classic buses, FLFs BUO203B and HEV995B. She was out of use by the end of the nineties. *(Clown Jewels)*

BELOW: In use as the control point for the Leicester Mercury Historic Transport Pageant in May 1989 is former 307 (FCD307D), when that newspaper's publicity vehicle.

HALESOWEN. Established successful Inn taking £190,000 ex VAT under management. 2 Bars, Central Servery, 2 Bedroomed Self Contained Flat. New Leasehold £30,000 (30/4462)

Queen Mary thrown in

ABOVE LEFT: 272's preservation was effectively financed for a while by her use as a mobile insurance advert.

CENTRE LEFT: 296 went on loan from Southdown to Tideway School in Newhaven in 1992 and was used as a 'residential centre' in the school grounds until 1997. Here it was visited by 422 after the day out described on p.111.

BOTTOM LEFT: The interior of 275 when in use as a furniture display bus.

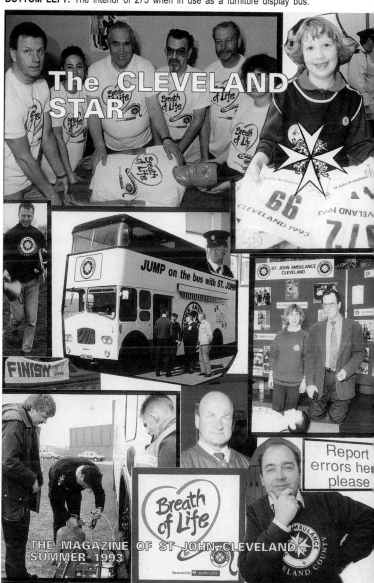

Overseas Marys

Which brings us back to the subject of overseas Marys, which we left in The Gulf on p.103. The post-1985 story beyond The Gulf is, on balance, also a positive one with some significant survivors and some expansion to new countries: 275 spent the mid-nineties as a mobile restaurant in south-east New Jersey, USA. In 1998 she was sold on to a Christian outreach group working in north-east Philadelphia but was never used by them (narrow streets and overhead railways posing big problems) and was put up for sale in 2001. 429, after use by Leisurelink Wales and a limbo semi-abandoned period went through London Bus Export in Lydney to Croatia where it worked as a display unit for a brewery. When Kenwood had exhausted all the PR possibilities of European travels for 402 from its Havant home, they sold it to their Turkish distributor (although it appeared to have had some difficulty actually entering that country). And 415 provided the Galway city tour for Lally's in Ireland for a while.

Having been bought with convertibility in mind, 415 was slightly late on stand on the day I visited in 1995 after a turn in the weather forced the rapid re-instatement of its roof: Lally's, like the chaps at its first Southdown garage (Portsmouth, where it, 408 and 423 were originally an isolated trio back in 1964) would dispute the Portslade Works claim that this operation could be accomplished

ABOVE: 402 on one of its tours around Europe for Kenwood pauses in Stockholm *(Kenwood)* RIGHT: 275 being hoisted aboard in Felixstowe *en route* to America. *(Maersk Lines)*

LEFT and BELOW: Kennedy Town by night April 1982 and Spot the QM: 930 withdrawn on the roof of Chai Wan garage April 1989 (third from right).

in twenty minutes! What the exercise proved in Galway was that no one ever got round to renumbering the roof: Southdown atypically branded the things to facilitate career-long partnerships but when the rest of 415 became 3215 the top retained its original gold-leaf pre-NBC 415 inside the front dome and still did in 1995. I had a most enjoyable day on (and off with camera) 415 in the company of Patsy the driver and Andrea the guide as it performed three tours and one special school contract sliding through the wonderfully efficient chaos of central Galway, out to Salthill sea front, up onto the higher ground to the west and back to town past the university and the cathedral. 415 later had its roof cut in half so it could work closed top or in three possible open-top configurations, usually appearing henceforth with its front half in place, 366 style.

In the Far East, things were less good. Restaurant Haya tried to move 284 and finding her disintegrating as they did, had to scrap her. And in that once main overseas gathering place of QMs only 50% of the 1985 remnants reached 1997. Most 1981 survivors found, as intended, their raison d'etre removed by the 1985 extension of the underground railway and went for scrap. However, one survived until 1988 working, with short wheel-base Guys, on the tortuous service across the Tai Tam Reservoir dam which has vehicle-size restrictions. This bus, once No 930, latterly PD525 and half-cab since 1984, survived in the possession of CMB until 1994. It and two Guys had been requested by the Hong Kong

ABOVE: Galway was the last major town in Ireland to retain the old Irish method of urban traffic management – chaotic illegal parking and comprehensive jaywalking. As a means of keeping vehicles moving at a sensible speed through the streets whilst not scaring life away from the shopping centre it worked wonderfully well – U.K. 'accelerate or coagulate' traffic planners please note; but to work it did require an element of give and take which might be difficult for some U.K drivers to understand, especially the infinite courtesy to pedestrians. Sadly progress reached Galway shortly after my visit. The clock saying Dublin Time is a legacy of the coming of the railways when for the first time a standard time regardless of the sun was needed throughout Ireland. The trains ran on Dublin Time – Galway's by the sun is fifteen minutes later.

Museum of History but CMB, as they had similarly done in the past in such circumstances, scrapped the things. The other survivor sold (still a proper full-front Queen Mary) for use as a site hut in 1983 remained as a scrapyard store in the New Territories, the very last survivor of the first 140. It was PD12, TCD 818, a member of the very first batch. Although in the early stages of reverting to nature, it survived to outlast all its contemporaries until 1998! I last saw it in November 1997 and at their suggestion photographed some old friends' eleven month old son in front of it to prove the date. What a fine and neat end to this story 818's survival would have made but, unfortunately, shortly after my visit the site was levelled and our story must seek a new ending. And there is a very positive one

BELOW: 818's last resting place near Sheung Shui. This picture was taken in November 1997.

Breeze Up To Devil's Dyke

Take the bus to explore the dramatic and historic scenery of Devil's Dyke

TAKE THE BUS FOR A WALK

Working in Partnership to Protect the South Downs

THE 3RD ANNUAL
**WORTHING RALLY
AND RUNNING DAY**
(IN ASSOCIATION WITH WORTHING SEAFRONT FAYRE)

SUNDAY 25 JULY 1999
SOUVENIR GUIDE & TIMETABLE
£2.50

ALL PROCEEDS IN AID OF THE
ST BARNABAS' CHILDREN'S HOSPICE

THE 4TH ANNUAL
**WORTHING RALLY
AND RUNNING DAY**
(IN ASSOCIATION WITH WORTHING SEAFRONT FAYRE)

SUNDAY 30 JULY 2000
SOUVENIR GUIDE & TIMETABLE
£3·00

ALL PROCEEDS IN AID OF THE
ST BARNABAS' CHILDREN'S HOSPICE

TOP LEFT: Worthing preservationists provided facilities for Corgi's designers when they were preparing their Queen Mary model range – here 416 is measured and photographed in Worthing garage on Monday 1st March 1999.

ABOVE LEFT: 406 back on Brighton's streets July 2000. **BELOW LEFT:** The Leicester Mercury making its own news April 2000.

ABOVE RIGHT & OPPOSITE PAGE: 401 and 416 hard at work at the 2002 and 1997 Worthing Running Days respectively.

Seaside Retirement

The remarkable Survivors phase of the Queen Mary story was coming to an end in the mid-nineties and what, realistically, is probably the final phase of their long history was beginning. By the Millennium, most surviving Marys were in the hands of preservationists and back in their old south coast operating area. After long and busy lives they were retiring to the seaside.

Oops! anthropomorphism...... Stephen Morris once commented that my original book on the Marys tended at times to such regarding of the buses as human. But in this last phase, not only were they behaving like many of their former passengers in home choice, some were eating the others. Most surviving Queen Marys were now in preservation, and split between Runners (or potential Runners) and Non-Runners (mainly as sources of spare parts) Things are not always cut and dried though – 418, for instance, was bought as a spare part source but found to be in such good nick that plans changed.

The first QM totally broken up to assist other preserved QMs was 360 and after that 296 and 421 were reduced to such shadows of their former selves as to be all but eliminated (see p.126). Others await similar fates or perhaps a sudden caving in after years standing in the open!

Ownership of preserved Marys changed over the years since the first few were earmarked in the late eighties and kept changing. The Southdown Historic Vehicle Group is, in 2004, a major player but it is a complex organisation and there are other people and groups. Suffice it to say that a dedicated band of enthusiasts is looking after fleets of these fine vehicles, often sharing facilities and generally assisting each other.

Whilst one or two never left, many of the Marys now back in the Sussex coast area have made long return journeys to be there. Chris Pearce went and brought 415 back from Galway for instance and 277 came from County Durham after many years in the careful hands of Mike Fishwick. 279 also came from County Durham but via East Anglia whence came 416 and 260. 292 and 404 (latterly the United Counties treelopper) came from Northamptonshire. Another Midland homecomer was 307 which the Leicester Mercury newspaper kindly donated to its new owners. I went with Chris and Richard Cossey to collect this one. QM model maker Corgi being based in Leicester, I suggested that they might also like to get involved and all this resulted in quite a handing over ceremony outside the Mercury offices with the newspaper subsequently featuring the event in their pages. Many Marys operated in Leicester in the 70s and 80s and so there was a sense of occasion as 307 crossed the city boundary heading south and Leicester was Maryless for the first time in 30 years. If you are of a nervous disposition don't look out the back of a vintage Mary trundling down the M1 on a Friday afternoon – the just-in-time overtaking philosophy of some lorry and indeed PSV drivers can be alarming to watch! In 1997 John Witt brought 972 all the way from Scotland, where it had worked for two more farmers after Frampton; since then he has transformed the vehicle, a recent high note being the re-energising of its illuminated offside advert panel. Fellow Frampton Mary 954 had made the journey south in 1991.

Because many of these Marys have been in continuous service since new and thus continuously maintained, most preservationists do not experience quite the problems that their colleagues restoring buses found in fields and quarries do. But there are some issues that

result purely from the vehicles' age. The aluminium body frames are almost indestructible but other bits are coming to the end of their lives – like the wood inserts in the frame to which the body panels are attached by screws and the foam sound-deadening equipment behind those panels. The decline of these two features means the panels rattle, displeasing MoT inspectors, and the

> Hong Kong's climate hastened such developments in the wood inserts of their Marys: CMB then welded steel straps to the pillars and riveted the exterior panels to them.

decay of the wood holds the possibility of the panels eventually falling off. Similarly life-expired are the very difficult to replace green window rubberings which disintegrate unpleasantly in preservationists' hands or in a tiresomely semi-adhesive way on one's clothing. The 'teeth' of the radiator grilles are finally in need of dentistry too with many working loose and rattling. Engine and chassis-wise the Marys are again almost indestructible – Chris Pearce assures me that, with regular water, oil and grease, they will go on for ever.

Of course the great thing about this particular accumulation of preserved vehicles is that most of them are runners and can regularly appear in service together. The open-toppers are very popular with enthusiasts and non-enthusiasts alike, especially when no fares are charged, and running days and special events all over Southdownland can usually produce half-a-dozen fully-loaded Marys bustling to and fro. They are not all free – one of Alan Elliott's Marys has been running in Class 6 service between Brighton and Devils Dyke as in days of yore. The usual bus has been 406, substituted by 350 on inclement days and for a while in 2000 by Eric Stobart's 410, when 406 became temporarily indisposed. My son Tim and I sampled the service in July 2000 and enjoyed the experience, although clearly it wasn't as nostalgic for Tim as his Dad. The blow on the descent was bracing to put it mildly with various items blown out of my pockets and away.

Because of the convertibles' resilience, their current activities are really the latest part of a continuous tradition rather than a recreation of the past – indeed, in earlier times such concentrations of Marys were relatively infrequent. The stuffing of Pool Valley with QMs in 1996 was wonderful but it was not how things ever were: we never had wall-to-wall Marys – unfortunately.

To really recreate the sixties we need other types as well and, we are gradually amassing that capability. Recently, the fifties have been yielding long-forgotten remnants: in 1995, our friend Danny Chabaud found a Beadle PD2/12 sitting beside the road south of Paris and contacted the Southdown Enthusiasts Club. In 2001 an all-Leyland PD2/12 (742) returned home after 30 years in a County Durham scrapyard and a utility Guy was repatriated from Denmark; we have Royal Tigers, Tiger Cubs, Commers and Leopards and the reasonable chance that in our dotage we really will be able to recreate our youth – only with potentially more interesting food.

But the more buses you have, the bigger problems with authenticity. The current collection of preserved Southdowns did not all operate together in Sussex – the utility, for instance, was well into its Danish career by the time Panoramic Queen Marys arrived in 1967 and, to be totally sensitive to a scene from that year, 742 would have to turn up in OK livery on some pretext or other. Actually it's rather a shame, I think, that none of the QMs that worked for

OK has been preserved in their colours: it was a nice livery and they worked for OK as long as they did for Southdown, longer in 279's case. But OK did change its livery during that time. What though of 272 which spent ten years in traditional green and cream, four in NBC green and fifteen in the black and grey of Confidence of Leicester?

Another area problematic for authenticity is the matter of blinds – whilst doing some research for Corgi, I came to the embarrassing conclusion that a significant proportion of Southdown buses operated with partially incorrect blinds – this is of course handy for preservationists in a way as long as some attempt is made. When we took Chris Pearce's 294 out for a photo shoot to cover missing sixties pictures in 1998, we were quite plausible with the blinds but in Brighton had to settle for one for the terminus away from which 294 was heading (not an unusual occurrence it has to be said) and on the A286, we didn't have a totally authentic via blind. But there have been occasions when we haven't made enough effort with blinds, displeasing the strategically placed photographers along the route – and sometimes that meant we'd blown it

completely because the route itself did not interest the running day riders aboard! Happiness can be increased greatly, whatever the problems, if an open-top is used!

Chugging about on Running Days trying to be authentic (or running in service) is not all these surviving Marys do – they're still in use at all sorts of special events and charity dos and a selection uphold tradition by visiting The Derby most years. I suppose there will be a final final phase to the story when the surviving survivors will be so old that they'll be static exhibits in museums but that day seems a way off yet. I need to date this, don't I? It's May 2004.

Photo: Authors' collection

With so many surviving Marys the ability to recreate the past is helped enormously – on running days there really can be another one along in a minute as there once was! In this Spread we see various QMs being prepared for service and then re-visiting their old haunts. Various rural premises house Marys. The rubbed-down one is 277 when with Mike Fishwick. 401, 294 – with 260 behind – and 416 (p.119) were all performing at the 1997 Worthing Running Day. The sad Mary donating bits to 419 in Trent's Langley Mill garage in 1996 was 963. Wallace Arnold 425 was the paparazzi bus ahead of 294 at the 1996 Rally whence came many of the pictures on p.58. 426 in Portsmouth Dockyard in 1999 could almost illustrate symbolically our "Early Days" pages.

Photo:
Richard J. Cossey

Photo: Authors' collection

Derby Day 1999 – and still they go.

Stagecoach continued to use 409 and 424 into the 21st century. By then 'Health & Safety' decibel warnings had to be put in the cabs but they still performed well. 424 got 296's engine in 2000 and was eventually sold – for further heritage work with Stephensons of Rochford – but 409 remained. The story is all but told: here by way of a summary then is the story of the one Queen Mary always owned by Southdown – illustrated by phases of 418's life.

How had 409 come to this point in its career from that heady day in 1964 when I first saw and snapped it (p.13)? In June 1964, 409 DCD was delivered and allocated to Eastbourne to begin a pretty uneventful life. There were the rites of passage of all the convertibles (a push-out window going off to be a dome ventilator in a Panoramic in November 1967, an NBC fleetname from May 1973, full NBC leaf green livery in November 1974, a subsequent multi-coloured double-N symbol, August 1977) but it seems to have done nothing else to attract attention during its early career. It spent most of its time working in the eastern part of the company's area, from Eastbourne or Brighton, and even after allocation to the spare pool in 1978 at about the time it became No 3209, it ventured west for only very brief stays. In December 1980 it was allocated to Brighton for the Marys' very last fling on Brighton town services (p.76). After 1981, No 3209 engaged in the special activities performed by all the remaining convertibles but did something distinctive for a change by adopting a special livery to commemorate Maritime England Year from 1982 to 1986. It returned to real Southdown livery and became a Company Preserved Vehicle just before the Stagecoach era and in that era continued as the company preserved bus, albeit licensed as a full PSV. For most of that period it was kept at Eastbourne but after the closure of Eastbourne garage (in which it was the last resident) it transferred to Chichester. It was the only QM to retain its original registration throughout.

BELOW: A fitting finale. In 2002, to withold it from competitors, Stagecoach decided not to surrender the name Southdown Motor Services and indeed to formally rename Coastline, Southdown. Thus 409 became once again legally a Southdown bus. At about the same time Stagecoach made available the original DCD registrations to QM owners. Here at Chichester in early 2004, Stagecoach South Managing Director Andrew Dyer symbolically hands owner Bob Jackson the "proper" plate for 419, allowing it to dispense with its Trent era Derby moniker. 409 attended as did the Dart which makes two QM links by being ex-Hong Kong and carrying a DCD mark – one that Stagecoach will probably retain, its original owner having been scrapped in 1990.

TOP LEFT: 418 at Worthing Pier in July 1965, working roofed on an ordinary service in only her second summer.
TOP RIGHT: In May 1978, she was working open-top but on an ordinary service – in Brighton.
MIDDLE: By April 1989, 418 was a driver trainer for United Counties stationed at Kettering.
BOTTOM: And in July 2001, preserved 418 was the control point for the Worthing Running Day.

Many thanks to Stagecoach South for assistance with this photo, not least bringing the Dart over from Havant for it. Thanks also to them for their permission to use copy from various Southdown Chronicles in the book. Part, I would suggest, of a great tradition of assistance to enthusiasts by Southdown and its successors, which is greatly appreciated.

Notes and Addenda

NBC Temporary transfers

Queen Marys 917, 929(?), 932, 938, 940, 950 to Crosville immediately prior to withdrawal Summer 1974. Used mainly at Rhyl. But possibly elsewhere – Manchester?

Queen Marys 3216, 3217, 3218, 3220 to United at Scarborough in summer 1979 (open top).

Queen Mary 3218 to United at Scarborough in summer 1980 (open-top)

Queen Marys 3213, 3214, 3216, 3217(?) to Devon General at Torquay in summer1983 (closed-top, working as conducted buses).

ABOVE: 933, 935 949 were sold to London Country in 1975 to help cover a vehicle shortage. They performed for a year on services 409 and 411 from Godstone garage and were then sold for scrap. *(John Bishop)*

Photo: Gary French

Photo: Authors' collection

Photo: Authors' collection

TOP LEFT: 417 was bought by Cleveland Transit in 1988 and thus passed into Stagecoach ownership five years after her sisters still in Sussex and six years after the first Stagecoach purchases which ended up with United Counties. Before and after joining Stagecoach, she was used on a variety of special bus services in the Tees-side area as well as in maintenance roles like checking bridge clearances. She attended the 1998 Worthing Running Day and in an example of intraStagecoach co-operation was driven to and from Bedford by her own crews and between there and the coast by Stagecoach United Counties ones. She is seen here pausing at Bedford. *(Gary French)*

UPPER RIGHT: 362's identity crisis(see p.107).

LOWER RIGHT: London Bus Export converted 413 and 414 to rightside loading. Rumours of sale followed regularly but they were still (or back) in the UK at the Millennium.

ABOVE: OPO conversion reversing window still in 831 Hong Kong 1979

25th March 1990 – 426 undergoing tilt-test at Wembley! *(Alan Snatt)*

QUEEN MARYS IN SUMMARY

In the following, scrap dates are, whenever possible, the date the bus ceased to exist but some such exact scrapping dates are unclear and for others grey areas of standing derelict prior make consistent application of our maxim difficult. Speculative purchases etc make precisely dating some preserved statuses similarly difficult.

Whatever happened to? (WEHT)

Gradually over the years some QMs have slipped out of sight, their disappearance from public view often not being noticed at first. I have gathered them together in this box. Can anyone out there shed any light? Have you, sir, got 845 in your back garden? Do you, madam, recall seeing 975 last time you were in Dhahran?

In compiling this list certain assumptions have been made, chief among them that any second owner within a 10-mile radius of Barnsley at any time means 'scrapped'.

No recorded final purchasers from these vendors

845 (West Auckland Junior Jazz Band 1984); 848 (Moffatt & Williamson, Gauldry 1983); 851 (Morris, Swansea 1981); 852/3/4/7 (second owner within a 10-mile radius of Barnsley but Sykes *Export Division* ex-British Shoe – however probably for spares); 869 (vanished from CMB 1981); 936 (Islington Bus Company); 955 (Wallace, Nottingham 1982). 285/8/90/9 (British Shoe 1984); 289 (Northern General 1982)

To dealers not in Barnsley then silence

977 Lister, Bolton 1984; 964 Rochdale dealer 7.83

252 APT Bracebridge Heath 1982; 261 Perrett Northampton 3.83

293 Ensign 1.91

Last heard of in Gulf, early 80s

957 969 Crescent Dhahran Saudi Arabia,

958 959 962 967 975 976 AMEC Dhahran Saudi Arabia

966 968 282 283 Dutco Dubai UAE Rumoured to have gone 'to Africa' possibly Egypt (Port Said)

Miscellaneous Missing Marys and other puzzles

402 Sold by Kenwood Havant to distributor in Turkey 1993. Refused entry to Turkey because too old; probably still on quay at Izmir.

405 Dixons – then what?

407 London Bus Export – then what?

257 Was as an office and lecture theatre on a Rare Breeds Farm in Ashdown Forest after 1986 (interim private owner) but then what? Last seen Christmas 1991 and farm no longer open to the public

264 Did it leave Dubai intact?

273 Burnt out 1993?

275 Sold on Ebay 2001?

284 School for Disabled?

315 Playbus Nottingham; last seen by me 1982

349 sold to Henderson, Elmsall (sic), Suffolk 1990. There is an Elmswell in Suffolk. Was a display unit: does 349 still exist?

353 359 only one Barnsley owner. Sold to Hartwood Export 1980. – then what?

361 Sundeckers. Seen in Lisbon Summer 1981. Turned up with Ripley, Carlton in 1994 via Weymouth dealer: anyone see it in the intervening years?

366 Sold by St Johns to a band in Newcastle. For sale again 10.00

368 Staff bus Food Factory Tunbridge Wells until early 80s – then what?

SMS number	Chassis number	Body number	Date delivered	1st re-registration	2nd re-registration	2004 status
813	571756	5221	10.58	AH 4183		sc 9.81 Hong Kong
814	571757	5220	08.58	AH 4184		sc .78 Hong Kong
815	571758	5228	12.58	AH 4188		sc 6.85 Hong Kong
816	571759	5223	11.58	AH 4186	DC 5003	sc .86 Hong Kong
817	571760	5226	11.58	AH 4190		sc 9.81 Hong Kong
818	571774	5222	08.58	AH 4187		sc .98 Hong Kong
819	571775	5229	12.58	AH 4185		sc 9.81 Hong Kong
820	571776	5224	11.58	AH 4191		sc by .88 Hong Kong
821	571777	5227	12.58	AH 4198		sc 9.81 Hong Kong
822	571778	5225	11.58	AH 4195		sc 9.81 Hong Kong
823	571818	5217	06.58	AH4189		sc 9.81 Hong Kong
824	571819	5218	06.58	BC1174		sc 9.81 Hong Kong
825	571820	5216	05.58	AH4196		sc 9.81 Hong Kong
826	571821	5219	06.58	BC4163	DA8035	sc 6.86 Hong Kong
827	571822	5215	05.58	BB9521		sc 9.81 Hong Kong
828	582544	5327	02.59	BB9767		sc 9.81 Hong Kong
829	582567	5326	02.59	AH4197		sc 9.81 Hong Kong
830	582581	5337	04.59	BE7787		sc 9.81 Hong Kong
831	582583	5328	02.59	BC7081		sc 9.81 Hong Kong
832	582545	5332	03.59	BC4162		sc 9.81 Hong Kong
833	582563	5338	04.59	BE2254		sc 9.81 Hong Kong
834	582564	5335	03.59	BB9519		sc 9.81 Hong Kong
835	582565	5329	03.59	BC4161		sc 9.81 Hong Kong
836	582566	5336	03.59	BD7332		sc 9.81 Hong Kong
837	582541	5331	03.59	BE2256		sc 9.81 Hong Kong
838	582542	5334	03.59	BE2257		sc 9.81 Hong Kong
839	582543		03.59			sc 2.70 Newhaven
840	582582	5333	03.59	AH4200		sc 9.81 Hong Kong
841	582584	5325	02.59	AH4199		sc 9.81 Hong Kong
842	582585	5324	02.59	BB9520		sc 9.81 Hong Kong
843	591965	5412	11.59	AH4180		sc 6.77 Hong Kong
844	591978	5413	11.59			sc 8.78 Bridgend
845	591977	5414	11.59			WEHT
846	591966	5415	11.59			sc 2.78 B arnsley
847	592078	5416	11.59			sc 7.79 Dunscroft
848	592062	5417	12.59			WEHT
849	592052	5418	12.59			sc 12.76 B.Auckland
850	592098	5419	12.59			sc 11.76 Dunscroft
851	592180	5420	12.59			WEHT
852	592196	5421	12.59			sc 9.78 Barnsley
853	592195	5422	12.59			sc 9.78 Barnsley
854	592140	5423	01.60			sc 9.78 Barnsley
855	592181	5424	01.60	AH 4181		sc 9.81 Hong Kong
856	592245	5425	01.60	AH 4179		sc 9.81 Hong Kong
857	592141	5426	01.60			sc 8.78 Barnsley
858	592042	5427	01.60	AH 4176		sc 9.81 Hong Kong
859	592051	5428	01.60	AH 4182		sc 9.81 Hong Kong
860	592061	5429	01.60	AH 4177		sc 9.81 Hong Kong
861	592079	5430	02.60	AH 4192		sc 9.81 Hong Kong
862	592097	5431	01.60	AH 4178		sc 9.81 Hong Kong
863	601446	5490	10.60			sc 8.79 Barnsley
864	602040	5493	01.61	BE 6652		sc 9.81 Hong Kong
865	602042	5491	01.61	BG 1715		sc 9.81 Hong Kong
866	602087	5492	01.61	BE 7789		sc 9.81 Hong Kong
867	602119	5495	01.61	BE 6653		sc 9.81 Hong Kong
868	602096	5494	01.61	BE 740		sc 9.81 Hong Kong
869	602041	5532	04.61	BE 4731		WEHT
870	602086	5528	04.61	BD 8820		sc 9.81 Hong Kong
871	602120	5539	05.61			sc .85 B Barnsley
872	602121	5538	05.61			sc .85 Barnsley
873	602122	5531	04.61	BE 741		sc 9.81 Hong Kong
874	602131	5536	04.61	BE 2638		sc 9.81 Hong Kong
875	602132	5534	04.61	BD 8821		sc 9.81 Hong Kong
876	602195	5535	04.61	BE 6654		sc 9.81 Hong Kong
877	602210	5525	04.61			sc 4.85 Barnsley
878	602234	5501	01.61	BE 7790		sc 9.81 Hong Kong
879	602268	5505	02.61	BE 4732		sc 9.81 Hong Kong
880	602269	5537	05.61	XUF 467A		sc 4.87 Barnsley
881	602291	5504	02.61	BE 7791		sc 9.81 Hong Kong
882	602292	5502	01.61			sc 8.79 Barnsley
883	602301	5503	02.61	BE6656		sc 9.81 Hong Kong
884	602359	5500	02.61			sc .70 Lewes
885	602209	5497	01.61			sc 8.79 Barnsley
886	602249	5496	01.61	BE4733		sc 9.81 Hong Kong
887	602302	5499	01.61	BG1716		sc 9.81 Hong Kong
888	602319	5498	01.61	BE1586		sc 9.81 Hong Kong
889	602085	5526	04.61	BD8823		sc 9.81 Hong Kong
890	602133	5529	04.61	BE6657		sc 9.81 Hong Kong
891	602143	5530	04.61	BE7792		sc 9.81 Hong Kong
892	602233	5533	04.61			sc 10.79 Barnsley
893	602250	5527	04.61	BE1587		sc 9.81 Hong Kong
894	602320	5524	03.61	BE4734		sc 9.81 Hong Kong
895	602358	5508	02.61	BE6658		sc 9.81 Hong Kong
896	602376	5509	02.61	BE4735		sc 9.81 Hong Kong
897	602377	5506	02.61	BE2639		sc 9.81 Hong Kong
898	602474	5507	02.61	BE4736		sc 9.81 Hong Kong
899	602475	5513	03.61	BE6659		sc 9.81 Hong Kong
900	602476	5510	02.61	BD9826		sc 9.81 Hong Kong
901	602509	5511	03.61	BD9827		sc 9.81 Hong Kong
902	602632	5512	03.61	BG1718		sc 9.81 Hong Kong
903	602488	5515	03.61	BG1719		sc 9.81 Hong Kong
904	602489	5517	03.61	BD7333		sc 9.81 Hong Kong
905	602376	5516	03.61	BE7793		sc 9.81 Hong Kong
906	602517	5514	03.61	BG1720		sc 9.81 Hong Kong
907	602518	5521	03.61	BE 7794		sc 9.81 Hong Kong

SMS number	Chassis number	Body number	Date delivered	1st re-registration	2nd re-registration	2004 current status
908	602543	5522	03.61	BE 7795		sc 9.81Hong Kong
909	602544	5518	03.61			sc10.79 Barnsley
910	602584	5523	03.61	BE 6660		sc 9.81Hong Kong
911	602585	5520	03.61			sc by 6.82 Barnsley
912	602631	5519	03.61	BE 742		sc9.81Hong Kong
913	611096	5647	06.62	BH 4764		sc .86 Hong Kong
914	611097	5642	02.62	BJ 340		sc .85 Hong Kong
915	611098	5646	06.62	BJ 2013	DA6421	sc .86 Hong Kong
916	611132	5632	12.61	BH 8901		sc 6.83 Hong Kong
917	611133	5648	06.62	BH 5939	DB9404	sc .87 Hong Kong
918	611134	5644	02.62			sc 5.80Barnsley
919	611146	5641	01.62	BJ 2014		sc 10.84 Hong Kong
920	611147	5643	02.62	BJ 3690		sc 10.84 Hong Kong
921	611158	5640	01.62	BJ 341		sc 6.85 Hong Kong
922	611159	5645	03.62	BH 8900		sc 9.81Hong Kong
923	611160	5639	01.62			sc 4.75 Chichester
924	611174	5638	01.62	BJ 342		sc . Hong Kong
925	611175	5636	01.62			sc 5.80 Barnsley
926	611176	5630	12.61	BJ 344	DA9638	sc 6.86 Hong Kong
927	611183	5635	01.62			sc 12.74 Chichester
928	611184	5631	01.62	BH 4765		sc 7.87 Hong Kong
929	611200	5633	01.62			sc 4.75 Chichester
930	611201	5637	01.62	BJ 2015	DA 8623	sc .94 Hong Kong
931	611229	5634	01.62	BJ 346		sc 10.84 Hong Kong
932	611185	5609	10.61			sc .86 Hong Kong
933	611186	5611	10.61	BH 5940		sc 2.77 Barnsley
934	611202	5615	10.61	BJ 3691		sc 9.81Hong Kong
935	611230	5610	10.61			sc 2.77 Barnsley
936	611274	5613	10.61			WEHT
937	611275	5612	10.61	BH 8902		sc 9.81 Hong Kong
938	611276	5614	10.61	BH 3756		sc .86 Hong Kong
939	611329	5616	10.61			sc 9.65 Sussex
940	611330	5628	12.61	BH 3757		sc 7.87 Hong Kong
941	611331	5625	12.61	BH 3758		sc .86 Hong Kong
942	611332	5624	12.61	BH 8903		sc Hong Kong
943	611338	5623	11.61	BJ 2016	DA 7829	sc 1.86 Hong Kong
944	611339	5617	10.61	BJ 347		sc 10.84 Hong Kong
945	611340	5618	11.61	BH 5941		sc 6.85 Hong Kong
946	611341	5619	11.61	BJ 348		sc 10.84 Hong Kong
947	611359	5627	12.61	BH 5942		sc .86 Hong Kong
948	611360	5626	12.61			sc 4.80 Barnsley
949	611373	5621	11.61			sc 2.77 Barnsley
950	611374	5629	12.61	BH3759		sc . Hong Kong
951	611465	5620	11.61	BJ 349		sc .Hong Kong
952	611466	5622	11.61			sc 4.80 Barnsley
953	L02483	5978	03.64			sc 2.79 Barnsley
954	L02484	6001	06.64			Preserved Sussex fr 1991
955	L02485	5979	03.64			WEHT
956	L02493	5998	06.64	75616	86809	sc .94 Dubai
957	L02494	6002	06.64	SA43264		WEHT
958	L02533	5984	04.64	SA42895		WEHT
959	L02534	5995	06.64	SA42896		WEHT
960	L02535	5983	04.64	HOO343B		sc 6.95Coventry
961	L02536	5985	04.64	YCV28B		(Mobile Stage) Highlands
962	L02537	5982	04.64	SA43085		WEHT
963	L02551	5999	07.64			sc .96 Yorkshire
964	L02552	5992	06.64			WEHT
965	L02553	5994	06.64			sc 3.83Barnsley
966	L02585	5981	04.64	75617	86003	WEHT
967	L02586	5996	06.64	SA43087		WEHT
968	L02587	5989	04.64		60897	WEHT
969	L02588	6000	07.64	SA43265		WEHT
970	L02596	5993	06.64			sc .79Barnsley
971	L02597	5980	04.64		60896	sc .94Dubai
972	L02598	5997	06.64			Preserved Sussex fr 1997
973	L02621	5986	04.64	HOO383B		sc by .94 W Midlands
974	L02622	5987	04.64			(Preserved) Sussex fr 1991
975	L02864	5991	06.64	SA43086		WEHT
976	L02865	5990	06.64	SA42894		WEHT
977	L02866	5988	04.64			WEHT
400	L02938	6014	05.64	PRX188B		sc 6.90 Whitehaven
401	L02939	6013	05.64	PRX206B		Preserved Sussex fr 1991
402	L02996	6021	05.64	AOR159B		Izmir WEHT
403	L02997	6016	05.64	WRU734B		(Preserved) Sussex fr 1996
404	L02998	6023	05.64	PRX191B		Preserved Sussex fr 2002
405	L03146	6022	06.64	PRX199B		Dixons WEHT
406	L03147	6024	06.64	WRU702B		Preserved Sussex fr 1988
407	L03148	6017	05.64	WRU703B		WEHT
408	L03224	6020	05.64	WRU701B		Lydney WEHT
409	L03225	6025	06.64			Stagecoach bus
410	L03226	6018	05.64	PRX207B	BHM 288 DHJ 301B	Preserved fr 1997
411	L03262	6015	05.64	AOR160B		sc11.92Barnsley
412	L03366	6007	03.64	AOR158B		Preserved Sussex fr 1991
413	L03367	6006	03.64	PRX201B		LBE Lydney
414	L03368	6008	03.64	PRX208B		LBE Lydney
415	L03397	6019	05.64	PRX187B	ZV1461	Preserved Sussex fr 2000
416	L03398	6003	03.64	PRX190B		Preserved Sussex fr 1995
417	L03502	6009	04.64	PRX189B		Preserved Sussex fr 2004
418	L03503	6012	05.64	PRX200B		Preserved Sussex fr 1998
419	L03504	6005	03.64	PRX186B	YRC182 DRR 153B	Preserved Sussex fr 97
420	L03505	6010	04.64	PRX219B		Commentary box Bucks
421	L03590	6026	06.64	PRX458B		(Preserved)Sussex fr 1995
422	L03591	6004	03.64	AOR157B		Preserved Sussex fr 1997
423	L03592	6027	06.64	WOW993T		Preserved Hants fr 1993
424	L03593	6011	05.64	AOR156B	424DCD	Stephensons Essex

424: two AOR–DCD cycles. Many preserved DCDs regained original regs in 2004.

SMS number	Chassis number	Body number	Date delivered	1st re-registration	2nd re-registration	2004 status
425	L24026	6170	05.65			W Arnold Torquay
426	L24027	6169	06.65			Preserved Sussex fr 1996(or 90)
427	L24028	6172	06.65			Restaurant Surrey
428	L24152	6171	06.65			sc8.95 Barnsley
429	L24153	6168	05.65			Exhib Unit Croatia
250	L22967	6188	03.65			sc 2.81 Barnsley
251	L22968	6187	04.65			sc 10.81 Rotherham
252	L23475	6204	06.65			WEHT
253	L23476	6186	03.65			sc 2.94 Yorkshire
254	L23486	6184	03.65			sc 2.81 Barnsley
255	L23487	6200	05.65			sc 2.81Barnsley
256	L23539	6179	03.65			sc 10.81 Rotherham
257	L23540	6207	10.65			WEHT
258	L23566	6178	03.65	70867		sc .96 Dubai
259	L23567	6185	03.65			sc .82 Weardale
260	L23678	6206	06.65			Preserved Sussex fr 1990(semi)
261	L23679	6205	06.65			WEHT
262	L23680	6180	03.65			sc 9.80Barnsley
263	L23738	6181	03.65	60358		sc .94Dubai
264	L23739	6199	05.65	71578	95693	WEHT
265	L23794	6203	06.65	60357		sc .94Dubai
266	L23795	6183	03.65			sc .96Barnsley
267	L23796	6201	05.65			W. Arnold Leeds
268	L23797	6198	05.65			sc by .92 Weardale
269	L23847	6197	04.65			sc Larkhall 90s
270	L23848	6196	04.65			sc 10.95 Barnsley
271	L23973	6202	05.65			sc 10.79 Barnsley
272	L23974	6194	04.65			Preserved fr 1993
273	L24401	6193	04.65			WEHT
274	L24402	6195	05.65			sc 10.93 Barnsley
275	L24417	6177	03.65			USA WEHT
276	L24418	6192	04.65			(Preserved) Sussex fr 1992
277	L24481	6189	04.65			Preserved Sussex fr 1992
278	L24482	6190	04.65	217UKL	BUF278C	Preserved Notts fr 1993
279	L24493	6191	04.65			Preserved Sussex fr 1993
280	L24494	6182	03.65	32842		sc .94 Dubai
281	L24605	6174	03.65			sc .81 Barnsley
282	L24606	6173	03.65	71295		WEHT
283	L24607	6176	03.65	71004		WEHT
284	L24608	6175	03.65			Japan WEHT
285	L45031	6389	05.66			WEHT
286	L45032	6378	03.66			(Preserved) fr 1991
287	L45033	6377	03.66			(Preserved) Sussex fr 1995
288	L45054	6382	04.66			WEHT
289	L45055	6374	03.66			WEHT
290	L45056	6376	03.66			WEHT
291	L45150	6381	04.66			sc 5.84 Barnsley
292	L45151	6379	04.66			Preserved Sussex fr 1998
293	L60163	6380	04.66			WEHT
294	L60164	6375	03.66			Preserved Sussex fr 1995
295	L60165	6383	04.66			sc7.95 Barnsley
296	L60452	6385	05.66			(Preserved)Sussex fr 1998sc .01
297	L60453	6386	05.66			sc 6.84 Barnsley
298	L60463	6387	05.66			sc .81 Barnsley
299	L60656	6388	05.66			WEHT
300	L60657	6384	05.66			sc .83 Barnsley
301	L61291	6390	06.66			sc .79 Sussex
302	L61529	6391	06.66			sc 8.91 Yorkshire
303	L61543	6395	09.66			sc 4.79 Sussex
304	L61728	6397	09.66			sc 1.80 Barnsley
305	L61729	6392	06.66			sc 2.84 Barnsley
306	L61901	6403	11.66			sc 4.79 Sussex
307	L61902	6399	10.66			Preserved Sussex fr 2000
308	L61944	6402	11.66			sc .87 Barnsley
309	L61544	6393	08.66			sc 3.82 Barnsley
310	L62115	6396	09.66			sc4.79 Sussex
311	L61945	6394	09.66			sc 5.95 Manchester
312	L62114	6400	11.66			sc by 6.82 Barnsley
313	L62180	6401	11.66			sc 6.82 Barnsley
314	L62181	6398	10.66			sc 7.83 Barnsley
315	L62116	6460	10.66			WEHT
346	L63673	6476	06.67			sc 4.79 Sussex
347	L63811	6467	03.67			Preserved Sussex fr 1992
348	L63895	6473	03.67			sc 4.79 Sussex
349	L63896	6481	06.67			WEHT
350	L63987	6484	07.67			PreservedSussex fr 92
351	L63988	6479	07.67			sc 4.79 Sussex
352	L63989	6471	03.67			sc 11.81 Barnsley
353	L64108	6465	03.67			sc .81Barnsley
354	L64109	6483	07.67			sc 5.79 Sussex
355	L64110	6469	03.67			sc .82 Leics
356	L64215	6482	07.67			Commentary box Bucks
357	L64216	6477	06.67			sc 4.85 Barnsley
358	L64340	6474	03.67			sc 8.94 Barnsley
359	L64341	6480	06.67			sc .81 Barnsley
360	L64455	6468	03.67			(Preserved)Sussex fr 93 sc .99
361	L64456	6478	06.67			sc .94 Barnsley
362	L64686	6462	02.67			sc 3.93 Barnsley
363	L64687	6461	02.67			(Preserved) Sussex fr 1993
364	L64944	6475	05.67			sc .93 Yorkshire
365	L64945	6463	02.67			sc .02 Aberdeenshire
366	L65087	6464				WEHT
367	L65088	6466	03.67	87894		sc by .97 Dubai
368	L65089	6470	03.67			WEHT
369	L65090	6472	03.67			sc 11.83 Barnsley

Preservation dates believed correct but original locations, if different, not shown. Book should tell life story of each Mary but not always explicitly.

MARY SCRAPPED!!!
Scrapping a bus is a reality that
of commercial scrap
to fi

Written by **RICHARD J COSSEY** *and reproduced from the Ian Allan*
publication, 'Bus & Coach Preservation', by courtesy.
Photographs by Richard J Cossey

Scrapping a bus is a reality that sometimes preservationists have to face. With the tidying up of commercial scrap yards in order to comply with environmental legislation many items are now hard to find or are expensive to buy. Such a decision had to be taken in 2001 by the West Sussex-based Southdown Historic Vehicle Group (SHVG) about one of their ex-Southdown 'Queen Mary' PD3/4s.

In 1998 the SHVG acquired former Southdown 296 (FCD296D) from a school in East Sussex and although it was structurally complete its interior had been subjected to a non-PSV makeover and had lost some engine parts and all cab fittings. The original complement of 69 seats had long been replaced by a dozen solidly built two-tier beds for use as a bunkhouse. Body modifications also included a large emergency exit cut into the rear of the upper deck, the panelling over of some windows and the installation of extractor fans in others. False floors were installed upstairs and down and carpet applied to all floors and ceilings for that 'soft trim' look. To finish the transformation the exterior had been painted in late 20th century playbus style. After seven years use the bus's condition deteriorated and it was acquired by the SHVG. With so many parts missing or modified it was decided to recover the remaining useful parts of 296 to benefit the remaining 'QMs' in the collection.

In late 2000 the 296 was towed to Stagecoach's former Southdown garage in Worthing where its engine was removed for use in the company's own convertible Queen Mary 424 (424DCD) which had suffered an engine failure in April 2000. 296 was then towed away to the group's store where a team of spanner and screwdriver wielding volunteers descended on it. All useful mouldings and trims were removed as well as window pans, light fittings, destination gear, and window glass. All the undamaged sheets of wood-effect Formica from the interior were saved and some exterior panels and the interior handrails were also retained. Even the plated brass screws securing the interior trim were kept as they're not cheap to buy. With the outer panelling removed the bus began to take on the appearance of a cut-away drawing.

Photographs were taken of the interior structure for future reference. A lot of effort was required to demolish the bus as Northern Counties had built them to last. The only areas that had really suffered were the wood inserts to which the exterior panels are attached and a few areas such as the cab floor where steel and aluminium came into contact – the rest

296's career

May 1966	Delivered new to Portslade Works in green & cream livery
June 1966	Prepared for service & allocated to Edward St garage, Brighton
August 1972	Re-allocated to Brighton Hove & District duties
January 1973	Re-allocated to Edward St. garage, Brighton
November 1974	Re-allocated to Brighton Hove & District duties
July 1976	Re-painted into NBC leaf green / white
January 1979	Converted to driver trainer and painted yellow and white
November 1990	Withdrawn for disposal
July 1991	To Tideway School, Newhaven, East Sussex for static use
June 1998	Acquired by Southdown Historic Vehicle Group
February 2001	Broken up for spares; remains scrapped

was as solid as when it left Wigan in 1966 albeit a bit dirtier. With the body off it was easy to cut out the transmission and running gear.

296 may now be but a memory but parts of it will live on allowing a longer life for its surviving sisters.

En France

Photo: Authors' collection

Photo: P.R.Kemp

LA VIE DE L'AUTO
Camions & Cie

" BUS PRIDE "

Organisé chaque année en juin, la Lesbian & Gay Pride connaît un succès populaire grandissant. La coutume veut que les associations organisatrices défilent sur des chars, généralement des camions à plateforme aménagés en pistes de danse. Cette année, nombre de ces chars étaient... des bus !
Quand on vous dit que les transports urbains sont à la mode !

↑ Ci-dessus, un Routemaster britannique transformé en impériale ouverte, affrété par un bar - restaurant.

← A gauche, un vénérable Leyland, toujours immatriculé au Royaume-Uni, abrite les employés d'un site internet
© Arnaud WADOUX

A droite, un bon vieux SC10UPF de → la RATP, confié par la Régie à une association interne à caractère communautaire, l'AHTP.
Noter que la SNCF avait, de son côté, prêté une camionnette TGV pour l'association interne Gare !

24

RÉSEAUX URBAINS N° 39

(Re) Découverte

Musée à bon port !

Various latterday French connections. 406 was the first double-decker bus through the Channel Tunnel.

Frédérique Chalm, secrétaire général d'IDéale DS Normandie, est aussi un passionné d'utilitaires. Il nous parle d'un charmant musée, situé dans le port de Portsmouth.

«Si vos lecteurs passent par Portsmouth, au sud de l'Angleterre, qu'ils ne manquent pas le "City of Portsmouth preserved transport depot" (secrétariat : Clive Wilkin, 94, Kings road, Cowplain Hampshire-PO8 8UT, Grande-Bretagne) !
Ce musée, consacré aux transports en commun anglais, est géré par une association de bénévoles veillant sur un patrimoine de 21 pièces (dont certaines dans leur jus ou en cours de restauration) : depuis un coach attelé Fawley Flyer de 1876 jusqu'à un Leyland AN68 de 1975. Celui qui figure au côté de mon ambulance ID 19 F de 1963 est un Leyland Titan PD3/4 de 1964 (69 places). Entre les deux véhicules, pose la sympathique responsable de l'association».

«J'ajoute que le musée, ouvert un dimanche sur deux, dispose d'un département miniatures (disponibles à la vente) et propose (pour une modique somme) une promenade en ville toutes les heures et à chaque fois avec un véhicule différent. Ce musée se trouve dans l'avant-port, au 48-54 Broad street, mais l'ensemble de la collection devrait bientôt être abrité dans un local à sa racine. Une visite à ne pas manquer pour ceux qui ont quelques heures à tuer avant d'embarquer pour le continent».
Rappelons qu'en mars 1996, un de nos lecteurs nous confiait déjà cette intéressante adresse (qui figure aussi dans Le Guide du Collectionneur). Comme quoi, il y a des musées qui charment plus que d'autres !

Frédérique Chalm incite les amateurs à s'arrêter à ce musée des transports de Portsmouth : son ambulance ID 19 F est ici garée à côté d'un Leyland Titan de 1964

SOUTHDOWN OWNERSHIP DURING PERIOD OF BOOK
1957-1969 Part of British Electric Traction group (privately-owned)
1969-1987 Part of National Bus Company (state-owned)
1987–1989 Privately-owned. Management buy-out. No group.
1989–2004 Part of Stagecoach Group (privately-owned)
'independent' operators in text are small independent firms not part of any grouping (the 1960s understanding of the term)

127

Continued from p.3 Much later QM days. Worthing May 2000. The author on 426. Which design has stood the test of time best?! (*Richard J Cossey*)

Who were those people?

RICHARD J. COSSEY

Saw his first QM (a TCD) on delivery on the A27 and what a big shiny beast it seemed. His local garage at Littlehampton eventually had an allocation and they became his transport home after Scouts - the regular bag of chips having to be consumed before boarding to avoid the conductor's wrath. Now after a Civil Service and privatisation career, he finds himself with a PSV licence and a share in a couple of these fine vehicles.

MIKE DAVIS

Mike spent fifteen of the years between 1964 and 1984 in Hong Kong, mainly in the British army but latterly in the bus industry. He became a founder director of a coach company in Croydon from which he resigned in 1991 to found DTS Publishing. Mike has been active over the years contributing articles, information and photographs to leading journals, including Janes Urban Transport Systems and Janes World Railways and has done consultancy work for Janes, Washington DC, and a number of other clients in the transport industry. Over a period of 25 years he gathered together material for inclusion in his books on the bus fleets of Hong Kong, where possible taking the photographs himself, latterly on regular visits to what is now the Special Administrative Region of China. Mike is a founder member of Buses Worldwide and for five years edited that group's journal.

MICHAEL DRYHURST

Michael Dryhurst works in the film industry in the United States and has written and published on motorbuses and trolleybuses for many years.

ALAN LAMBERT

Started the Southdown Enthusiasts Club whilst still at school and on leaving joined Southdown as a Traffic Clerk. Left in 1966 to 'sort out' East Suffolk County Council's School Transport and after six years (job done) became Traffic Manager for Basil Williams' Southern Motorways. Joined West Sussex County Council when the Public Transport Unit was set up, later becoming Head of the Unit. Retired in 1998 and is currently Chairman of the Southdown Omnibus Trust at Amberley Museum and Consultant to Emsworth & District Motor Services (who use the old Southdown green and cream livery).

BRUCE A. MACPHEE ENG.TECH, M.I.R.T.E.

Life's earliest recollection is of the new '300' PD2s on service 12, this starting an undivided interest in Southdown. Served apprenticeship at Portslade Works and studied for HNC at Brighton Poly, but was more interested in '300s', in their twilight days, passing by the window on service 49A. Looked forward to 21st birthday for sole reason of being able to take PSV driving test; turned back on career prospects in order to be a driver. Later, resumed engineering career, on buses without wheels (i.e. ships). Recently returned to bus driving after break of over 30 years. Pleased to find that there were still Northern Counties bodied Leylands, but less pleased that engines were at the wrong end and that driver now had to collect fares. Favourite colour: green. Favourite animal: Tiger PS1 (green)

STEPHEN C. MORRIS

Although a music graduate from London University, Stephen Morris made a career as a professional bus journalist, having accepted the post of assistant editor of Buses in 1979. He became editor the following year and left the magazine in 1999 to become Ian Allan's magazine publishing manager. However his interest in writing about buses led him to set up as a freelance transport writer in 2000, and his freelance contributions include *Bus & Coach Preservation*, of which he is consulting editor, the trade weekly *RouteONE*, and the National Federation of Bus Users' quarterly magazine, Bus User. He undertakes other consultancy work. He is married with one son, still enjoys music – he plays the bassoon and sings, though not at the same time – and takes a leading role at Shepperton Community Church, but escapes to the Pembrokeshire coast at the drop of a hat.

The QMs' twilight may have turned to night but it's going to be a long one! 903 at Worthing Pier February 1968.